DECENTRALIZED A.I.

Decentralized A.I.

Proceedings of the First European Workshop on Modelling Autonomous Agents in a Multi-Agent World
Cambridge, England, August 16–18, 1989

Edited by

YVES DEMAZEAU

Chargé de Recherche au Centre National
de la Recherche Scientifique
Laboratoire d'Informatique Fondamentale
et d'Intelligence Artificielle
Grenoble, France

and

JEAN PIERRE MÜLLER

Professeur à l'Université de Neuchâtel
Institut de Mathématiques et d'Informatique, IMI
Neuchâtel, Switzerland

1990

NORTH-HOLLAND
AMSTERDAM • NEW YORK • OXFORD • TOKYO

ELSEVIER SCIENCE PUBLISHERS B.V.
Sara Burgerhartstraat 25
P.O. Box 211, 1000 AE Amsterdam, The Netherlands

Distributors for the United States and Canada:
ELSEVIER SCIENCE PUBLISHING COMPANY, INC.
655 Avenue of the Americas
New York, N.Y. 10010, U.S.A.

Library of Congress Cataloging-in-Publication Data

European Workshop on Modelling Autonomous Agents in a Multi-Agent World (1st : 1989 : Cambridge, England)
Decentralized A.I. : proceedings of the First European Workshop on Modelling Autonomous Agents in a Multi-Agent World, Cambridge, England, August 16-18, 1989 / edited by Yves Demazeau and Jean-Pierre Müller.
p. cm.
Includes bibliographical references.
ISBN 0-444-88705-9
1. Artificial intelligence--Congresses. I. Demazeau, Yves. II. Müller, Jean-Pierre. III. Title.
QC334.E99 1989
006.3--dc20 90-39141
CIP

ISBN: 0 444 88705 9

Printed in the Netherlands

Foreword

The papers in this book have been first presented at the 1st European Workshop on Modelling Autonomous Agents in a Multi-Agent World, held in King's College at Cambridge, England, in August 1989. The format of this book is based on the collection and categorization of these papers that have been revised by the authors after the workshop. The reasons that guided the choice of both the title and the structure of this monograph are explained in the first paper.

The idea for the workshop originated in the COST-13 MAGMA Project (Modelling an Autonomous aGent in a Multi-Agent world) which contributed to recent developments in Decentralized Artificial Intelligence. The project took place in the framework of the European COST-13 Action (Commission of the European Communities, DG XIII). We are grateful to Jean-Claude Latombe who inspired this project and we would like to thank the Commission for supporting it.

We would like to thank John Campbell for organizing the workshop, the Commision of the European Communities for both contributing to the genesis of this workshop and supporting it, and every participant in the COST-13 MAGMA project for their continuous and valued help.

We are grateful for the support of our institutions, the "Centre National de la Recherche Scientifique", the "Laboratoire d'Informatique Fondamentale et d'Intelligence Artificielle" in Grenoble, the "Université de Neuchâtel", and the "Institut d'Informatique et de Mathématiques", for providing us with an excellent research environment for many years.

The first editor also thanks the Artificial Intelligence Laboratory at the Vrije Universiteit Brussels and the SWIFT company for providing the environment and support for Decentralized Artificial Intelligence which made this compilation possible.

Yves Demazeau
Jean-Pierre Müller

Introduction

DECENTRALIZED A.I.
Yves DEMAZEAU & Jean-Pierre MÜLLER (Eds.)

DECENTRALIZED ARTIFICIAL INTELLIGENCE

Yves Demazeau[1]

LIFIA-IMAG/CNRS
46, av. Félix Viallet,
F-38031 Grenoble Cédex
FRANCE
demazeau@lifia.imag.fr

Jean-Pierre Müller

Université de Neuchâtel
Chantemerle, 20
CH-2000 Neuchâtel
SWITZERLAND
inmuller@cnedcu51.bitnet

Decentralized Artificial Intelligence (DzAI) is concerned with *the activity of an autonomous agent in a multi-agent world.* Since DzAI focuses on modelling an agent we introduce a very simplified model of an agent to highlight some essential features of an autonomous agent in a multi-agent world. The consideration of both the *locality of a task* and the *capabilities of an agent* to achieve a task, allows us to distinguish four *kinds of behaviour* : cohabitation, cooperation, collaboration, and distribution. The consideration of the *kinds of information that can be exchanged* between several agents allows a fine-grained description of the *interactions between agents.* Such considerations, by emphasizing the agent modelling, offer an interesting and systematic framework for studying multi-agent problems [2] .

1 Scope and Goal

This paper is an attempt to structure the activity in multi-agent modelling by an approach that is different than classical Distributed Artificial Intelligence (DAI) : Decentralized Artificial Intelligence (DzAI). We first introduce a definition of these two points of view and compare them.

1.1 Distributed versus Decentralized Artificial Intelligence

DAI, as defined in [13], is concerned with the *collaborative solution of global problems by a distributed group of entities.* The entities may range from simple processing elements to complex entities exhibiting rational behaviour. The problem solving or task performing is *collaborative* in the sense that mutual sharing of information is necessary to allow the group as a whole to produce a solution, or to successfully accomplish a *global* task. The group of entities is distributed in that both control and data are logically, and often geographically, distributed.

---

[1]The author is currently at the Vrije Universiteit Brussels, Artificial Intelligence Laboratory, Pleinlaan 2, B-1050 Brussels, demazeau@arti.vub.ac.be, with the support of CNRS, and having a SWIFT AI chair.

[2]This work has been done in the framework of the European CEC COST-13 Project MAGMA "Modeling an Autonomous Agent in a Multi-Agent World".

DzAI is concerned with the *activity of an autonomous agent in a multi-agent world.* The word "agent" is used in a broad sense to designate an intelligent entity, acting rationally and intentionally with respect to its own goals and the current state of its knowledge. By "autonomous" agents, we mean that each agent has its own existence, which is not justified by the existence of other agents. We consider several autonomous intelligent agents which coexist and may collaborate with other agents in a common world. Each agent may accomplish its own tasks, or cooperate with other agents to perform a personal or a global task.

In the light of these definitions, DAI and DzAI have a common interest in the behaviour of distributed entities. However, in DAI, a global task is initially defined and the problem is then to design the distributed entities to enable the performance of this global task. The main issue is to study the distribution and the collaborative resolution of the given task. In DzAI, the decentralized autonomous entities are initially defined. We then study how these entities are able to achieve tasks that may be personal or may interest several entities. The main issue is to study the structure of the autonomous entities to provide insights into what kinds of problems these entities are able to solve or what tasks they are capable of performing.

1.2 Motivations for DzAI

Most research works in AI have considered a single agent having complete control over the world. To design one agent having full capability to control its environment appears a difficult task.

- the agent has to deal with multiple, uncertain, contradictory sources of information
- the agent has to deal with multiple, contextual, conflicting goals
- the agent has to map its goals into its restricted perception and acting capabilities

To consider a multi-agent world is an improvement from the point of view of both a single agent and a society of agents :

Designing more powerful and more autonomous agents : through developing new planning or solving methods that process incomplete and uncertain knowledge by communication with other agents, DzAI can provide insights into improving and increasing the reasoning and decision capabilities of each agent for the achievement of its own goals. The maintenance of incompatible information or goals, and the resolution of the incompatibilities when necessary, occur naturally in a multi-agent framework.

Understanding social behaviour : through collaboration between autonomous agents, DzAI can not only improve the intrinsic power of the capabilities of each agent but also model social behaviour emerging from the agent interactions. DzAI can provide keys for understanding the interactions among intelligent beings who belong to various groups or societies, since it is based on the very structure of the interacting entities.

Since in the DzAI approach the agents are defined first, we begin by introducing a very simplified model of an agent. Based on this description, we propose some criteria on which the multi-agent problems can be classified, and use them to describe different papers in this field.

2 A generic agent

Our intention in describing a generic agent is to define the minimal features from which we can explain the various interactions in a multi-agent world. The purpose of the following description is not to specify what the architecture of an agent is or should be but to illustrate in which terms its behaviour can be described.

Any agent can be thought of as having representations of the world or of the problem it has to solve. Let us just call these representations *knowledge* whatever form, implicit or explicit, they may take. This knowledge can be given or acquired through perception or communication with other agents. A good discussion of the nature of knowledge can be found in [20].

It is always possible to abstract *goals* from the observation of the behaviour of agents. These goals do not need to exist explicitly inside the agent. The goals can be encoded in the algorithms or explicitly given or acquired by the context or by communication with other agents.

From knowledge and goals, an agent can be thought of as having to consider a set of possible solutions or plans to acheive its goals. For the sake of generality, let us call it the set of *possible solutions*. An agent does not need to be able to derive all the possible solutions but only a part of these depending on its *reasoning capabilities*. This last notion allows us to take into account limited reasoning [14,7].
When various possible solutions (or plans) are potentially applicable, a decision must be made among them to choose the best one from the point of view of the agent. Let us call it the *choice* of the agent. For planning agents, this choice is called the intention of the agent. Due to agent limitations, the choice can be wrong from an external point of view. The limitations can be taken into account by introducing a model of the *decision capabilities* of the agent.

This proposal is illustrated by the following figure 1.
In the following paragraphs, we detail some features of the autonomous agent in a multi-agent world and show how this generic agent can be used to explain interactions between more or less autonomous agents.

3 Some features of the autonomous agent

3.1 Dynamics of the world

Each agent has at best incomplete, uncertain and partly erroneous knowledge about the world and about other agents. As a consequence, it is not possible for an agent to safely plan actions or to find solutions that are applicable in the long term. Un-

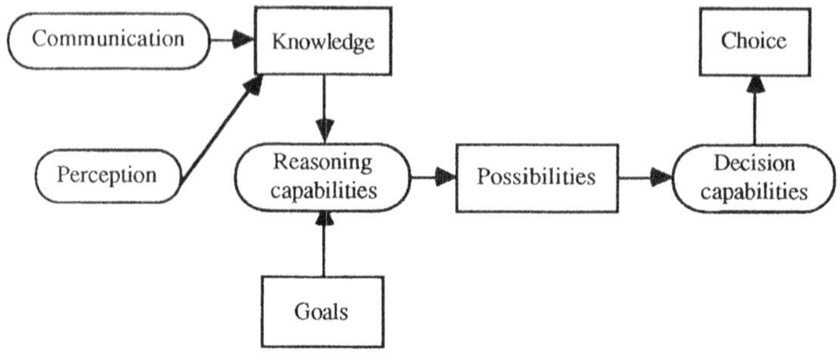

Figure 1: Agent model

certainty about the actual choices of other agents requires that an agent carefully monitors plan execution, interweaves plan generation and execution, and frequently updates its knowledge, goals, and choices. In the case of DzAI, the models used to update knowledge about the changing environment will be expressed in terms of agent behaviour.

3.2 Kinds of agent behaviour

Each agent may anticipate the actions to be executed by other agents, and may interact with them in order to satisfy its goal with respect to the choices of the other agents. Our presentation of the several kinds of agent behaviour is based on the two following criteria :

the locality of the task to be performed by the agent : *personal* (local) or *interpersonal* (global)

the capability of the agent to perform the task alone : *able* or *unable*

According to these criteria, there are naturally four ways to describe how to take into account the other agents evolving in the same world :

Cohabitation : the agent has to successfully accomplish a task and it is able to execute it alone. This point of view is equivalent to classical AI problems of planning in a mono- agent environment, but whose dynamic behaviour can be explained in terms of actions of similar entities with which conflicts may occur.

Cooperation : in order to perform a personal task, an agent will have to cooperate with others either because it is not able to accomplish it itself (restricted possible solutions), or because others can successfully accomplish it more efficiently (e.g. within a shorter interval of time). This is something deductible by the decision process of the agent.

Collaboration : some global goals may concern all agents and may be realized individually by several agents. The main problem deals with electing one of the agents to carry out the task. The redundancy of the capabilities of these agents contributes to the robustness of the whole system.

Distribution : finally, some global goals can only be achieved by several agents collectively. The main problem deals with splitting the global task and distributing it to the cooperative agents. This kind of behaviour, increasing the effectiveness of the entire system, can be observed in DAI systems.

Obviously, other dimensions of the multi-agent problems can be taken to classify the kind of agent behaviour. As an example, Werner [23] describes various styles of cooperation between agents ranging from the totally cooperative and selfless to the absolutely selfish.

3.3 Kinds of information exchange

One way for exchanging information with other agents is to communicate with them. An agent may also perceive the world through sensors such as visual sensors. Both the perception and the communication acts may be considered as actions to be planned. Through acquiring knowledge about other agents, an agent may be able to recognize the actions, and eventually will be able to infer the choices of, other agents (plan recognition). We can distinguish three types of exchange (through perception or communication) between agents evolving in a common world, according to the type of information that is effectively exchanged.

Knowledge : due to differences and due to the incompleteness in perceiving the environment, two agents may have either complementary or conflicting descriptions of a shared situation. In the first case, reasoning about the knowledge of other agents can be useful for supporting exchange of information as pointed out in [1]. Conflicts arise in the case where contradictory descriptions are present ; the problem is to negotiate in order to decide which description better matches reality. This last problem has been pointed out in [9], and its resolution involves exchanges of justifications.

Possible solution : the exchange of possible solutions arises when two or more agents have to agree on a common solution or plan. The process can be thought of as finding the intersection of the possible solutions issued by each agent. Due to different reasoning capabilities, this intersection can be empty ; in this case, reasoning about the reasoning capabilities of other agents may be useful to deduce which knowledge must be communicated to produce other possible solutions. This kind of protocol has been suggested by [19].

Choice : given a set of common possible solutions, one has to agree on a common choice when cooperation is needed. One possibility is to avoid the problem by agreeing on choosing the first solution uttered in the intersection of possible solutions. A more elaborate but passive solution requires reasoning about the decision capabilities of each agent. For example, a possible solution which is very highly rated by an agent may be rejected because the conjoined income from the point of view of both agents is in fact less interesting than the single income of each solution [10]. The communication of choice also occurs when an agent requests another agent to do something. However, when a choice is not accepted by another agent, negotiation must occur [3].

4 Interaction between several agents

4.1 Strong interaction between decision capabilities

Interaction between several agents cannot only be described by single message exchange. Usually, communication occurs through sophisticated protocols for informing, requesting or convincing. For example, requesting is not only composed of an order to do something but is usually followed by an acknowledgement of the acceptance of the request or even a set of exchanges to agree upon the intended meaning of the request. These protocols can be described from an external point of view as in [2].

They also can be explained in terms of conflicts between what the agent wants to do or more specifically about what the agent considers as most important. This last point requests reasoning about the decision process of each other [10] and about the influence each agent can have on the other (social power) [3]). A protocol for decision making in distributing tasks among several agents based on the contract net paradigm is described in [22].

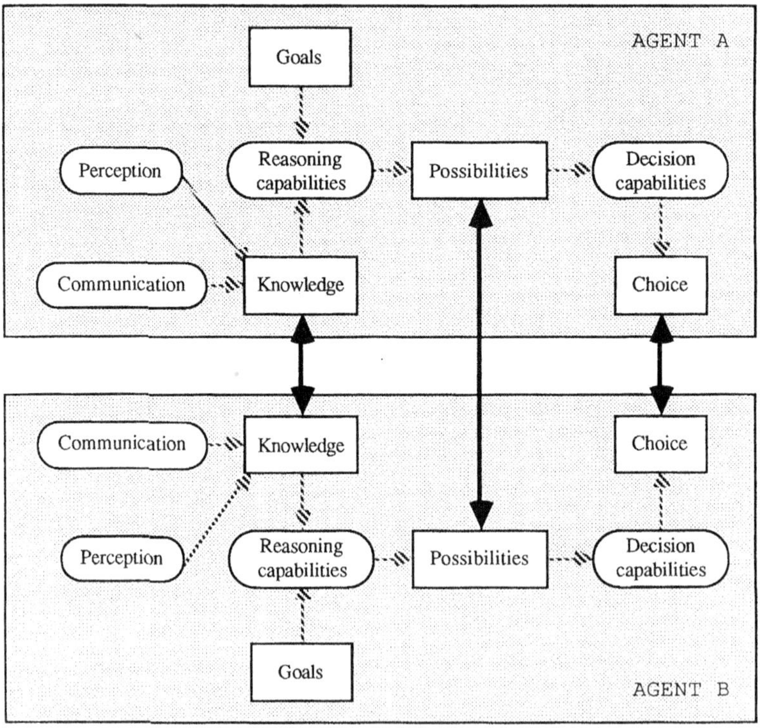

Figure 2: Strong interaction between decision capabilities

4.2 Medium interaction between reasoning capabilities

A weaker interaction than a full protocol for influencing each other occurs when the agents want to simply take into account what the other agents intend to do. One example is the simplified protocol where agents try to produce multi-agent plans (plans with actions from both agents) by using the model they have of their own reasoning capabilities (i.e. their capability to infer possibilities from their knowledge). Such a simplified protocol is illustrated in [8] through the interactions between a set of controlled agents and several autonomous uncontrolled ones. These multi-agents plans may be exchanged until a common plan is found [19].

Another case which requires reasoning about the reasoning capabilities of other agents is plan recognition [6]. In both cases, a model of the possible interactions (both positive and negative) between various possible plans is necessary. A taxonomy of such interactions is described in [17]. An architecture to produce plans dealing with time and goal interactions is described in [15].

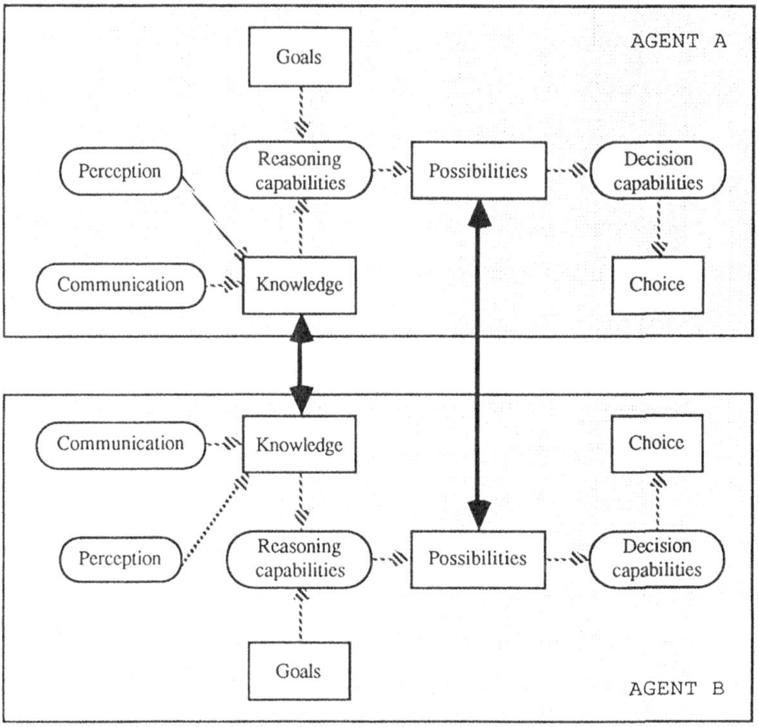

Figure 3: Medium interaction between reasoning capabilities

4.3 Weak interaction between perceiving capabilities

The weakest interaction which can be found among several agents is to use the external world to exchange information. In fact, as we said it before, behaviour can be described as deriving directly or not, from the knowledge an agent has about its environment. Sending information to an agent (communication case) or modifying the environment (world used as a blackboard) are two means by which cooperative behaviour can be achieved among loosely coupled autonomous entities [21]. In fact, no common plans have to be exchanged or even derived explicitly since they do not need to be communicated and no decisions have to be explained because convincing other agents is not part of this paradigm. Another example of this paradigm is in [4] where the environment has been extended to include utterances but in which the agents are described as reactive to changes (situated actions).

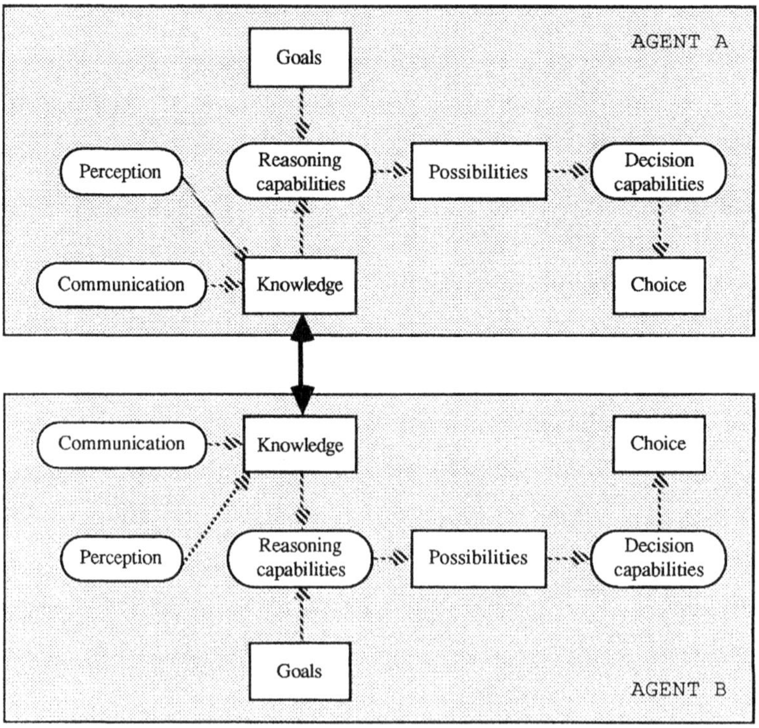

Figure 4: Weak interaction between perceiving capabilities

4.4 Practical considerations for information exchange

All these considerations need strong computational models and a lot of work is focused on providing a framework for designing communicating agents. Two paradigms emerge :

- the *actor* paradigm
- the *blackboard* paradigm

The actor paradigm is based on an object-oriented language where each object has an independent life and communicates with others by sending messages [12]. Various kinds of message passing mechanisms can be imagined as direct addressing, local or global broadcasting [18]. An extension allows typed messages by using abstract descriptions of their structure [11]. The implementation can be either a single machine or distributed.

The blackboard paradigm makes agents communicate by writing on a shared structure called a blackboard. The blackboard can be structured for organizing communication at various levels of abstraction. An agent communicates with another one by writing on the blackboard. Agents are activated when given patterns of information are present on the blackboard [16].

5 Conclusion

By starting from a simple agent description, we have covered a substantial part of possible social behaviours. The consideration of both the locality of a task and the capabilities of an agent to achieve a task, allows us to distinguish four categories of behaviour : cohabitation, cooperation, collaboration and distribution. The consideration of the kinds of information which can be exchanged between several agents seems to allow a fine-grained description of the multi-agent interactions. These results suggest that Decentralized Artificial Intelligence, by emphasizing agent modelling, offers an interesting and systematic framework for studying multi-agent problems.

6 Acknowledgements

Recent developments in DzAI have been and are being performed through an European Action, the Project MAGMA (Modelling an Autonomous aGent in a Multi-Agent world) [5]. This project is part of the COST-13 action of the Commission of the European Communities. The main goal of the program is to study a system architecture, reasoning models and knowledge representation schemes in order to allow problem solving or planning in a multi-agent world. Clearly, this program does not deal with developing a centralized problem solver or planner that will distribute sub-problems or actions to be performed among the agents ; it is concerned with developing the knowledge representation capabilities, the reasoning capabilities, and the decision capabilities which make each agent autonomous in a complex and dynamic multi-agent world. Mobile robots evolving in restricted office environments have been selected as a testbed. We want to thank Pr. Jean Claude Latombe who inspired this work and the Commission of the European Communities for taking the decision to support it.

REFERENCES

[1] D. E. Appelt, "Planning English Referring Expressions", in Artificial Intelligence, vol. 26(1985), pp. 1-33.

[2] J. A. Campbell and M. P. D'Inverno, "Knowledge Interchange Protocols", in this book.

[3] C. Castelfranchi, "Social Power", in this book.

[4] D. Connah and P. Wavish, "An Experiment in Cooperation", in this book.

[5] Y. Demazeau, "The COST-13 MAGMA Project", CEC-DG XIII report, AI-Lab/VUB AI-Memo, Spring 90.

[6] M. Di Manzo, A. Cucchiarelli, and S. Valenti, "A Framework for the Recognition of Actions and Plans from Visual Information", in this book.

[7] R. Fagin and J. Y. Halpern, "Belief, Awareness, and Limited Reasoning", in Proceedings of IJCAI-85, pp. 91-99, Los Angeles.

[8] Th. Fraichard and Y. Demazeau, "Motion Planning in a Multi-Agent World", in this book.

[9] J. R. Galliers, "The Positive Role of Conflict in Cooperative Multi-Agents Systems", in this book.

[10] M. R. Genesereth, M. L. Ginsberg, and J. S. Rosenschein, "Cooperation without Communication", Research Report HPP-84-5, Stanford, March 1984.

[11] H. Hammainen, J. Alasuvanto, and R. Mantyla, "Experiences on Semi-Autonomous User Agents", in this book.

[12] C. Hewitt, "Viewing Control Structures as Patterns of Passing Messages", in Artificial Intelligence, vol. 8(1977).

[13] M. N. Huhns (Ed.), "DISTRIBUTED ARTIFICIAL INTELLIGENCE", Morgan Kaufmann, 1987.

[14] K. Konolige, "A Deduction Model of Belief and its Logics", Reserach Report, TN 326, SRI, August 1984.

[15] M. Lizotte and B. Moulin, "A Temporal Planner for Modelling Autonomous Agents", in this book.

[16] B. Maitre and H. Laasri, "Cooperating Expert Problem-Solving in Blackboard Systems : Atome Case Study", in this book.

[17] F. v. Martial, "Interactions Among Autonomous Planning Agents", in this book.

[18] T. Maruichi, M. Ichikawa, and M. Tokoro, "Modeling Autonomous Agents and Their Groups", in this book.

[19] J. S. Rosenschein and M. R. Genesereth, "Communication and Cooperation", Research Report HPP-84-5, Stanford, March 1984.

[20] J. S. Rosenschein, "Formal theories of Knowledge in AI and Robotic", in New Generation Computing, vol. 3(1985), pp.345-357.

[21] L. Steels, "Cooperation between Distributed Agents through Self-Organisation", in this book.

[22] V. D. Parunak, "Distributed AI and Manufacturing Control : some Issues and Insights", in this book.

[23] E. Werner, "Distributed Cooperation Algorithms", in this book.

Features of the Autonomous Agent

DECENTRALIZED A.I.
Yves DEMAZEAU & Jean-Pierre MÜLLER (Eds.)
Elsevier Science Publishers B.V. (North-Holland), 1990

DISTRIBUTED COOPERATION ALGORITHMS

Eric Werner *

University of Hamburg
Distributed Systems Research Group
Department of Computer Science
Bodenstedtstr. 16, 2000 Hamburg 50
WEST GERMANY

werner%rz.informatik.uni-hamburg.dbp.de
werner@ddagmd11.bitnet, werner@unido.uucp

A class of distributed algorithm types is explored that describe various degrees of cooperation between autonomous agents. Each algorithm type describes a style of cooperation. The styles range from the totally cooperative and selfless, to the absolutely selfish. The algorithms are goal based, modifying the intentional state of the agent. Goal relaxation, goal removal and goal formation are used to resolve conflicts.

1 Introduction

What is cooperation? When autonomous agents attempt to achieve social goals, cooperation is necessary so that the actions of the agents are coordinated. An agent B cooperates with an agent A by adjusting his goals and intentions to help agent A achieve his goals. There are styles of cooperation. These styles range from being totally cooperative to being completely selfish. Any given agent B has a particular style, and this style may vary with context. For example, the agent may be cooperative with some agents and not at all with others. The style of cooperation is in part determined by the conditions for being cooperative at all and in part by the willingness to compromise intentions and goals. Cooperation algorithms describe the cooperation styles of an agent. The interactions among autonomous agents are guided by their cooperation algorithms.

In this paper a class of cooperation algorithms is explored that describe a whole range of cooperation styles from selfless to selfish. To accomplish this we first develop a formal theory of the cognitive structure of the agents. In particular we describe the agents intentional states and show how such states interact to achieve agent goals. The cooperation algorithms describe how the goals and intentions of the agents are updated. We develop a general structure that specifies cooperation algorithm types. Then, we look at some typical styles of cooperation as instances of the general cooperation algorithm structure. Finally, we make some observations about the interactions between cooperation styles.

2 Cognitive States of Situated Agents

The agents that are governed by cooperation algorithms are situated in an historical and informational context. These agents have partial state information about the world as well as partial strategic information about the goals and intentions of other agents. Furthermore, they have their own goals and intentions. We first formally define the temporal situations which determine the theater of action for distributed agents.

While we are in agreement with Winograd and Flores [86] that situation theory cannot account for and ignores the social aspects of language, Barwise and Perry have been prematurely accused of "naive realism" by Winograd and Flores [86]. Situation theory can be used as a theory of representation. It is so used here. The definitions of cognitive states of agents make use of situations as basic partial state and event representations.

Winograd and Flores also argue against the use of cognitive states, e.g., intentional states, and argue for a "social dimension" as opposed to a mental one that uses mental states. However, they propose a naive symbolic interactionism without mental states that cannot explain the intricacies of cooperative action. On the contrary, we propose that social phenomena are supported by social minds, i.e., agents with a social competence. A theory of mental states is needed to account for cooperation and how cooperation is related to communication [Werner 89b]. Furthermore, we propose that something like a theory of intentional states is needed to give a rigorous account of the notion of structural coupling between agents. In Winograd and Flores structural coupling is left ill-defined, vague, and virtually without content. Finally, as argued in [Werner 88b] the very notion of speech act force requires the notion of intentional state for its deeper pragmatic meaning. We now outline a theory of cognitive states that can be used as a basis for understanding cooperation and cooperation algorithms.

2.1 Temporal Situations

Let P, $P_1, \ldots$, be *properties*, and R^n, R^n_1, $\ldots$, be *n-ary relations* for $n \geq 2$. Let O be the set of *individuals*. Let T be the set of *time instants* ordered by a relation $<$. The elements of T will be denoted by t, t', t_1, etc. Let TP be the set of *time periods*. Elements of TP will be denoted by τ, τ'.

A *situation* s is a set of objects in O that have properties P and that stand in various relations R^n to one another. For example, $s = \{Pa; yes.\ Qa; no.\ R(a,b); yes.\}$ is a situation where property P holds of a, a does not have the property Q, nothing is said about b's properties, and a is related to b by the relationship R. Let *Sits* be the set of all possible situations.

A *state* σ is a complete, static situation where all properties and relations are specified for all objects in O. Let Σ be the set of all states. *Histories* or *worlds* are series of states. More formally, a *history* H is a function from times T to the set of states Σ. Let H_t be the value of the function H at t. H_t is state of the world H at time t. Let Ω be the set of all possible *histories* or *worlds* H. Let H^t be the *partial history* of H up to and including the time $t \in T$. Let $Hist(\Omega)$ be the set of possible *partial histories* H^t for all times $t \in T$. Partial histories H^t are then partial functions where $H^t_{t_0}$ is the state of the partial history at time t_0. *Events* are dynamic situations over a time period τ, i.e., events are functions taking times $t \in \tau$ to situations $s \in Sits$. *Actions* a are events with agents given by the function $Agent(a)$. $Time(event)$ is the time period of the event. An event e is *realized* in H at τ if e is contained in H and the domain of e is time period τ (See Barwise and Perry [83]).

2.2 Information States

An *information state* I is a set of partial histories that are possible given the available information. Each information set I has an associated set of alternatives or choices *Alt(I)*. Each *alternative* is a set of possible histories leaving I. $Time(I)$ is the time indicated by the information I. We assume $Time(I)$ is unique. The possible information states of an agent A in the environment Ω form an *information partition* Ξ_A (see [Werner 89a]).

2.3 Intentional States and Goals

The intentions of an agent control the actions of that agent. The intentional state of an agent is the overall state that specifies what the agent would do in various contexts. Such intentional states are normally partial or incomplete, because the agents will usually be uncertain in advance as to what actions to take. Moreover, the strategic knowledge an agent has of another agent's intentions will normally also be incomplete. The formal definition of intentional state makes use of the notion of strategy. We define an intentional state as a class of strategies S where any strategy π in S is a possible candidate that may be, given the strategic knowledge available, controlling that agent's actions. A strategy π' that is not in S is known not to be controlling the agent's actions.

We distinguish between *active goals* that actually guide an agent's actions and goals that are only being considered as possible candidates for becoming active goals of an agent. Wants, for example, can be nonactive goals. An agent can have conflicting wants as long as they are not simultaneously active goals.

We now define these ideas more precisely: A *strategy* π is a function from information states I to the alternatives at I. $STRAT$ is the set of all possible strategies. Let $STRAT_A$ be the set of all possible strategies for agent A. π^* is the set of possible histories consistent with the strategy π, i.e., $\pi^* = \{H : H \in \pi_A(I), \forall I \in \Xi_A(H)\}$. $\Xi_A(H) = \{I : I \in \Xi_A \text{ and } \exists t \in T, H^t \in I\}$. We refer to π^* as the *potential* of the strategy π.

An *intentional state* S_A of an agent A is defined to be a class of strategies that govern the actions of the agent where $S_A \subseteq STRAT_A$. The uncertainty of one agent A about the intentions of another agent B can also be defined as a class of strategies. S_A^B represents agent A's knowledge and uncertainty about B's intentions.

A goal g generates a set g^* of possible worlds H that are compatible with g. g^* consists of all those histories where the goal g holds. Formally, the *potential* g^* of a goal g is a subset of the class of possible histories Ω, i.e., $g^* \subseteq \Omega$. A *goal combination* gc is an ordered set of goals. gc is ordered by a *goal ranking relation* $<_{rank}$. Let *Goals*(gc) be the unordered set of goals in gc.

The *potential of a class of strategies* S is the set of all histories that are compatible with at least one of the strategies in S. It is defined as follows: $S^* =_{df} \bigcup_{\pi \in S} \pi^*$.

A strategy π *satisfies* a goal combination gc relative to the intentions S_A^B if the strategy together with the intentions brings about the goals in the goal combination gc.

Formally, *Satisfies*(π, gc, S_B^A) holds if and only if $\pi^* \cap S_B^{A*} \subseteq \bigcap_{g \in Goals(gc)} g^*$

In terms of a satisfaction relation $\Vert\!\rightarrow$ satisfaction can be equivalently expressed as follows: $\pi_B \otimes S_B^A \Vert\!\rightarrow gc$. This states that the composition $\pi_B \otimes S_B^A$ *satisfies (guarantees)* gc. In [Werner 88a, 89b] we used the term *forces*, but this sometimes led to the unintended misinterpretation that one agent attains cooperation from another agent only under duress. All that is meant is that the intentional states together insure that the goal will hold. It says nothing about how the cooperation was obtained.

A class of strategies S_B satisfies a goal combination gc relative to agent B's knowledge of A's intentions S_B^A if those two strategy classes together bring about the goals in the goal combination. More formally,

Satisfies(S_B, gc, S_B^A) holds if and only if $S_B^* \cap S_B^{A*} \subseteq \bigcap_{g \in Goals(gc)} g^*$. In terms of the satisfaction relation this can be equivalently stated as: $S_B \otimes S_B^A \Vert\!\rightarrow gc$.

A class of strategies $\hat{S}_B$ is *maximal* for gc relative to S_B^A, if for all π that satisfy gc, then $\pi \in S_B$, i.e., $\hat{S}_B = \{\pi : Satisfies(\pi, gc, S_B^A)\}$. Thus a class of strategies $\hat{S}_B$ is maximal for a goal combination gc if the class contains all strategies that satisfy the goal combination, relative to what B knows about A's intentions.

2.4 Representational States

The *cognitive* or *representational state* R of an agent is described by three components $R = <I, S, V>$. I is the *information state* of the agent. S is the *intentional state* of the agent. S is a set of possible strategies that guide the actions of the agent. S includes the goals g that are active in controlling the agent. V is the *evaluative state* of the agent. V represents the agent's evaluation and focus on situations. The evaluations in the evaluative state include the ranking of goals as well as the knowledge about the rankings that other agents make of their goals. The representational state R_A may include the agent A's representation of B's representation, R_A^B. It may also include the agent A's representation of B's representation of A's representation, R_A^{BA}. Thus we can represent arbitrary levels of nesting of representations. Let INF, INT, and EVAL be the set of all possible information, intentional and evaluative states, respectively. Let the *representational capacity*, *Rep*, be the set of all possible representational states of an agent. For the theoretical foundations and some of the principles interrelating intention, information and ability, see Werner [88d].

3 The Preconditions to Cooperation

Cooperation is a kind of agent interaction. It is a process. Many authors confuse cooperation with the preconditions for cooperation. While the preconditions for an agent being cooperative are a part of the cooperative or noncooperative nature of the agent, the coordination of multiagent action is produced through an active process of cooperation and not by the preconditions to that process.

The conditions under which an agent will cooperate in part determine the cooperativity of the agent. If, for example, an agent will not cooperate under any conditions, then, no matter how nonselfish the agent's cooperation algorithm may be, the agent is in effect noncooperative. The more stringent the preconditions to cooperation the less cooperative the agent. The more generous the conditions under which an agent will cooperate, the more cooperative we judge the agent to be.

Cooperation rules can be used to describe the conditions under which an agent will cooperate. Consider a cooperative situation involving a computer system and a user. The rules may be of many different forms: *If Want(User, Goal) then Want(System, Goal)*. This is a (simplified) rule for adding new goals to the system goals. Here, the system adds the user goal as one of its own goals. Under this rule the system is slaved to user wants and cannot deny user wants. Furthermore, using this rule, duplication of effort, interference, etc., are possible shortcomings.

Another rule might be: *If Want(User, Goal) and Not Can(User, Goal) and Co-can(System, User, Goal) then Cooperate(System, User, Goal)*. Here, the system first makes sure the user cannot achieve the goal alone and that the system and user together cooperatively can [Werner 90] achieve the goal before invoking a cooperation procedure to help the user achieve the goal. A little thought will convince the reader that there are many shortcomings with this rule as well. For, here again, the system is slaved to user wants. However, this effect can be ameliorated if the system has a semiself-interested cooperative style (see below). In spite of these shortcomings we presented these rules here to illustrate how such rules might be used to add new goals and to invoke cooperation procedures. Furthermore, we want to show the difference between such rules and the cooperation process itself.

Cooperativity is a property of agents. The ascription of the predicate '*is cooperative*' is in part determined by the preconditions to an agents being cooperative and in part by the cooperation style of the agent. Having briefly looked at the preconditions to cooperation, the rest of the paper will concentrate on the process of cooperation.

4 The Structure of Cooperation Algorithms

A cooperation algorithm describes a cooperation style of an agent. The algorithm takes the perspective of the agent it governs. We call the agent that the algorithm governs the *active* or *cooperating agent.* When an active agent B is controlled by an algorithm, we will say the algorithm takes B's *perspective.* In this paper we assume that there are two agents A and B who are interacting and each controlled by their own cooperation algorithm. The results can be generalized to an agent cooperating with n other agents since the intentions of groups of agents can be taken into consideraton as well [Werner 90].

If the active agent is B, i.e., the cooperation algorithm takes B's perspective, then the input to the algorithm is a set of new active and not yet active goals in the goal sets G_A and G_B of agents A and B. Additional input is what the cooperating agent B knows about the intentions of the other agent A. The output is a maximal partial intentional state $\hat{S}$ that achieves some, possibly compromised, subset of the goals of A and B. When this maximal partial intentional state is composed with the agent's given intentional state S_B, a new intentional state S'_B is formed that describes the new intentions of the agent B.

A cooperation algorithm is thus part of a complex operator on the intentional states of the agent it governs. Since a cooperation style forms intentions, it can be viewed as a *meta-intentional state* of an agent. The cooperation style described by a particular cooperation algorithm is a dynamic, context dependent meta-intentional state. The cooperation style of an agent will vary with context, including the agents that the cooperating agent is interacting with.

4.1 Cooperation Procedures

Let G_A and G_B be the set of goals of two agents A and B. The algorithm takes B's perspective. The algorithm assumes that A's goals are known to B by some prior process, e.g., by communication and through a model that B has of A. Note, we do not assume that B has perfect information about A's intentions, i.e., the strategies and plans that guide B's actions.

We now describe the general structure of cooperation algorithms by looking at the key procedure types that constitute such algorithms. In the procedures below we assume the following variable type declarations with the interpretations specified above: A, B: agent; G_B, G_A: goal-set; $\hat{S}_B$, S_B^A: strategy-class; gc: goal-combination.

Procedure *Cooperation*$(B, A, G_B, G_A, \hat{S}_B, S_B^A)$
begin
    Initialize(gc, G_A, G_B);
    Cooperate$(B, A, gc, \hat{S}_B, S_B^A)$
end.

The procedure *Cooperation* consists of two core procedures: an initialization procedure which ranks the goals of the agents and a procedure *Cooperate* that attempts to come up with an intentional state that satisfies as many goals as possible given the priorities inherent in the ranking of goals. A key feature is the way goals are compromised when all the given goals are not simultaneously satisfiable.

Procedure *Initialize*(gc, G_A, G_B)
begin
    Rankgoals(G_A, G_B);
    Let $gc := \{G_A \cup G_B, <_{rank}\}$;
    Return gc
end.

The procedure *Initialize* ranks the goals in G_A, G_B by a goal ranking relation $<_{rank}$ and assigns the goal combination gc the combined set of goals ordered by the ranking relation $<_{rank}$. It then returns the goal combination gc.

Procedure *Cooperate*$(B, A, gc, \hat{S}_B, S_B^A)$
begin
    Find a maximal $\hat{S}_B$ that *Satisfies*$(\hat{S}_B, gc, S_B^A)$;
    if $\hat{S}_B$ not found **and** *Compromise*$(gc) \neq$ *empty set*
    then *Cooperate*$(B, A,$ *Compromise*$(gc), \hat{S}_B, S_B^A)$;
    if $\hat{S}_B$ found **then** *Return* $\hat{S}_B$

else *Return fail*
end.

The procedure *Cooperate* tries to find a set of strategies $\hat{S}_B$ that satisfies as many of the goals of A and B as possible. If there is no such set of strategies to be found, then it compromises and tries to cooperate with the compromised set of goals.

The set of strategies $\hat{S}_B$ is *maximal.* What that means is that the procedure finds a whole set of strategies each of which satisfies the goals in gc. Thereby, the procedure makes the minimal commitment as to which strategy will actually be followed. The set of strategies $\hat{S}_B$ is, in effect, a partial or general plan that is minimally constrained. Because the generated partially specified strategy $\hat{S}_B$ makes minimal commitments, it avoids overcommitment. As a result, it can be combined with other constraints on intentions to form new intentional states in the agent with a minimal chance of conflict.

The agent B cooperates using his knowledge of A's intentions, since the general plan $\hat{S}_B$ satisfies the goal combination gc relative to B's information S_B^A of A's intentions.

Function *Compromise*(gc)
begin
Generate the next goal combination gc' from gc;
$gc := gc'$;
Return gc
end.

The compromise algorithm generates the next goal combination gc' and returns it. Given a linearly ordered *compromise graph CompGraph* $= \{gc_1, \ldots, gc_n\}$ of all goal combinations gc, then *Compromise*(gc_i) $= gc_{i+1}$. Thus, given an ordered compromise graph of goal combinations, we can define a compromise function, *compromise*(gc), and, vice versa, given a compromise function we generate a compromise graph of goal combinations.

4.2 An Alternative Top-Down Cooperation Algorithm

In the cooperation procedures described above together with the compromise functions described below, we start with the largest goal combination $gc := \{G_A \cup G_B, <_{rank}\}$. If this is not consistent with S_B^A, then we take out the lowest ranked goal combination gc (an individual goal at the outset) and see if we get a conflict free goal set. If not, we take out the next lowest ranking goal combination, etc., until we find a conflict free goal set. In effect, all combinations are considered, the largest first and then we systematically try to find the minimal reduction of that set.

We now describe a different approach. We start with the highest ranked goal and try to satisfy it, then we proceed to the next highest goal and try to satisfy it and the previously satisfied goals. If we fail at any point, we simply drop that goal, keeping the higher ranked goals and go on to try to satisfy the next highest ranked goal.

More specifically, given goal sets G_A and G_B at a given time t, agent B can cooperate with A in that he chooses strategies π_B that do not conflict with his knowledge of A's goals and intentions. B's representation of A's goals and intentions is given by G_A and

S_B^A, respectively. Let $G_A = \{g_A^1, \ldots, g_A^n\}$ and $G_B = \{g_B^1, \ldots, g_B^n\}$. A can sequentially process the goals in G_A and G_B, keeping his strategy S_B as open as possible. B can do this as follows:

He successively takes goals g off the top of the ranked list of goals, finds the maximally open S_B such that $S_B \otimes S_B^A \Vert\!\rightarrow g$ where $S_B = \{\pi_B : \pi_B \otimes S_B^A \Vert\!\rightarrow g\}$. Each new goal g leads to a reduction of S_B, since we take the given goal g and the given intentions S_B and update S_B to $S'_B := \{\pi_B : \pi_B \in S_B \text{ and } \pi_B \otimes S_B^A \Vert\!\rightarrow g\}$.

If the new goal g conflicts with the given set S_B, i.e., $\neg\exists\pi_B \in S_B$ such that $\pi_B \otimes S_B^A \Vert\!\rightarrow g$, then the goal g can be relaxed or dropped. If g is relaxed to $relax(g)$ we attempt to satisfy it by setting S_B to $S_B := \{\pi_B : \pi_B \in S_B \text{ and } \pi_B \otimes S_B^A \Vert\!\rightarrow relax(g)\}$. If no relaxation of g works, then g is dropped and we proceed to the next highest ranking unprocessed goal. Note, g can be dropped because further interactions with other goals do not occur. For, if some later lower ranked goal g' makes g possible, then g was possible all along since S_B is maximally open. Even if some goal g fails at rank n, lower ranked goals are still processed since they may still be satisfiable. The output of the algorithm is a class of strategies S_B that satisfies the maximal set of goals relative to the highest rank.

It should be noted that the Top-Down Cooperative Algorithm ignores lower ranked conflicting goals even if the sum of the ranks of those goals is greater than the rank of the higher conflicting goal. A more subtle approach would take into consideration both the rank and the value of the goals. We will not consider the Top-Down Algorithm further in this paper.

5 Styles of Cooperation

Various styles of cooperation come about through the unique characteristics of the compromise procedure. How much an agent is willing to give up and how much an agent is willing to take on in terms of other agents' goals gives that agent an individual style of interaction. Fundamental to the compromise procedure is how the goals of the agents are ranked. Then, given a ranking of the goals, the graph of goal combinations determines the unique compromise style of the agent.

The graph of goal combinations is generated by the function *Compromise* which takes a goal combination gc and generates a new goal combination gc'. A goal combination gc is just a sequence of goals whose members come from the goal sets G_A and G_B. The set of goal combinations form a graph and not a sequence because the ordering of goal combinations is a partial ordering. It is partial because some goal combinations are of equal value. Since the order of equally valued goal combinations makes no difference for the algorithms at this level of abstraction, we simplify matters by replacing the goal combination graph with a sequence of goal combinations that maintains the order of the graph for nonindifferent goal combinations.

We now will describe different goal combination sequences (compromise graphs) which result from different compromise functions. Alternatively, we could take the sequence as given and use it to define the compromise function where *Compromise* $(gc_i) = gc_{i+1}$ in the compromise graph. In these examples we restrict the algorithm to two agents A and B where B is the agent that the algorithm is describing. The first goal combination in the compromise graph is the result of the ranking procedure. It is the first input to the compromise function and the first compromise is then the second member gc_2 in the compromise graph.

5.1 Total Cooperation with Secondary Self-Interest

The totally cooperative agent B always puts the other agent A's goals G_A ahead of his own goals G_B. If the agent has self-interest, he will still try to satisfy his own goals, but only if that does not interfere with the attainment of A's goals. The following compromise function in the context of the cooperation algorithm will generate totally cooperative behavior with secondary self-interest. Let $G_A = \{g_A^1, g_A^2\}$, $G_B = \{g_B^1, g_B^2\}$.

Recall, that the procedure *Cooperation*$(B, A, G_B, G_A, S_B, S_B^A)$ begins by ranking the goals where $gc :=$ *Rankgoals*(G_A, G_B). Ranking yields: $gc = gc_1 = < g_A^1, g_A^2, g_B^1, g_B^2 >$. The procedure *Cooperate*$(B, A, gc, \hat{S}_B, S_B^A)$ is then called. It finds a maximal $\hat{S}_B$ that *Satisfies*$(\hat{S}_B, gc, S_B^A)$. If no such $\hat{S}_B$ is found, then *Cooperate*$(B, A, Compromise(gc), \hat{S}_B, S_B^A)$ is recursively called on the compromised set of goals.

The function *Compromise* generates the following compromise graph:

1. Initially $gc = gc_1 = < g_A^1, g_A^2, g_B^1, g_B^2 >$
2. $Compromise(gc_1) = < g_A^1, g_A^2, g_B^1 >$
3. $Compromise(gc_2) = < g_A^1, g_A^2, g_B^2 >$
4. $Compromise(gc_3) = < g_A^1, g_A^2 >$
5. $Compromise(gc_4) = < g_A^1, g_B^1, g_B^2 >$
6. $Compromise(gc_5) = < g_A^1, g_B^1 >$
7. $Compromise(gc_6) = < g_A^1, g_B^2 >$
8. $Compromise(gc_7) = < g_A^1 >$
9. $Compromise(gc_8) = < g_A^2, g_B^1, g_B^2 >$
10. $Compromise(gc_9) = < g_A^2, g_B^1 >$
11. $Compromise(gc_{10}) = < g_A^2, g_B^2 >$
12. $Compromise(gc_{11}) = < g_A^2 >$
13. $Compromise(gc_{12}) = < g_B^1, g_B^2 >$
14. $Compromise(gc_{13}) = < g_B^1 >$
15. $Compromise(gc_{14}) = < g_B^2 >$

In this method of generating compromises the least ranked goals are given up first. We, therefore, will refer to this method as the *minimal modification method* of generating compromises.

5.2 Complete Selfishness with Secondary Cooperation

The completely selfish agent A will place his own goals G_A first. He will rank his own goals ahead of the goals G_B of another agent B. Any cooperation he displays will be secondary to the achievement of his own goals. Interestingly, the selfish agent will rank the goals in G_A and G_B exactly as the cooperative agent does. This is because, when A puts himself first and B puts himself last, we get the same ranking in the case of two agents. For similar reasons, the compromise function will also be exactly the same. While the selfish agent A always compromises the other agent's goals, the cooperative agent B always compromises his own goals. Thus, the selfish agent and the cooperative agent both compromise the same set of goals first, namely, the cooperative agent's goals G_B. The following describes how the cooperation algorithm works for the selfish agent with secondary cooperation: Let $G_A = \{g_A^1, g_A^2\}$ and $G_B = \{g_B^1, g_B^2\}$.

Now, when the procedure *Cooperation* is called the following occurs:

- $Cooperation(A, B, G_A, G_B, S_A, S_A^B)$ is called.
- Ranking yields the same combination as for cooperative agents with secondary self-interest: $gc = gc_1 = < g_A^1, g_A^2, g_B^1, g_B^2 >$.
- Then the subprocedure $Cooperate(A, B, gc, \hat{S}_A, S_A^B)$ is called.
- It finds a maximal $\hat{S}_A$ that $Satisfies(S_A, gc, S_A^B)$.
- If no such $\hat{S}_A$ is found, then *Cooperate* is called on the compromised goal combination as follows: $Cooperate(A, B, Compromise(gc), \hat{S}_A, S_A^B)$.

5.3 Complete Selfishness with no Secondary Cooperation

In this algorithm A follows his own goals ruthlessly taking no consideration of B except to use B if that furthers his ends. A totally selfish agent may not even make secondary compromises, except incidentally, in so far as they are generated as a side effect of achieving his own goals. His compromise function would yield a compromise graph of the following sort for two agents:

1. Initially $gc = gc_1 = < g_A^1, g_A^2 >$
2. $Compromise(gc_1) = < g_A^1 >$
3. $Compromise(gc_2) = < g_A^2 >$

Let us call a totally selfish agent with no secondary cooperation a *self-centered agent*. In other words the self-centered agent A would not even think of satisfying the goals of other agents even if the satisfaction of those goals G_B would not harm his own goals. The self-centered agent would not even rank, let alone compromise, those goals since he is oblivious to the needs of other agents. Note, although the self-centered agent does not consider the goals of other agents when forming his plans, the self-centered agent still makes use of his knowledge of the intentions S_A^B of other agents. Thus, the self-centered agent uses other agents to attain his goals. In the case of more than two agents, an agent A may be self-centered with regard to B, but cooperative with respect to C. Indeed, the agent may use the knowledge of B's intentions S_A^B to help agent C attain his goals.

5.4 Total Cooperation with No Secondary Self-Interest

An entirely similar compromise style governs the selfless agent B that ignores his own goals and considers only the goals of other agents. Indeed, the ranking and compromise functions are identical to the completely self-centered agent. The selfless agent and the self-centered agent are the complements of one another. Fascinating, is the thought that just a switch in perspective changes a self-sacrificing agent to a self-centered agent.

5.5 Mixtures of Cooperation and Self-Interest

Between the extremes of pure cooperation and complete selfishness there is every possible mixture of cooperativity and self-interest. The degree of cooperativity depends on the ranking function and the compromise function. How the goals are ranked and how the goal combinations are then generated determines the extent to which the given agent is cooperative or not.

5.5.1 Cooperativity within Rank

For example, an agent B might rank the goal sets $G_A = \{g_A^1, g_A^2\}$ and $G_B = \{g_B^1, g_B^2\}$, as follows:

$$Rankgoals(G_A, G_B) = gc_1 = < g_A^1, g_B^1, g_A^2, g_B^2 >$$

If the goal combinations are generated by the above minimal modification method, then, depending on who is the active agent, this leads to cooperativity or selfishness within a given rank or level n. Thus, the attempt is made to satisfy all goals of rank n whether these are the agent's own goals or another agent's goals of rank n.

In this mixture the cooperative agent B still maintains his interests up to priority n. Still the agent B may not satisfy any of his goals if it so happens that at each level n his goals g_B^n conflict with A's goals g_A^n.

On the other hand, the selfish agent A is no longer completely selfish. Indeed, at each rank n he puts his interest above the other agent's. However, the other agent's higher prioritiy goals g_B^n are always given preference to his own lower priority goals g_A^k for $k < n$. From that perspective agent A is very cooperative.

5.5.2 Cooperativity up to Rank

Another form of mixing cooperation and self-interest is cooperation up to a certain level or rank and after that placing one's own goals ahead of the other agent's goals. For example, let the goal sets $G_A = \{g_A^1, g_A^2, g_A^3\}$ and $G_B = \{g_B^1, g_B^2, g_B^3\}$. Let the ranking function produce the following:

$$Rankgoals(G_A, G_B) = < g_B^1, g_A^1, g_A^2, g_A^3, g_B^2, g_B^3 >$$

Let the goal combinations be generated by the minimal modification method.

If B is the active cooperating agent, then with this compromise style B is very cooperative for all lower level goals up to rank n. Still, B preserves his interests for his high priority goals, those at level n and above. ($n - 1$ in this example).

If A is the active agent, then by this ranking and compromise method A is cooperative for important goals but selfish for unimportant goals. This sort of cooperative style may seem irrational. Yet, some might describe this agent as the sort that will help when one really needs him.

6 Relaxation and Alternatives to Resolve Conflicts

Beyond simply dropping a goal when it conflicts with higher priority goals, one might relax the goal or one might replace the goal with an alternative. Relaxation involves the abstraction of some of the features of the goal making it less specific and, thereby, more easily satisfiable. For example, the goal g_2 of going down Oak Street may conflict with the higher priority goal g_1 of seeing Mary. If we relax the goal of walking down Oak Street to that of going to the store $relax(g_2)$, then the relaxed goal may be satisfiable if, for instance, Mary lives on Elm Street, which is also on the way to the store.

6.1 A Relaxation Hierarchy

One approach for the generation of alternatives is to postulate a *relaxation hierarchy* where more abstract goals are higher up on the relaxation tree. Going back down the tree by a different branch yields an alternative goal of the same type. Another approach to generating alternative goals is to associate a set of alternatives directly with a given goal instead of indirectly through a relaxation hierarchy.

Clearly, we could extend the above compromise functions to included relaxation and the generation of alternatives. The compromise function would first go through various relaxation steps and possible alternative generation steps before finally dropping a goal. We now get more subtle forms of cooperation and selfishness depending on the willingness of an agent to relax his goals or come up with alternative goals.

6.2 Selfish Relaxation

Another style of cooperation results from agents that use relaxation and alternatives for themselves more than for others or vice versa. For example consider the following partial compromise graph:

1. Initially $gc = gc_1 = < g_A^1, g_A^2, g_B^1, g_B^2 >$
2. $Compromise(gc_1) = < g_A^1, g_A^2, g_B^1 >$
3. $Compromise(gc_2) = < g_A^1, g_A^2, g_B^2 >$
4. $Compromise(gc_3) = < g_A^1, g_A^2 >$
5. $Compromise(gc_4) = < g_A^1, relax(g_A^2), g_B^1, g_B^2 >$
6. $Compromise(gc_5) = < g_A^1, relax(g_A^2), g_B^1 >$
7. $Compromise(gc_6) = < g_A^1, relax(g_A^2), g_B^2 >$
8. $Compromise(gc_7) = < g_A^1, relax(g_A^2) >$
9. $Compromise(gc_8) = < relax(g_A^1), g_A^2, g_B^1, g_B^2 >$

. . .

In this case the selfish agent A relaxes his own goals, but not those of B. If B is the active agent, then B is even more cooperative than before. He not only ranks the other agent's goals ahead of his own, he further attempts to satisfy those goals by relaxation while not relaxing his own goals. This is a truly accommodating agent.

7 Interactions Among Cooperation Styles

When two agents A and B with cooperation styles C_A and C_B interact, the goals that are achieved will depend on those styles. A selfish agent A interacting with a totally cooperative agent B will result in each agent satisfying the same goal combination as the other agent.

Two selfish agents will each attempt to satisfy their own goals first. If their goals are not in conflict, then both will satisfy their goals. If their goal sets conflict, then one or the other or both will not be able to satisfy all of their goals.

Of special interest is the fact that two totally cooperative agents will have an interaction result that is equivalent to the interaction result of two completely selfish agents. For the cooperative agents will attempt to satisfy the other agents' goals as if they were their own goals. In effect, the agents will be competing as noncooperative agents except that they have switched roles. One way to resolve this sort of *overcooperativity* is to have the agents recognize their cooperation styles and then form a new compromise on that basis.

8 Knowledge of Cooperation Styles

When persons get to know one another they also get to know the cooperation styles of the other. They come to know in what contexts and with whom a given person is cooperative, noncooperative, indifferent or competitive. Such knowledge of cooperation style may be placed in the representation of that agent's intentional state. The intentional state guides the agent's actions and in this case is decomposable into distinct cooperation styles. Which subintentional state (cooperation style) is active will depend on complex factors that include the social relations and other goals of the given agent. Looked at dynamically, given a new set of goals G_A and G_B, the cooperation style generates a new intentional state S_B in the cooperating agent B. Whether we place the cooperation algorithms within the intentional state of the agent or view them as *meta-intentions* that operate on simpler intentional states is a methodological and theoretical issue which may depend on other theoretical or practical system design constraints.

Whichever approach we choose, the agent must have a way of representing partial knowledge of cooperation styles. Given that that is the case, an agent B will be better off knowing that agent A is noncooperative than not knowing the cooperation style of the agent at all. We can then also investigate the dynamics of uncertainty and information about cooperation styles.

9 Limitations and Extensions

9.1 Multi-Rankings

The ranking of the goals in G_A and G_B may be different for each agent. In this paper we consider only the ranking that the active agent gives to the goals. We assumed that B's ranking of A's goals corresponds to the ranking made by the other agent A. A possible extension is to allow an agent a partial representation of another agent's ranking function. A further measure of cooperativity would then include the extent to which the active agent is willing to assume the same ordering of goals.

9.2 Metaknowledge About Intentions

The knowledge that one agent has about the intentions of another can significantly affect the intentions of both agents to the degree that there is metaknowledge about that knowledge. In our algorithms we have implicitly assumed that during the construction of the intentions $\hat{S}_B$ the intentions of the other agent are not affected either by metaknowledge or knowledge about intentions. Thus, we assumed that the process of finding a partial strategy $\hat{S}$ which forms new intentions in the active agent B does not effect the intentions of the other agent A. For the agent B considers only his knowledge S_B^A and not what happens to the intentions S_A (and, hence, to S_B^A) when agent A attains knowledge about B's newly formed intentions $\hat{S}_B$.

9.3 Communication, Roles and Social Context

Closely related to and a way out of the problem about metaknowledge and the resulting unwanted interactions between the intentional states of agents is communication. Not considered in this paper is the communication necessary to avoid duplication of effort, to avoid the undoing of actions and to insure the necesarry coordination. For more details see [Werner 88a,b; 89b]. Implicitly, communication is part of the strategies in $\hat{S}$ generated by the procedure *Cooperate*. However, the coopertion algorithm as it stands assumes the intentions of the other are constant. Therefore, communication and social roles (contractual agreements as to who does what) are necessary to avoid overcooperation between agents. Communication and cooperation algorithms need to be integrated.

Also not considered in this paper is the social context within which the agents find themselves. The assumption of a cooperative style by an agent may well depend on the power relations in which the agent finds himself. (See Castelfranchi and Parunak this volume). Thus the preconditions to cooperation may well need to consider the social roles of agents [Werner 88c, 89b]

10 Conclusion

What is cooperation? We see that cooperation is composed of a multiplicity of factors. First, the preconditions to an agent's being cooperative determine the readiness of an agent to assume a particular cooperative style. This may vary with the situation and the agents. Second, the cooperative style is in large part determined by nature of the willingness of the agent to compromise. And, this in turn depends on how the agent ranks his and others goals. Third, the actual process of cooperation involves the construction of an intentional state that, in context of the other agent's intentions, satisfies the goals as much as possible relative to their ranking.

We have described a whole range of types of cooperative and noncooperative behavior by way of describing the algorithms that govern the cooperative style of an agent. These algorithms transform the cognitive states of agents, in particular, the intentions of such agents. The process of cooperation (noncooperation) is generated by the ensuing harmonious (disharmonious) intentional states that govern the actions of the agents. Many open problems remain. We regard this as a first step in the analysis of high-level algorithms that underlie cooperative behaviour.

References

[Agha 86] Agha, G.A., ACTORS: A Model of Concurrent Computation in Distributed Systems, MIT Press, London 1986.

[Barwise & Perry 83] Barwise, J., and Perry, J., SITUATIONS AND ATTITUDES, Bradford Books/MIT Press, 1983.

[Bochmann 83] Bochmann, G.v., Concepts for DISTRIBUTED SYSTEM DESIGN, Springer-Verlag, Berlin 1983.

[Bratman 87] Bratman,M., INTENTION, PLANS, AND PRACTICAL REASON, Harvard University Press, London 1987.

[Milner 1980] Milner, R., A CALCULUS OF COMMUNICATING SYSTEMS, Springer-Verlag, New York 1980.

[Werner 88a] Werner, E., "Toward a Theory of Communication and Cooperation for Multiagent Planning", THEORETICAL ASPECTS OF REASONING ABOUT KNOWLEDGE: Proceedings of the 2nd Conference, Morgan Kaufman Publishers, pp. 129-142, 1988a.

[Werner 88b] Werner, E., "A Formal Computational Semantics and Pragmatics of Speech Acts", COLING-88, Proceedings of the 12th International Conference on Computational Linguistics, Budapest, Hungary, 1988b.

[Werner 88c] Werner, E., "Social Intentions", Panel on Interaction Among Intelligent Agents, Proceedings of the 8th European Conference on Artificial Intelligence, Munich, Germany, pp. 719-723, 1988c.

[Werner 88d] Werner, E., "Intention, Information and Ability: Outline of a Unified Theory", WISBER Report Nr. B37, University of Hamburg, West Germany, 1988d.

[Werner 89a] Werner, E., "The Modal Logic of Games", WISBER Report Nr. B48, University of Hamburg, West Germany, 1989a.

[Werner 89d] Werner, E., "Cooperating Agents: A Unified Theory of Communication and Social Structure", *Distributed Artificial Intelligence, Vol. 2*, M. Huhns & L. Gasser (eds.), Morgan Kaufmann and Pitman Publishers, London, pp. 3-36, 1989b.

[Werner 90] Werner, E., "A Semantics of Cooperative Ability", to appear, 1990a.

[Winograd & Flores 86] Winograd, T., and Flores, F., UNDERSTANDING COMPUTERS AND COGNITION: A New Foundation For Design, Ablex Publishing Corp., Norwood, New Jersey, 1986.

DECENTRALIZED A.I.
Yves DEMAZEAU & Jean-Pierre MÜLLER (Eds.)

THE POSITIVE ROLE OF CONFLICT IN COOPERATIVE MULTI-AGENT SYSTEMS

Julia Rose GALLIERS

University of Cambridge Computer Laboratory
Cambridge CB2 3QG, (ENGLAND)

This paper describes some of the primary theoretical concerns of a research project recently completed at the Open University, England. A theoretical framework for computer models of cooperative multi-agent dialogue was developed as a preliminary to future implementations which use negotiation and the resolution of differences in cooperative activity [15,16]. The envisaged applications encompass both human computer interaction (HCI) contexts, and distributed artificial intelligence (DAI). The aim of this paper is not to describe the entire framework, but to focus only on the results of the entailed investigations into the nature of multi-agent cooperation. These investigations were predicated upon initial assumptions about the autonomy of agents.

1 Introduction

In a recent collection of papers on DAI, multi-agent systems are described as being concerned with

> 'coordinating intelligent behaviour among a collection of (possibly pre-existing) autonomous intelligent "agents" how they can coordinate their knowledge, goals, skills and plans jointly to take action or to solve problems' [4].

The operative word here is "coordination". Multi-agent systems are comprised of agents who can coordinate their behaviour, goals, plans and so on. This coordination must be grounded in a cooperative rationality, just as goal-directed behaviour is an expression of a purposive rationality. Whether explicitly stated as properties of agents or implicit in their design, some theory of cooperative rationality is inevitably incorporated into any multi-agent system. Human cooperativity is suggested here as a paradigm for the modelling of cooperativity in multi-agent systems.

Cooperative multi-agent systems are envisaged for future applications requiring joint execution, management, allocation of tasks, between several automated agent(s) (DAI), or between one or more of such agents and human agent(s) (HCI). For many of these applications, the multi-agent systems will be open systems, as characterised by [18]. This means that each agent will be processing information concurrently, with new information entering the system at any time, with each only knowing its own state and communicating what is necessary....in other words, a constantly changing and unpredictable environment where centralised control over the entire system is impossible. In such environments inconsistencies within the system are inevitable. Conflict situations will arise, just as they do in human open systems.

Social psychologists studying human social groups consider conflicts to be an essential and positive force in the maintenance and emergence of cooperation and stability. This is an idea now firmly embedded in current theory, having been revived in the fifties by [8], from the classical work of Simmel [28], and others who wrote at the turn of the century. In artificial intelligence (AI) however, most existing research involving aspects of cooperative multi-agent interaction, has assumed that being a cooperative agent means being benevolent; cooperative agents are always in agreement and ready to adopt each others goals. Conflicts either simply never arise, or are alternatively avoided when they do arise.

If conflicts are understood as playing a positive role in the maintenance of multi-agent cooperation, then AI must reconsider it's ideas about agent design. Cooperative rationality is not comprised of benevolence or conflict avoidance.

Thirty years of conflict studies in social psychology endorse such a dialectic approach to cooperation. Autonomous agents expressing conflicts and resolving them without imposed benevolence, can be flexible in their dealings with unexpected events. Multi-agent systems thus designed can evolve appropriately to changing and unpredicted circumstance, and cooperation be maintained. In contrast, existing AI frameworks and systems are rigid in being constrained by assumed omniscience of some or all agents, centralised control, imposed benevolence or conflict avoidance.

The aim of this paper is to justify and expand upon the position stated above. Firstly, cooperation and conflict are introduced in section 2 as propositional postures[1]. The suggested nature and role of these as representations for autonomous agents in the multi-agent context is outlined, and contrasted with AI's existing notions of cooperation. Section 3 then elaborates the notion of conflict as a positive force in cooperative multi-agent systems.

2 Propositional postures — conflict, cooperation and indifference

Posture is a collective term denoting alternative characterisations of the social concepts, conflict, cooperation and indifference. Each is defined according to a pattern of mental states. Beliefs and goals are mental states; primary cognitive and conative

[1]Acknowledgements to George Kiss for suggesting the term "posture".

propositional attitudes from which models of agents and multi-agents can be derived, as for example in [15,16,5,6]. Beliefs and goals express a relation between an agent and some proposition. Mutual belief is another mental state, one which specifically relates to the multi-agent situation. It expresses a type of cognitive relation between more than one agent and a proposition. Postures define alternative relations also between more than one agent and a proposition, but they are molecular representations built up out of both cognitive and conative elements. For example, (CONFLICT x y p) describes a conflict relation between agents x and y, with respect to the proposition p. It represents a pattern of beliefs and goals reflecting x's attitudes to p and to y's attitudes to p, or a mutual belief about this. Postures generally specify the nature and distinctions between an agent's own attitudes to a proposition and the attitudes believed to be held by another agent with respect to that same proposition. Importantly they must include a conative element or goal related to the believed attitude of the other agent. An explanation for this will be given in the subsection 2.2.

The importance of the representation of posture is in its enablement to potentially then manipulate its maintenance or change. From experience, human agents build up beliefs concerning the effects or consequences of the various postures. Perhaps, for example, having a belief about the divisiveness of conflict between two parties being in a third parties favour, may lead to a goal for this to occur. An example of this is Iago recognising the benefits to himself of conflict over love and loyalty between Othello and Desdemona in Shakespeare's "Othello". More usually, the same belief about the divisiveness of conflict may lead to a desire for its resolution. Automated agents with such beliefs should similarly be able to generate and act according to these goals.

Imagine an example agent x, with a goal for another agent y to perform an action a. However, y is busy with another task. This is a situation of inconsistent goals or (CONFLICT x y (DONE y a)). With a representation of this conflict and a goal for cooperation, x has a prescription of a pattern of mental states she wants to effect in y. Similarly, if y has a representation of a conflict between them with respect to (DONE y a) and also a goal for x's cooperation in the matter, this goal will direct her actions. She has the possibilities of achieving cooperation by either agreeing to do a, or trying to change x's mind, to dissuade x that she wants y to do a. She may indicate to y that she is too tired to do a, for example. Since x not only has the goal (DONE y a) but also (COOPERATION x y (DONE y a)), she also then has a choice. She can drop her goal (DONE y a) thus instantly achieving (COOPERATION x y (DONE y a)), or she can try to achieve both by changing y's mind. For both x and y, there is a choice; they must reason which choice is *preferable*. Preferences are briefly discussed in subsection 2.3. Choices between alternatives are made according to maximal satisfaction of multiple goals, taking their strength or centrality to the agent into account. In this case, it may satisfy more and/or stronger goals in x to be kind to y, and achieve cooperation by dropping the goal (DONE y a), for example.

Without such representations, x and y's actions would be according to the immediate goal (DONE y a) only. y can only agree to x's request or refuse it. There is no mechanism for flexibility and adaptation in the fuller context of the particular relationship and contexts of x and y at that time. For example, in existing AI approaches, y may have been designed as a benevolent agent, in which case she would always take on x's goal unless she had an existing contradictory goal. In this case she has an existing contradictory goal. Alternatively, x may have been designed as a dominant agent and y as subordinate, in which case y always acknowledges x's authority. Alternatively again, another "supervisor" agent might determine whether and how the conflict can be resolved/managed/avoided. This latter approach needs at least one agent to be omniscient, knowing all about all aspects, and all *possible* aspects of the joint environment, (including each other's mental states). It therefore has only limited applicability to closed systems [18].

In human societies there is no overall "controller". Cooperation emerges from selfish agents, each with only partial knowledge of their whole system, and each with their own concerns and responsibilities. My suggestion is that automated agents be modelled similarly. Each should have representations of the benefits (to themselves) and nature of cooperation, the benefits and nature of conflict, and an understanding of the mechanisms by which these postures can be achieved, one from another. To achieve cooperation from conflict for example, may involve deciding a mutually preferred compromise solution [24,7] and/or persuasion to the validity of another position [15,16,29]. Either may involve dialogue as a means of changing mental states, and hence of altering posture.

In summary: By representation of the alternatives, both x and y have a means of recognition of what posture exists, as well as a prescription for alternative postures and changes in attitudes. With the appropriate mechanisms for each autonomous agent to potentially carry out such changes, the multi-agent environment as a whole can function and evolve flexibly in contexts unsuited to the imposition of centralised authority.

2.1 Existing notions of cooperation in artificial intelligence

Cooperation is an issue in any area of artificial intelligence research which involves multi-agent planning or joint problem-solving. Frequently, the principles are not rigidly thought out and explicitly expressed; they are implicit in systems and theories whose emphasis is elsewhere.

> 'Previous DAI work has assumed that agents are mutually cooperative through their designer's fiat'. [24,25].

The accepted notion of cooperation which is so implicitly encoded, involves agents firstly having a common goal. In some cases this may involve each agent in a multi-agent system individually holding a goal to achieve the same end result. In other cases, the goal may be initially held by only one of those agents but on recognition of this, other agent(s) then take on that goal as their own. Taking on another's goal as one's own implies an element of "helpfulness". Even if each agent individually and independently has the goal p, this "helpfulness" component must be present, if there is to be actual cooperation between them to achieve p. In other words, the reason for having the goal must be at least in part because another agent has it as a goal. Power refers to the situation of more than one agent independently having the same goal, and yet unaware of each other's goals, as "accidental coordination" [23]. He offers as an example two art enthusiasts who independently arrive at an art gallery with the goal of destroying a particularly shocking picture. One is intercepted by a guard, but the other succeeds in tearing the picture. The one agent achieved the goal state of both of them, and yet unaware of the other's goal, he was not actually cooperating to achieve it. If however, they had collectively possessed the intention to damage the picture, they would have had a mutual intention [23].

Allwood also characterises cooperation as including a "mutual consideration" as well as a common purpose [1]. In fact, he goes further by defining mutual consideration as not merely an awareness of the existence of another agent's goal. That is just the cognitive consideration component. In addition he suggests an ethical consideration which states that agents should not do anything which would prevent one another from acting in accordance with the rules of rational agenthood. For example, they should not prevent each other from acting intentionally and purposefully according to their will, or from acting normally according to their motives, or from being rational.

Previous computational research in cooperative interactions however, has embodied the notion of helpfulness in cooperation merely as the recognition of another's goal. Agents are also designed to be *always* cooperative - always helpful and therefore ready to take on other agents' goals. This assumption is generally built in to the system architecture. One agent merely needs to communicate her goal to another agent, for cooperation in the form of joint planning, to ensue.

Is there any condition, any circumstance, in which helpful agents in existing research, do not necessarily adopt other agents' goals by virtue of merely recognising their existence? Yes. Cohen and Levesque define agents as helpful in adopting others' goals, but only as long as they do not have any existing contradictory goal of their own [6]. Perrault also stipulates this condition [22]. In fact, this condition is most probably true in other work as well. However, if it is not explicitly stated it is because the implicit assumption is that agents simply do not have conflicting goals of their own.

There are only a few examples of previous work in artificial intelligence, which acknowledge the existence of conflicting goals between cooperative agents. Firstly, the work of Georgeff which concerns the synchronisation of robots with existing plans. However, he uses a "supervisor process" which enables potential conflicts to be successfully avoided; they are not dealt with directly [17]. The most notable work is that of Rosenschein [24,25].

Rosenschein's thesis "Rational interaction: cooperation among intelligent agents", is aimed towards the design of machines for DAI which can plan cooperative action, yet acknowledging the existence and ubiquity of multi-agent conflict. The premises from which he starts are firstly, that

> 'the vast majority of real-world interactions lie between the two extremes of total conflict and absence of conflict' [24]

and if machines are being designed to operate in the real-world, then they cannot

> 'operate under restrictive, crippling assumptions' [24].

Secondly, given the unpredictable nature of real-world domains, performing well requires 'sophisticated and flexibile interaction capabilities' [24].

Agents being assumed to have identical goals, and carrying out any task requested of them, is termed *the benevolent agent assumption* [25]. They offer example application scenarios where this assumption creates systems simply not flexible enough to realistically function successfully. One is that of an automated personal secretary interacting with another automated or human secretary, in order to schedule a meeting. In order to be practical, the private interests of the human boss must be protected. Another example concerns robots constructing a space station. Unpredicted occurrences such as fuel running low, or drifting objects in space cause conflicts between the building agents, each of which is assigned a different task.

2.2 The nature of multi-agent conflict

Agents operating cooperatively in the real world, must have an understanding of the nature of cooperation. This involves understanding the nature and role of multi-agent conflict.

In attempting to define conflict as a property of multi-agents, it is firstly assumed that multi-agent conflicts have certain generalisable properties. These properties should characterise each and every conflict, and are therefore entirely discernable from the context.

> '... there are enlightening similarities between, say, maneuvering in limited war and jockeying in a traffic jam, between deterring the Russians and deterring one's own children, or between the modern balance of terror and the ancient institution of hostages.' [26].

There are a number of such properties which have been compiled from various sources amongst the social psychology literature on this subject:

- (i) Social conflict requires at least two parties, or two analytically distinct units or entities. Even one party conflict is analysed according to actor versus the environment, or actor versus nature [20].
- (ii) Mutually exclusive and/or mutually incompatible values and opposed values are inevitable characteristics of conflict [20].
- (iii) Mutually exclusive, mutually incompatible and opposed values arise from resource limitations. These can be divided into two categories. Firstly, "resource scarcity" occurs when the supply of desired objects or states of affairs is limited, so parties cannot have all they want of anything. Secondly, "position scarcity" describes truths such as that an object cannot occupy two places at the same time, an object cannot simultaneously serve two different functions, a role cannot simultaneously be occupied or performed by two different actors, and different prescribed behaviours cannot be carried out simultaneously [20].
- (iv) The incompatibility which arises can be either of goals (referred to as conflicts of interests or "ends") and which are described as motivational factors to

conflict [21], or of beliefs. The latter are referred to as conflicts of "means" and are the cognitive factors to conflict [3]. There may be an interplay between these two factors, such as conflicts of interests deriving from ideological differences or contrasting ideologies developing out of a conflict of interest [12].

- (v) There must be contact between the parties. This does not necessarily have to be "face to face", but involves a "visibility" or awareness of the situation [20].
- (vi) A conflict relationship always involves the attempt to acquire or exercise power, or the actual exercise or acquisition of power. Power is defined as control over decisions, or the disposition of scarce resources, and the basis of reciprocal influence between or among parties [27].
- (vii) Conflict cannot exist without action [19]. An action/reaction/action sequence must embody this pursuit of power.
- (viii) Conflict relations "constitute a fundamental social-interaction process". They have important functions and consequences [13].

From (iv) above, there are two types of conflict: conflict of beliefs and conflict of goals. Point (i) also specifies that there should be more than one agent. Conflict is correspondingly defined as a type of relation between more than one agent and a proposition.

Points (ii), (iii), and (iv) in the previous section, all refer to "mutually exclusive", "mutually opposed" or "mutually incompatible" values. These are terms used in the context of studies in social psychology, and refer to the causes of a conflict. "Mutually exclusive values" in their terms, refer to the desires of two agents to simultaneously possess the same object, or occupy the same space at the same time, for example. It is obviously the case that two agents cannot physically ever occupy the same space at the same time, and that this expresses a notion of mutual exclusivity BUT, the beliefs about or desires for these states are not mutually exclusive. They can and do co-exist. They are not logically incompatible. The definition of conflict is a description; it describes such a state of affairs. It merely describes the mental states of an agent regarding her beliefs about her own and another's beliefs or goals with respect to the proposition in question. The primary (but not sole) condition of conflict is therefore that the other agent is believed to have a belief or goal which is in opposition to her own. For example,(BEL x p) and (BEL x (BEL y $\neg$p). These beliefs comprise the element of "visibility" or "awareness of the situation", as suggested in point (v) in the previous section.

Finally, and most importantly, a committed goal to change the other's mind is essential to the characterisation of conflict. This reflects points (vi) and (vii) above. If such a goal is abandoned, whether because it has been achieved, is now believed impossible to achieve, or no longer desired for some reason, the conflict is over. I may believe that my colleague believes there is a God, and I believe there is not. If I have no desires to change his mind on the issue, we are not in conflict over this. We are agreed to differ. A particular incident of conflict is over when no agent in the system has a goal for further change with respect to the issue in question, whether the goal has in fact been satisfied or not. What is achieved from such a resolution of the conflict is a renewed, temporary stability of the multi-agent system; there is currently no goal for change. This ties in with point (viii) concerning the functions and consequences of conflict.

It is important to note that conflict is defined here as being subjective. In other words, x only needs to believe that y believes a proposition which is the opposite to her own belief or goal with respect to that same proposition, and have a committed goal to change this. The reality of y's belief in relation to p is irrelevant.

The definition of multi-agent conflict therefore is [2]:

conflict of goals or conflict of beliefs exist between one agent and another, when the agents' beliefs or goals with respect to the same proposition are believed by the one agent to be in opposition, and this agent is also committed to a goal to change the other's belief or goal. Alternatively, there may be a mutual belief about the difference in belief or goal between the participating agents, in which case, conflict exists if either or both also has a committed goal to change the other's belief or goal.

2.3 The nature of multi-agent cooperation

To summarise what was said in subsection 2.1, previous work in artificial intelligence has considered the following to be characteristic of cooperative interaction:

- (i) a common goal exists between cooperating multi-agents,
- (ii) at least a component of possessing the goal is an awareness that another agent has it as a goal,
- (iii) recognition of another's goal is sufficient to adopt that goal as one's own, assuming no contradictory one already in existence, and
- (iv) if the attainment of the common goal requires the attainment of sub-goals, these are adopted and shared out between the interacting parties, on the same basis as above.

The claim is that this characterisation is one of benevolence, not cooperation. Truly autonomous agents adopt other's goals not merely because they are made aware of their existence and as long as they are not doing anything else, but also based upon their own preferences. Cooperation can therefore be achieved even in contexts involving conflict, by the creation of circumstances (using dialogue) which conform to another's preferences. In such circumstances, one alternative maximally satisfies multiple goals taking their relative strengths into account. For example, x has a goal of staying home and working this evening and y requests x to go out with her instead. x has other goals such as for y to like her, for y to ask her out again, for her not to be viewed as a "stick in the mud", and so on. The reasons for the goal to be working are still all true, but if the satisfaction of these other goals overrides them then on recognition of the request, x's preferences dictate that she drop her original goal and cooperate with y [15,16].

[2]formal definitions and examples of their use in Galliers, 1989

Cooperation by an agent x with respect to another autonomous agent y and some proposition p, alternatively then has the following characteristics:

- (i) cooperation requires a common goal between agents. Recognition of another's goal may lead to this situation of a common goal, but this is dependent also upon the preferences of the receiving agent. Alternatively, it may be mutually believed that there is already a common goal in existence
- (ii) an essential component of x's cooperation is her awareness that her goal is relative to y's having the goal. In this way cooperation is more than mere accidental coordination, as described in subsection 2.1, but incorporates an element of helpfulness
- (iii) cooperation can be partially summarised as a recognition or belief about another's goal and a personal preference for this goal state to be achieved, and as a consequence of both of these conditions, there is a commitment to achieving the common goal, and
- (iv) if attainment of the common goal requires the attainment of sub-goals, these are adopted on the same basis as above.

The complete definition of cooperation between multi-agents is [3]: *cooperation exists between one agent and another with respect to some proposition when one agent recognises the other's goal that this proposition be realised and, as a consequence of also a personal preference for this goal state to be achieved, is committed to achieving it as a common goal, relative to the other agent having it as a goal. Alternatively, cooperation exists between one agent and another with respect to some proposition if one or both is committed to achieving the goal for this proposition to be realised relative to the other agent having it as a goal, as a consequence of it being mutually believed that they have a common goal.*

3 The positive functions of conflict

> 'Conflict is a pervasive and inevitable aspect of life. Its pervasiveness suggests that conflict is not necessarily destructive or lacking in pleasure. Conflict has many positive functions. It prevents stagnation, it stimulates interest and curiosity, it is the medium through which problems can be aired and solutions arrived at; it is the root of personal and social change. Moreover, conflict is often part of the process of testing and assessing oneself and, as such, may be highly enjoyable as one experiences the pleasure of the full and active use of one's capabilities' [11].

In the above quote, Deutsch stresses especially the personal gains from conflict. He appeals to the fact that individuals actively seek out conflict in competitive games, at the theatre, in novels, in intimate encounters, at work and so on, to suggest that such conflict is beneficial to those individuals. It is not a "villain",

[3]formal definitions and examples of their use again in Galliers, 1989

> '... the cause of psychopathology, social disorder, war' [11].

Psychological utopia is not a conflict-free existence.

A broader and more complete description of the positive functions of social conflict is provided by Coser [8]. He derives his ideas from the classical work of Georg Simmel (1858 - 1918). It is interesting to note that whilst commenting that early American sociologists such as Charles Cooley, Edward Ross, William Sumner and others, also regarded conflict as constructive and functional, Coser expresses concern that his contemporary sociologists viewed conflict as dysfunctional. He refers to the work of Talcott Parsons, Elton Mayo, George Lundberg as focussing on maladjustment and tensions, and these as interference to concensus. However, by the time Coser's second book appeared [10], a decade later and of course a well established time after the Second World War, his views were being widely endorsed. Nowadays he is rarely quoted in literature on social conflict; his ideas are assumed. The following is a list of Coser's views on the positive functions of conflict :

Conflict exerts pressure for innovation and creativity in social systems [8] . It thereby enables a shift in the governing norms and expectations; it revitalises existent norms or contributes to the emergence of new ones. This is important to the maintenance and evolution of social systems because such systems are dynamic; survival in constantly changing conditions requires regular reevaluation and rebalancing [8]. This principle is also applied in biological theories of social adaptation, evolution and survival. Male stags fighting each year for example, is a regular conflict ensuring that either the existing power structure is reestablished by the same male remaining dominant, or else he is overthrown and a new order established.

> '... social conflict is a mechanism for adjustment of norms adequate to new conditions. A flexible society benefits from conflict because such behaviour, by helping to create and modify norms, assures its continuance under changed conditions. Such mechanisms for readjustment of norms is hardly available to rigid systems: by suppressing conflict, the latter smother a useful warning signal, thereby maximising the danger of catastrophic breakdown.' [8].

Internal conflicts therefore ascertain the relative strengths of antagonistic interests within a structure, and thus are a mechanism for the adjustment or maintenance of the balance of power. The resolution of such conflicts establishes a new equilibrium. [9] quotes a natural scientist Kaemfert, who in an article in the New York Times in July 1952, put forward similar views with respect to the functions of earthquakes. Earthquakes were suggested as being the earth's way of maintaining equilibrium, an adjustment enabling the crust to yield to stresses which may reorganise or redistribute materials.

Intergroup conflicts set group boundaries by strengthening group cohesiveness and separateness. Conflicts involving associations or coalitions provide a bond between the members, uniting and removing social isolation. A social structure in which a multiplicity of conflicts can exist with associations whose

> 'diverse purposes crisscross each other' prevents 'alliances along one major line of cleavage' . [8]

Conflict also reduces tension and permits maintenance of social interaction under stress. It clarifies objectives. It allows agreement rather than subordination. Coser concludes:

> 'conflict tends to be dysfunctional for a social structure in which there is no or insufficient toleration and institutionalization of conflict ... What threatens the equilibrium of such a structure is not conflict as such, but the rigidity itself which permits hostilities to accumulate and to be channeled along one major line of cleavage once they break out in conflict' . [8]

Axelrod has examined the question of the evolution of social cooperation,

> 'in a world of egoists without central authority' [2].

In other words, if each member of a multi-agent system has their own self-motivated goals, and there is no central authority exerting insistencies concerning benevolence towards others, can cooperation emerge? According to Axelrod, the answer is "yes". Axelrod's theory is based upon investigations into individuals pursuing their own self-interest without any enforced cooperation. His research included the instigation of a computer tournament for the Prisoner's Dilemma Game. The programs were designed to select moves according to a history of the game so far, in a variable number of games. Each entrant was programmed to use a different strategy. The outright winner each time was the simplest; it was a program written by A. Rapaport comprising a TIT FOR TAT strategy. This starts with a cooperative choice and after that simply does what the other player did on the previous move. Axelrod also investigated the evolution of cooperation in animals, such as symbiotic relationships and those based on kinship. Further investigations involved trench warfare experiences in World War 1, and the tacit cooperation which evolved from one side being the first to cooperate and then an arrangement of reciprocation continuing [2].

4 Conclusions

The volume of research into the structures of multi-agent systems and the nature of multi-agent interactions is currently increasing, especially for distributed processing applications. Important issues for example, relate to the possible characterisations of the nature of organisations of agents - should there be hierarchical structures such as "master/slave" relationships between nodes, what is the distribution of control and decision-making, how are resource limitations to be coped with, what are the alternative structures and means of communication, and so on. Many researchers have considered human societies to be examples of organisations from which potential solutions can be found to these issues, for particular applications and domains. Human society can be taken as a paradigm for generating a model of distributed systems. An example is the work of Fox, who suggests that the designers of distributed systems should draw upon the ideas of other fields

> 'which have considerable experience with their own distributed systems',

such as biology or management science [14]. This paper also suggests that automated systems operating as agents in open multi-agent environments will be subject to the same constraints as are human agents. For this reason, an investigation has been carried out into the nature of human cooperation; it's maintenance and evolution. Current theory suggests that an essential and very positive force in that maintenance and evolution, is the acknowledgement of conflicts. This allows adaptation and flexibility in a changing and unpredictable environment. Self-interest as a motivating force can be demonstrated as a component of developing cooperation. Imposed benevolence or the incorporation of some omniscient "overseer" agents in artificial systems therefore, is considered not only unnecessary and impractical, but in fact a rigidifying and constraining force to social development in the context of a dynamic environment.

References

[1] Allwood, J. Linguistic Communication as Action and Cooperation - A study in Pragmatics. Gothenburg Monographs in Linguistics 2, 1976.

[2] Axelrood, R. The evolution of cooperation. Basic Books Inc. N.Y., 1984.

[3] Brehmer, B. Cognitive Factors in Interpersonal Conflict. In Druckman D. (Ed.) Negotiations Social-Psychological Perspectives. Sage Publications, Beverley Hills/London, 1977.

[4] Bond, A.H. and Gasser, L. (Eds.) Readings in Distributed Artificial Intelligence. Morgan Kaufmann, California, 1988.

[5] Cohen, P. and Levesque, H. Persistence, Intention and Commitment. Technical Report No. 415, AI Centre, SRI International, California, U.S.A.,m 1987a. Also: Proceedings of the 1986 Workshop at Timberline Lodge, Reasoning about action and plans. Kaufmann Inc., 1987a.

[6] Cohen, P. and Levesque H. Rational Interaction as the basis for Communication. Technical report No. 89, Centre for the Study of Language and Information, Stanford University, California, U.S.A., 1987b.

[7] Conry, S.E., Meyer, R.A., and Lesser, V.R. Multistage Negotiation in Distributed Planning. Tech. Report No. 86-67, Dept. of Computer and Information Science, University of Massachusetts, Amherst, MA, 1986.

[8] Coser, L. The Function of Social Conflict. Glencoe Ill. Free Press, 1956.

[9] Coser, L. Social Conflict and the Theory of Social Change. The British Journal Of Sociology, Vol. 8, pp 197-207, 1957.

[10] Coser, L. Continuities in the Study of Social Conflict. The Free Press, New York, 1967.

[11] Deutsch, M. Conflict and its Resolution. In Smith, C.G. (Ed.) Conflict Resolution: Contributions of the Behavioural Sciences. University of Notre Dame Press, London, 1971.

[12] Druckman, D. Conflict of Interest and Value Dissensus: Two Perspectives. In Druckman, D. (Ed.) Negotiations: Social-Psychological Perspectives. Sage Publications, Beverley Hills/London, 1977.

[13] Dubin, R. Power and Union-Management Relations. Journal of Conflict Resolution, Vol. 1, Adm. Sci. Quarterly No. 2, pp 60-81, 1957.

[14] Fox, M.S. An organizational View of Distributed Systems. Proceedings of IEEE Transactions for Man, Systems and Cybernetics, Vol. SMC-11, No. 1, pp 70-80, 1981.

[15] Galliers, J.R. A Strategic Framework for Multi-Agent Cooperative Dialogue. Proceedings of the Eighth European Conference on Artificial Intelligence, Munich, pp 415-420, August, 1988.

[16] Galliers, J.R. A Theoretical Framework for Computer Models of Cooperative Dialogue, Acknowledging Multi-Agent Conflict. Cambridge University Computer Laboratory, Tech. Report No. 172, and HCRL Tech. report No. 51, Open University, 1989.

[17] Georgeff, M.P. Communication and Interaction in Multi-Agent Planning. Proceedings of the National Conference in Artificial Intelligence, American Association for AI, Washington D.C., pp 125-129, August 1983.

[18] Hewitt, K. Offices are Open Systems. ACM Transactions on Office Information Systems, 4(3) pp 271-287, 1986.

[19] Kerr, C. Industrial Conflict and its Mediation. American Journal of Sociology LX, pp 230, 1954.

[20] Mack, R.W. and Snyder, R.C. The Analysis of Social Conflict- Toward an Overview and Synthesis. In Smith, C.G. (Ed.) Conflict Resolution: Contributions of the Behavioural Sciences. University of Notre Dame Press, London, 1971.

[21] McClintock, C.G. Social Motivations in Settings of Outcome Interdependence. In Druckman, D. (Ed.) Negotiations: Social-Psychological Perspectives. Sage Publications, Beverley Hills/London, 1977.

[22] Perrault, C.R. An application of Default logic to Speech Act Theory. Report No. CSLI 87-90, CLSI, SRI International, California, U.S.A., 1987.

[23] Power, R. Mutual Intention. Journal for the Theory of Social Behaviour, Vol. 14, pp 85-101, 1984.

[24] Rosenschein, J.S. Rational Interaction: Cooperation Among Intelligent Agents. Ph.D thesis, Stanford University, California, U.S.A., 1985.

[25] Rosenschein, J.S. and Genesereth M.R. Deals among rational agents. Proceedings of the 9th International Joint Conference of AI, Los Angeles, pp 91-99, 1985.

[26] Schelling, T.C. The strategy of Conflict. Harvard University Press, Camb., Mass., 1960.

[27] Sheppard, H. Approaches to Conflict in American Sociology. British Journal of Sociology V, pp 324-342, 1954.

[28] Simmel, G. Conflict. New York Free Press. 1955.

[29] Sycara, K. Resolving Goal Conflicts via Negotiation. Proceedings of 7th AAAI, Saint Paul, Minnesota, 1988.

Interactions between Decision Capabilities

DECENTRALIZED A.I.
Yves DEMAZEAU & Jean-Pierre MÜLLER (Eds.)

SOCIAL POWER
A Point Missed in Multi-Agent, DAI and HCI

Cristiano CASTELFRANCHI *

Social Behaviour Simulation Project
Istituto di Psicologia
Consiglio Nazionale delle Ricerche
Rome, Italy

The predominance of the logical and engineering mind of A.I. over that of cognitive modelling and simulation has led to serious lack of realism in Multi-Agent and interaction studies. The sociality of the agents is merely postulated rather than explained in terms of their **dependence**; the adoption of goals (usually called "cooperativeness") takes place by magic. In other words, **the problem of the agent's power** is ignored. Their lack of power concerning their own goals, which makes them dependent; the power they have to influence someone else and to be adopted by a truly autonomous agent. The present paper discusses recent attempts to solve the problem of adoption between autonomous agents, emphasizing the critical point of **reciprocation**. The following proposals are made: a theory of individual and social power of agents; the **basic strategies of influencing power** (as seen in the relations between State and citizen); the postulates referring to the definition of **truly autonomous agents**.

1. The two minds of the Multi-Agent

1.1. The society metaphor

Introducing a panel on "Interaction Among Intelligent Agents" H.Coelho [5] raised the question of whether "The society metaphor is put forward by many authors to discuss and introduce new models about intelligent interactions. Is it appropriate and enlighting? Or, on the contrary, such metaphor can frame and prevent us to generate new ideas ?"
In order to answer this we think that a distinction must first be made between two different minds or "projects" within the framework of A.I. studies on social

* Istituto Psicologia CNR
Viale Marx 15 - 00137 Rome, Italy
tel: +39-6-8292626 Fax: -824737 ; E-mail PSCS @ IRMKANT.BITNET

interaction (from Distributed Artificial Intelligence, Multi Agent systems to Human-Computer Interaction):

A) One project is concerned with intelligence, with problem solving, with systems architecture (for the sake of conciseness we shall call this trend *Distributed Intelligence Approach*) (e.g. [10] [20]).
Essentially, in this approach the mind (natural or artificial) is studied and society is used (usefully, we think) as a metaphor.

B) The other trend is (or should be) more concerned with social interaction per se (*Social Simulation Approach*) (e.g. [6] [22] [1]).
Any confusion between these two approaches is detrimental. We believe that if the mind can be a society, society (although probably an autopoietic system [16]) certainly is not a mind nor does it possess a mind [8] [11]. Therefore, if our object is the *Social Simulation Approach*, the comparison with the mind may frame us nagatively: it may give us *a too rational view of social functioning*.

1.2. Pre-established harmonies

The society-mind comparison and the failure to distinguish between the two approaches can lead to misunderstanding. In the case of the *Social Simulation Approach* it is not a question of making models of "intelligent interactions", nor of necessarily assuming the existence of a rational outcome, a distributed intelligence or a cooperative functioning. DAI and Multi-Agent studies, as well as logics of social action [6] [7] still remain in a world of "pre-established harmonies" as a result of their architecture and simplistic postulates. As Galliers [12] says:"..previous work in A.I. which deals with multi-agent interaction, has ignored [conflict] by assuming that cooperative agents are simply benevolent towards each other; they are ever ready to adopt each others goals. Negotiation has so far been considered to be simply the sharing out or delegation of tasks between such benevolent agents in a system e.g. [10] [9]".
The recent work of Galliers [12] and Werner [22] [23] represent significant progress in the direction of a more realistic and direct approach to social interaction. However, despite this, and despite the introduction of "self interested" agents [21] with non-identical interests, or the development of theories of intentions or commitment [7], we remain in a word of "pre-established harmonies". The conflict is nevertheless a temporary one leading to cooperation (as in the sociological functionalism). The overall outcome is coherent and of common interest. Above all, goal adoption, although the agents are more "autonomous", remains a mechanical process.
In other words, the fundamental question we face when dealing with several agents is not "how to get those agents to achieve a social goal" [22] (1) , but:
"why does an autonomous agent enter into social interactions ?" (**Sociality Problem**);
"how does an agent get his problem to become social, i.e. get it adopted by other agents ?" (**Adoption Problem**).
As we shall endeavour to show, the answer to the first question is "dependence"; the answer to the second question is "power". We will focus our attention mainly on the second point.
The predominance of the *Distributed Intelligence Approach* over the *Social Simulation Approach* and the harmonic and cooperative outlook which derives naturally from studies on conversation, have led to the power problem, which is central to social interaction, being neglected.
The importance of power relations could easily be overlooked in the study of **conversation** for three reasons: a) the primary goal of the communicative act ("that the listener assumes that the speaker wants the listener to assume that

the speaker wants.....") is attained automatically, without any adoption decision by the listener except to listen; b) the real adoption requested by the speaker (to converse together) is often a spontaneous adoption (see below) which does not require any special negotiation; c) the exercise of *influencing power* (which is used, for instance, to convince the other of the truth of a statement) is not based on conspicuous threats or promises, but adopt the strategy which will later be called "search for cooperation", as well as rhetorical arguments.
It is essential to tackle the power problem explicitly for the purposes of a more realistic *Social Simulation Approach*, but also for a more efficient *Distributed Intelligence Approach*, in which control can be decentralized and negotiated, the agents become more autonomous and cooperation relations can be tailored to suit the tasks and the circumstances.

2. Adoption

2.1. Adoption vs Cooperation

The term "adoption" is to be preferred to that of "cooperation", widely used in A.I. and social psychology to refer to a wide range of social phenomena.
We consider **goal adoption** to occur each time Ag1 takes over a goal because he knows that it is one of Ag2's goals, i.e. to allow Ag2 to attain it.
In other words: Ag2 has the goal that Ag1 reaches a goal.
The first definition is more "cognitive": it implies that agents understand goals of other agents; the second one is more general: it applies also to animal social behavior, at any level. What is needed for this powerful account is an unified theory of goals (or better of teleonomic phenomena), which relates "external goals" (biological and social functions) with "internal goals" (goals consciously or unconsciously represented within minds: purposes, desires, intentions, ...).

For adoption to occur, there *is not necessarily any communication or request.*
There are different kinds of adoption, based on the different reasons for adopting, but , in any case, the adoption is performed as a means to an end: *to attain one's self-interested goal*, or for altruistic reasons (affection, love, pity: because the final goal of the one is that the other attain his goals).
Cooperation is merely a special case of instrumental adoption: Ag1 adopts Ag2's goals because they both share a common goal in view of which they help each other out. It implies also coordination.

2.2. Magic goal adoption

The weak point in the present approaches is the transition from the goal of agent 1 (Ag1) to the goal (and action) of agent 2 (Ag2) who must act in Ag1's interest and with Ag1.
As Werner [22] rightly states :"this communication must be able to change the intentions of other agent". He goes on to discuss a particular type of information (different from information on current events and evaluations), i.e. "process information" : "about intentions of an agent. It modifies the intentional state of an agent " .
In Werner's system, however, this modification continues to occur only because it is mechanically postulated as the effect of the comunication.

Galliers [12] proposes a correct analysis: "utterances are speech actions planned to convey the information that the speaker is in a particular mental state which relates to the fact that the speaker has the goal to induce a particular mental state in the hearer". However, even this is very vague and inadequate. How does this "induction" of mental states in the hearer come about ? What strategies does the speaker use and what powers does he rely on to achieve this?
In most cases the transition takes place as if by magic, i.e. it is merely postulated, not explained. A rule is made by means of which "if Ag2 comes to know that Ag1 has a goal G, he adopts it (unless it clashes with other goals, or if he prefers it to other goals)".
In some cases [21], Ag2 more correctly starts from his own personal interest and calculates whether he stands to gain or not. But even this is not enough. Agents are "self-interested", but they are located in a system architecture which is by nature cooperative: very little individual understanding of social process is required as the rationality model is imposed from the outside through the establishment of a market mechanism. The agent must just place his demand and supply on the market, then checking whether they correspond to someone else's. Rationality is assured by the "hidden hand" postulated by Adam Smith, which in this case is the hand of the designer.
In this approach, the agent does not have to solve the problem of *how to induce others to adopt his goals.*

What would be needed in the first place is a broad-based phenomenology of the reasons for which Ag2 adopts Ag1's goals, and therefore a detailed analysis of Ag2's reasoning and decision-making processes. Are the goals adopted on his own initiative or at someone elses's request ? Does Ag2 adopt the goal out of motherly love or altruism, or with a gun pointed at her/him, or under a commercial contract or because ordered to do so by her/his superior ?
These problems are dodged in the approaches of Cohen e Levesque, Galliers and Werner. In Rosenschein-Genesereth's approach the utilitarian flattening is accepted so that the whole social interaction is likened to an exchange. Such a viewpoint is reductive for anyone interested in cognitive science who can theorize on the *various* mental states of the agents.
In the second place a theory of plans is required, a theory of Ag1's strategies to obtain from Ag2 what he wants. Ag1 cannot limit himself to "expressing wishes" or to put himself on the market, but calculates the various reasons for which Ag2 could adopt his goal and makes complex plans to influence the other.
Ag1's *power over* Ag2 is the most neglected factor (see section **3**).

2.3. Inadequacy of current adoption theory

As mentioned earlier, Werner's work [22] [23] places communication capable of modifying Ag2's "intentional state" as the centre of the social interaction. However, it is not enough to "modify" it; it is necessary to state the direction in which it is modified. It is modified in order to adopt Ag1's goal. Werner's adoption theory (that I use as an example of an advanced theory) is inadequate:

1) The phenomenon of adoption extends *beyond Ag1's requests* and also *beyond the communication* between the two. For instance, there are **spontaneous adoptions**, which are usually indicative of the maximum willingness and helpfulness.
Ag1 asks Ag2 to pass him the hammer and Ag2 replies "here's the riveter, it's easier".
Ag2 has not only understood the goals that Ag1 was communicating to him so that he could adopt them, but also Ag1's supergoals [3], i.e. his overall plan:

G1: attach the cloth
↑
G2: drive in the nails
↑
G3: get the hammer ↑ = *for, in order to*
↑
G4: Ag2 gives the hammer to Ag1
↑
G5: ask Ag2 for the hammer
↑
sentence

Ag2 does not adopt the sub-goal suggested to him (G4) but rather the goal G1, and suggests another plan to Ag1 (other actions and tools). The same limitation is present in the definition of the predicate HELPFUL in [6].

2) Ag2's change of mind does not come about by chance (nor is it sufficient to postulate it as a rule). The basis of Ag1's capacity to change Ag2's intentions (influence him) is the knowledge of Ag2's mental mechanisms which decide whether to adopt or not.
"Agents need knowledge of the other agent intentions", although:
- not only and not principally, as Werner says, to coordinate the actions towards a shared goal (cooperation), but before being able to influence the other agent;
- the agents must not only know the *intentions* but, more general, the *goals* of the other agent. In the example of the hammer Ag2 not only adopts the intentions of Ag1 but also the permanent goal [3] of "making the least possible effort". When a mother says to her child "If you do your homework I'll take you to the cinema" she is not working only on the child's *intentions*, to influence him, but also more in general on his *goals*, both active and inactive (*sleeping goals*) (2).
In Werner's approach, induction and adoption seem to occur automatically: one pragmatic effect of the communicative acts is the dawning of Ag1's goal in Ag2's mind; this goal is "forced" by the communication. It is not clear where Ag2's decisions and utility are. Where is the negotiation, confidence, persuasion, commitment, etc.; and what about the pitfall of reciprocation ?

2.4. The reciprocation problem: the uncertainty of social exchange

If one does not suppose the existence of automatic adoptions or of generalized "benevolence", or of "inborn" rules (like Axelrod's "tit for tat"), the problem of adoption runs into the pitfall of reciprocation.
Let us assume we have two agents in a block world (fig.1).

CLEARTOP(Ag,X,Y) = take one block away from another block and put it on the table. Both CLEARTOP and PUTON presuppose GRASP, i.e. to have X in one's hand; they also presuppose that X is FREE; PUTON requires also Y to be FREE.
Neither of the agents has the power to attain its goal: Ag1 lacks the action CLEARTOP, and Ag2 lacks the action PUTON.

However, let us assume that communication and social interaction take place; let us also assume that the agents each know the other's goal and powers and are able to understand whether, by *including an action of the other agent* in their own plan, they can attain the goal.

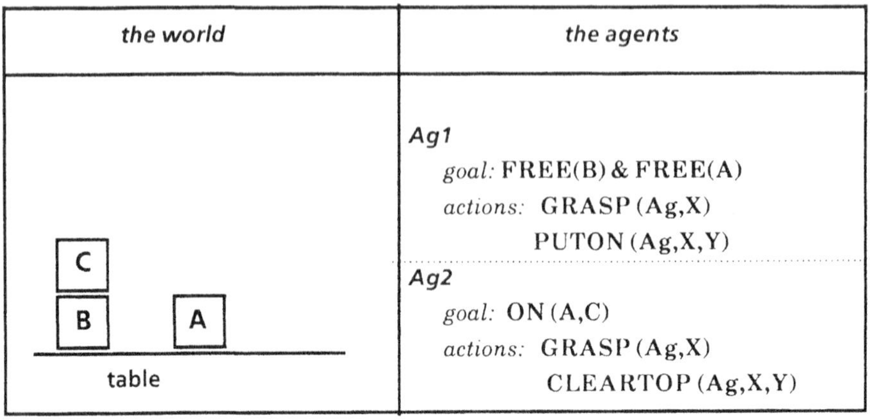

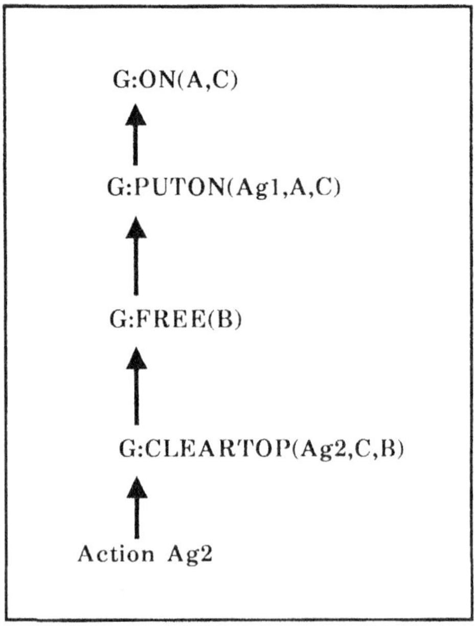

Ag2 therefore has the goal of PUTON (Ag1,A,B) and will try to find a way of getting Ag1 to adopt this goal. Let us assume that Ag2, knowing that Ag1 wants FREE (B), promises Ag1 that "IF (PUTON (Ag1,A,B), CLEARTOP (Ag2,C,B)", and also that Ag1 accepts this, i.e. he decides it is in his interest to adopt what Ag2 is asking him (PUTON) so that Ag2 will do something that is useful to him

(CLEARTOP). We obtain (skipping many cognitive steps) the classic "social exchange" situation. Fig. 2 shows the "unnatural" plan within Ag2 mind.
There has therefore been a common plan, an agreement to cooperate, a rational and distributed intelligent solution to each agent's problem. But let us examine what is happening. Ag2 removes C from B as promised, Ag1 sees his goal realized: FREE (B) and *stops there, as he is satisfied!* The goal of PUTON, which was instrumental for him in order to obtain FREE (B), no longer applies.
There is no point in inventing permanent or compulsory goals: a rational agent must stop when he no longer has any autonomous motives for doing something.
If reciprocation is often involved in real social interactions and promises are kept, etc., it is not as a result of absurd automatisms but because other goals are involved, which make it useful to reciprocate:

- either there exists a moral imperative (a final goal) to reciprocate;
- or the goal is to avoid a sense of guilt (internal punishment for harming someone else);
- or there is a fear of being punished by society which prescribes reciprocation and keeping one's word;
- or there is a fear of someone's anger and of their retaliation;
- or one wants to retain the confidence of that person or of others with whom one expects to have other exchanges in the future;
- or some or all of these conditions apply simultaneously in various combinations according to the circumstances.

In any case reciprocation (the basis of functioning social exchange) is not a trivial problem. It requires the representation of the *agreement* within the mind of the partners, and the strategies to reach it. The maintenance of the agreement demands a complex motivational structure on the one hand, and on the other a sophisticated control by the first adopting person. This is why social image and the confidence inspired thereby, and the checking of the guarantees and the reliability are so important.

3. Power

Basically power is not a social concept; it relates an agent to his goal (individual power - Hobbes, Russell):

Power of

Ag has the *power of* G1 if he can (doing or being something) ultimately attain G1.

Power is not defined in terms of the agent's beliefs. However, the agent's assumption concerning his own or other agent's power are very important in social interaction. In order to get one's own goals adopted it is more important that the other agent *believes* that we have a certain power than actually possess it (e.g. the holdup man's toy or unloaded gun; false teeth, wigs, make-up, etc.).
In evaluating the Ag's *power of*, it is of fundamental importance in a naive judgment to make a distinction between internal bases (capacity, skill, organs) and external bases (means, resources) of power (**attribution problem**).
The **evaluation** (assumption concerning the power of Ag or of a means[17]) is central to social interaction and adoption. For instance, a REQUEST plan within an EXCHANGE plan implies that the listener is evaluated as being capable and able to perform the required action or assigned task [15] (3). It further implies that he will be evaluated as a possible reciprocator or as someone who will keep faith with his commitments (*social image* : the goal to be well evaluated).

3.1. Social power

Dependence

Ag1 depends on Ag2 if Ag1 does not have the *power of* G1 and Ag2 does; or if Ag1 has the power of G1 unless Ag2 prevents him from attaining it.
If Ag1 assumes he is dependent on Ag2 (with regard to goal G1) this belief makes him dependent upon Ag2 with regard to G1 in actual fact. *Assumptions change powers* (whether social or not); knowledge forms part of our powers.
Dependence forms the basis of and the reason for sociality. Society was invented to multiply agents' powers of achieving their goals (using the powers of other agents). A consequence of the foregoing (and the other side of dependence) is *power over*.

Power over

Ag1 has power over Ag2 (with regard to G2) if he can help Ag2 to attain his goal, or else to prevent him from doing so (Ag2 depends on Ag1 with regard to G2).
In the example of the two agents in the block world, Ag1 was dependent on Ag2 with regard to the goal FREE (B) and had power over Ag2 with regard to the goal ON (A,C); and vice versa.

Possess

Possess is a social relation. It presupposes the concept of power, and it is the basis of a dependence relation. It implies the notion of *resource*, which is just a condition (normally an object endowed with some *power of*) necessary for Ag2 to reach a goal.
Ag1 possesses X if
a) he has the *power of* preventing Ag2 from having access to or using X (this presupposes that Ag2 has the goal to have access to or use X);
b) he has the *power of* having access to and using X.

Ag2 depends on X and so depends on Ag1. Ag1 has which possesses (control) X, gains *power over* Ag2.

Influencing power

This is what is normally meant by "power" with reference to the social field.
Ag1 has the *power to influence* Ag2 with regard to G2 if he has the power to increase or reduce the probability that Ag2 will pursue G2 (i.e. has some intention to do so). In other words, if he has the *power of* getting him to do or to refrain from doing something.
The *power to influence* other normally requires a capacity on the part of Ag1 to act on Ag2's mind, i.e. to modify his goals, assumptions, or emotions (4). To achieve this, communication is *normally* used.
The basis on which the *power to influence* rests is usually the *power over* Ag2: by communicating or exerting his *power over* Ag2 with regard to G2, Ag1 gains the *power to influence* Ag2 with regard to G3 (cf. the mother, using her *power over* the child with regard to the movie child's goal, gains the *power to influence* her child with regard to the homeworks goal).

3.2. Three very basic strategies of influencing power

Let us suppose that the Indian government decides to induce Mr Shastri not to have more than two children. The motives of the Indian government (i.e. the super-goals of this goal) are: to limit demographic increase and to encourage economic development and prosperity.

INDIAN GOVERNMENT'S MIND

G: India's welfare
↑
G: reduce demografic increment
↑
G: people should have no more
than two children
↑
G: Mr Shastri has no more children (**goal to be adopted**)

The indian government does not necessarily communicate its reasons or its plan. It merely wishes to obtain a certain behaviour from Mr Shastri and the other citizens.
Mr Shastri must carry out the "task" for his own reasons (goals). Therefore, the government must find out about Mr Shastri's goals, reasoning and decision making processes.

Promise of prizes

The government assumes that Mr Shastri's mind works according to the following goal-generating rule (planning rule):

BEL (Ag , IF (p, q)) & WANT (Ag, q) = = = > WANT (Ag, p)

It also assumes that Mr Shastri pursues the goal of making money (or at least more money than he has now), otherwise he would not be tempted by the government's offers. Let us further assume that the goal of making money (quantified as 500 rupees) is worth more to Mr Shastri than the goal of having many children (5). The government thus issued the following decree:
"Those having not more than two children (= p) will receive a prize of 500 rupees (= q)".
The indian government wants Mr Shastri to adopt its goal of "not having more than two children" in order to "have more money":

MR SH.'S MIND

G: to have money
↑
G: to have the prize
↑
G: to have no more children

Threat of sanctions

The government assumes that Sh.'s mind works according to the following "avoidance rule" (a corollary of the preceding rule):

BEL (Ag, IF (p q)) & WANT (Ag, NOT (q)) = = = > WANT (Ag, NOT (p))

It also assumes that Mr Sh. pursues the goal of having money (or, more exactly, of not having less money); it assumes that this goal is more important for Mr Sh. than that of having more than two children; it assumes that Mr Sh. will adopt the government's goal solely for his own purposes, which are different from the public goals. Therefore, the government issues the following order:
"Those having more than two children (= p) will have to pay a fine of 500 rupees (= q)".

MR SH.'S MIND

G: to have money
↑
G: not to pay a fine
↑
G: to have no more children

It should be noted that, for the same monetary value, the fine is much more "coercive" (i.e. leaves less freedom of choice). If Mr Sh. does not pursue the government's goal, in the case of the prize (at least with regard to the goal of having money) he will have *the same power as before the interaction* with the government, whereas in the case of the fine if he does not obey he will have less power than at the beginning.

Search for cooperation

Let us now assume that the Indian government does not consider its citizens to be incapable of understanding and sharing the reasons for its decisions, that it makes such decisions in the public interest and that these decisions can thus be considered shareable. Let us assume that the government does not consider its citizens to be capable only of making choices in their own individual (and economic) interest, or of acting solely to gain prizes or avoid fines. In this case the government can adopt a different strategy.
It can assume that Mr Sh. too pursues the goal of "India's welfare" and that he can understand and agree that the population increase threatens its welfare, that it is desiderable to keep the birth rate down and therefore that also Mr Sh. himself should not have more than two children. In other words, the government both predicts that Mr Sh. will have the following mind and plan and wants him to have them:

MR SH.'S MIND

G: India's welfare
↑
G: reduce demografic increment
↑
G: to have no more children

Mr Sh.'s mind is the same as the Indian govenment's: the government is counting on true *cooperation*, i.e. on the fact that Ag1 and Ag2 *share a goal from the outset* and that to achieve this goal one will adopt the goals of the other (and possibly viceversa).
Also in this case the government is guided by the above-mentioned rules, but on the assumption that the goal is shared, it must communicate its thinking to Sh. and account for its decisions. It communicates to Sh. that "if Sh. (and all the other citizens along with him) has more than two children (=p) there will be a large demographic increment (=r), and that if this were to happen (=r) this would jeopardize India's prosperity (=q)".
The government evidently assumes that the latter goal will be more important for Mr Sh. than his individual goal of having many children.

4. Our notion of an autonomous agent

In order to be autonomous an agent must make real decisions and have real preferences. That is, he must:

1) Have his own goals: an autonomous agent has autonomous goals!
2) Be able to make decisions concerning his own goals (internal conflicts).
3) Adopt other agents' goals only making his own choice among them: (adopting is thus neither automatic nor rule-governed, and it is not simply required that the goal should not be inconsistent with the preceding ones).
4) See adoption as a way of enabling the agent to achieve some goal.
5) Control the acquisition of beliefs, their "credibility", in relation to previous beliefs: an agent that swallows everything may be influenced to do everything.

It is correct to say that to be "autonomous", agents must have "control over their acquisition of mental states, i.e. their belief and goal adoption... Agents decide autonomously on the basis of their own preferences, and not benevolently" [12]. However, the theory of preference must not be an *ad hoc* theory.
Preferences are not just a sub-set of beliefs: in general, goals are not a sub-set of beliefs (this is a bias due to the fact that social theory in A.I. derives from speech act theory!).
Agents are not logicians; they want and act, without believing everything.
An agent is conceived of more as a very simple and idealized "problem solver planner - decision-marker" than as a "theorem prover about action" [13].
Preferences must be defined as they would be in a non-social system capable of making decisions concerning its own goals; not with a pre-established list of goal comparisons, therefore. Conflicts and outcomes cannot all be predicted; and the outcomes of decisions are not stable and automatic, but depend on the context. In a real decision-maker, goals have values (which derive also from the beliefs concerning their utility and probability) and, on the basis of these values (which can be modified according to the context) they can always be compared when a choice is to be made.

It is not sufficient to postulate that Ag prefers a goal and therefore adopts it: the problem is "why does he have this preference ?".
In order to be autonomous he must adopt a goal in accordance with his own goals, insofar as the goal can become *part of his own plan*
Essentially we adopt the following postulates concerning autonomous agents:

POSTULATE 1: **each new goal in an agent derives from his pre-existing goals** (and assumptions).

This happens in three main ways:

- *instantiation* of a generic goal in a particular case;
- *planning* (sub-goals);
- *means-end analysis* based on causal theory of the world.

POSTULATE 2: **every modification of the goals of another agent is achieved by modifying his assumptions**

Agents use various levels of communication, or alterations of the external world.
It is not possible to modify goals directly (6).
This is not because the goals are sub-set of beliefs but because their activation, generation and value depend on super-goals and assumptions (what he believes, knows, supposes, etc.). We saw one example of this in the three basic strategies of *influencing power* outlined above.

With these postulates we hope to reduce automatisms in social interaction, to make the process of goals adoption more complex but realistic. So we want to oblige ourselves to cope with the problems of personal and social powers, and of the representation of the other agents' reasons and reasoning.

5. Conclusion

In our view, though a simulative approach entails some degree of simplification and idealization, this does not necessarily imply a reduction of social interaction to mechanisms of forced cooperation, to "agents" lacking in real **autonomy** (which consists of having goals of one's own, and *adopting other's goals in view of one's own*, including altruistic impulses), to narrow utilitaristic models.
We deem it crucial -either to the cognitive and social simulation or to build up flexible applicative systems- to model power relationships between agents, cognitive strategies for influencing others, the decisional processes of the influenced person.

Notes

(1) The very concept of "social goal", as defined by Werner [22], implies harmony and cooperation. In fact a goal is always pursued by somebody in particular, and the fact that an agent cannot attain one of his goals and needs others (*dependence*) does not thereby make the goal a "social" one. Why should this fact concern the other agents ? This is precisely the problem of social power: *how to make Ag1's goal also that of Ag2.*

(2) Although it may appear surprising there is no comprehensive theory either in psychology or A.I. to account for the way goals are activated or inactivated. For some attempts in this direction see [13] [14] [24] [2].

(3) The prerequisite that Ag2 should have the *power of* doing what is requested guides the actual decision making of the partners in social interactions; or else it regulates plans aimed at giving the other the power which will be useful to us (e.g. education).

(4) However, see postulate 2 below concerning autonomous agents as well as note (6).

(5) The coefficient of value (CV) of a goal depends on how many super-goals it is assumed can be attained through it, or that it prevents from being attained (as well as on the CV of these super-goals). The Indian government (Ag1) increases the CV of the goal desired by Ag2, letting Sh. know that by means of this goal he will be able to attain another, or else Ag1 reduces the CV of Sh.'s goal, which it disapproves of (i.e. having more children), by informing him that this goal would prevent him from attaining another one (i.e. having money).

(6) This is not always true, although it is the most frequent case and the most significant for cognitive simulation. It is not true in animal social interaction (and partly in human social interaction) which is based more on "key stimuli" and "releasers" than on knowledge, nor in any case in which the aim is to elicit a reaction rather than to give rise to an intention: Ag1 tickles Ag2 to make him drop something he is holding. Moreover, it is not true in the rare cases in which it is possible to modify goals or their value directly by acting on the soma, e.g. lobotomy, drugs, etc.

References

[1] Castelfranchi,C. *Paradisi Artificiali: prolegomeni alla simulazione dell'interazione sociale*, **Sistemi Intelligenti**, I,1, 1989.

[2] Castelfranchi,C., Conte,R., & Miceli, M. *Emotions and Goals*, Symposium **Emotion und Handlung**, Bad Homburg, March, 1986 (T.R. Istituto Psicologia, CNR, Roma).

[3] Castelfranchi,C. & Parisi,D., *A goal analysis of some pragmatic aspects of language*, in H.Parret, M.Sbisa' & J.Vershueren (eds.), **Possibilities and Limitations of Pragmatics**. Studies in Language Companion Series (Vol.7). Amsterdam: John Benjamins, 1981.

[4] Castelfranchi,C. & Parisi,D., *Mente e scambio sociale*, **Rassegna Italiana di Sociologia**,XXV,1,1984.

[5] Coelho, H., *Interaction among intelligent agents*, **ECAI- 88**, Munich, WG, pp. 717-718, 1988.

[6] Cohen, P. & Levesque, H., *Rational interaction as the basis for communication*, T.R. n.89, CSLI, Stanford University, California, U.S.A.

[7] Cohen,P. & Levesque, H., *Intention = Choice + Commitment*, **AAAI-87**, Seattle, WA, pp.410-415, 1987.

[8] Conte, R., *Institutions and Intelligent Systems*, in **Operational Research and the Social Sciences**, Proceedings, Cambridge, UK, April 1989.

[9] Davis, R. & Smith, P.G., *Negotiation as a metaphor for Distributed Problem Solving*, **Artificial Intelligence**, 20 (1), pp.63-109, 1983.

[10] Doran, J., *The computational approach to knowledge communication and structure in multi-actor systems*, in G.N. Gilbert & C. Heath (eds.), **Social Action and Artificial Intelligence**, 1983.

[11] Douglas, M., *How Institutions Think*, Routledge & Kegan Paul, London, 1986.

[12] Galliers, J.R., *A strategic framework for multi-agent cooperative dialogue*, **ECAI-88**, Munich, WG, pp415-420, 1988.

[13] Georgeff, M.P. & Lansky, A.L., *Reactive reasoning and planning*, **AAAI-87**, Seattle, WA, pp.677-682, 1987.

[14] Heckausen, H. & Kuhl, J., *From wishes to actions: the dead and short cuts on the long way to action*, in M. Frese & J. Sabini (eds.) **Goal-directed behavior: The concept of action in psychology**, Hillsdale, New Jersey, Erlbaum, 1985.

[15] Hopkins, C., DePlan: *Enabling Agents to Produce Plans that Achieve Cooperative Problem Solving*, **ECAI-88**, Munich, WG, pp.421-425, 1988.

[16] Maturana, H.R. & Varela, F.J., *Autopoiesis and Cognition. The Realization of the Living.*, Reidel, Dordrecht, Holland, 1985.

[17] Miceli,M. & Castelfranchi,C., *A Cognitive Approach to Values*, **Journal for the Theory of Social Behaviour**, 19, 2, pp.169-193, 1989.

[18] McDermott, D., *A Critique of Pure Reason*, **Computational Intelligence**, 3, pp.151-160, 1987.

[19] Parisi,D. & Castelfranchi,C., *Potere*, in **Rassegna Italiana di Sociologia**, 19, pp.555-592, 1978.

[20] Rosenschein, J.S. & Genesereth, M.R., *Communication and Cooperation*, T.R.-HPP-84-5, Stanford University, California, U.S.A., 1984.

[21] Rosenschein, J.S. & Genesereth, M.R., *Deals Among Rational Agents*, in B.A.Huberman (ed.) **The Ecology of Computation**, Elsevier, North-Holland, 1988.

[22] Werner, E., *Social Intentions*, **ECAI-88**, Munich, WG, pp.719-723, 1988.

[23] Werner, E., *Toward a Theory of Communication and Cooperation for Multiagent Planning*, M. Vardi (ed.), **Theoretical Aspects of Reasoning about Knowledge**, Morgan Kaufman, pp. 129-143, 1988.

[24] Zukerman, I., *Goal-based Generation of Motivational Expressions in a Learning Environment*, **AAAI-87**, Seattle, WA, pp.327-331, 1987.

DECENTRALIZED A.I.
Yves DEMAZEAU & Jean-Pierre MÜLLER (Eds.)

KNOWLEDGE INTERCHANGE PROTOCOLS

John A. CAMPBELL and Mark P. D'INVERNO

Department of Computer Science
University College London
Gower Street
London WC1E 6BT

The interchange of information among autonomous agents, or cooperating parts of a distributed system computation in artificial intelligence, is likely to cause heavy demands on resources for communication in the computing systems that support it. This is even more likely to be true when what is interchanged is knowledge rather than data. It is proposed that a good way to keep the demands under control is to structure the possible acts of communication in advance, in the way that communication and actions are structured in formalised public activities, like traditional ceremonies, behaviour by diplomats etc. The word 'protocol' is used in this sense, and the ideas of protocols from diplomacy and behavioural psychology are exploited in connection with distributed computing in artificial intelligence. A taxonomy of protocols is outlined, and the structure of typical protocols is illustrated by informal examples.

1 Background

As far as we know, 'knowledge interchange protocols' is not a standard AI phrase, but we hope that it will find its way into the AI vocabulary in the future. We use the phrase to label a concept that has a practical use and justification, as indicated below.

The etymology of the phrase itself is interesting. The first appearance of 'knowledge interchange protocols' that we have seen in print was in a B-project section (where no explanations of the project headings are given) in an ESPRIT Call for Proposals. If the phrase survives and prospers it may be the first AI term invented by a collective made up of civil servants.

The justification for considering protocols for knowledge interchange is as follows. Even in ordinary AI computations (search, planning etc.) that involve communication between different entities, communication overheads can dominate the presumably more useful work in finding answers. (This is the main reason why AI searches do not map effectively onto homogeneously parallel computer architectures : identical agents or processors can start a search by doing the same things to copies of a common picture of the world, but searches that are that are going well imply a need for individual agents which make interesting discoveries to announce these to other agents and change their pictures, which can easily saturate the communication facilities or divert much of the processor power from 'useful' work to servicing communications). Where the computations are carried out by distributed and/or autonomous agents, the load imposed on communication channels is at least as heavy as in the non-distributed case. In distributed AI computations where autonomous agents are involved, the world that an agent is exploring includes complex and changing phenomena like the behaviour, beliefs, knowledge bases etc. of the other agents. The 'communication' mentioned above then includes communication of knowledge, e.g. for replication in order to make collective computations more efficient. To avoid excessive communication, and to keep discussion among agents under control, we claim that the best method that humans have evolved is the use of 'protocol' (in the sense of diplomacy, behaviour in public ceremonies etc.). Exchanging knowledge is likely to be the most complex form of communication among agents, and therefore the communication that has the greatest need of regulation and of formal (even stylised) behaviour by the agents. Moreover, there is obviously no single magic formula for regulation of communication: the agents' contributions to a dialogue or public debate depend mainly on what they regard as the purpose or intention (see section 3 below) of an exchange of information. Hence 'knowledge interchange protocols', with different protocols referring to different intentions.

1.1 Outline of the paper

For use in applied AI, the general idea for the above needs to turned into a set of particular examples of protocols or scripts for acts of communication among agents. To do this systematically, what is required is a taxonomy of protocol types. We approach this by identifying the different purposes for which two or more agents are likely to need to communicate. This information is laid out in section 3 below.

There are multiple dimensions of organisation or use of such a taxonomy. This point is mentioned briefly in section 3; more detailed treatment will follow in a later paper.

The basic intention is to use the primary labels for types of protocol to prompt detailed development of protocols (including alternatives and branches) for each type. In section 4 we give examples of the kind of discussion or reasoning that can be used to refine and fill out individual protocols.

Each protocol can be seen as a sequence of general statements by agents taking part in an interchange of information. For a particular instantiation of that protocol in a computation, well-defined slots in sequence will be filled by the particular information that an agent has to contribute. Thus the actual amount of information communicated is minimised. There is no need for an agent to say things that are redundant given that all agents know what protocol is being used, and the protocol itself ensures that risks of loops, long and useless conversational excursions etc. in unstructured attempts at logic-based collective planning are absent. These targets of simplicity are intended to make communication overheads as small as possible.

An agent initiating an exchange in the picture of communication, should choose an appropriate protocol and send the 'slot' information in the first line of the protocol, plus some header code that identifies this protocol to the other agents. They can then retrieve their own copies if they conclude that they wish to take part in the exchange. They can of course choose to ignore the initiating message or even (in a world closer to everyday reality) argue with the sender about the relevance of using that protocol.

We begin with an informal discussion of acts of communication, in section 2.

2 Communication between Intelligent Agents

It is natural to begin from assumptions that have been made in the past about communication between humans. At least since the time of Aristotle, the code model of verbal communication has been accepted as true. According to the model, when we have thoughts they are encoded into linguistic elements (speech) which are then transmitted through a medium (commonly air), decoded by the audience and then held as thoughts which one hopes are in some relation to the thoughts held by the communicator. The code model, though, has many defects and is now considered by many as not flexible enough to describe human verbal communication.

In 1957, H.P. Grice [1] suggested an alternative approach to understanding how a speaker manages to mean something. He argued that speaker meaning was logically prior to sentence meaning. He defined meaning in terms of intention. While many philosophers have argued about the specific definition [2] [3], it seems that for a speaker S to mean something by the utterance U, the speaker must intend at least

1. S's utterance of U to make more manifest a set of assumptions I to a hearer H.

2. for the hearer H to recognise S's intention in (1).

This definition is now considered to be the starting-point for a general theory of communication. Particularly in cognitive science where the search is for a psychologically plausible (and incidentally computationally plausible) account of communication (rather, that is, than talking about the necessity of mutual knowledge or discussing an infinity of intentions (which philosophers seem to enjoy no end)). The basic idea is that if we see humans as information processors then the mind will focus its attention on that which appears to be most relevant, and when we communicate we guarantee a tacit degree of relevance [4]. In other words, we are suggesting that what we have to say is more relevant than anything else that is in the present cognitive environment.

2.1 Speech Acts

To go one step further with the understanding mentioned above, we need to determine a classification or taxonomy of utterances. In this respect, the territory has already been defined, and partially mapped out, by the English linguistic philosopher J. L. Austin, who has produced extensive work on "speech acts" [5]. A speech act, or illocutionary act, in his view, carries some propositional content plus "illocutionary force", where that term is just another name for membership in some category. These categories obviously make the basis for a taxonomy.

As a simple example, consider the statements the statements "Close the door" and "You will close the door". They have identical propositional content, but the first is most likely to carry the illocutionary force of an order, and the second, prediction.

Later, Searle [6] classified illocutionary acts into five categories.

1. Assertive : Statements that commit the speaker to the truth of the assumption expressed.
2. Directives : Attempts to get the hearer to do something.
3. Commissives : Statements which commit the speaker to the performance of a future action.
4. Directives : Statements which bring about the state of affairs described in the assumption expressed.
5. Expressives : Which convey the emotional attitude to the assumption expressed.

It will be useful to bear this categorisation in mind when considering our protocols.

The discussion of protocols that occurs below is based on the assumption that any interchange between agents is governed by those agents' goals and their plans for realising the goals. In particular, the first utterance of an agent initiating a communication will be governed by what that agent sees as its currently most important goal. We do not try to set up a categorisation or taxonomy of goals as such, but we use the idea of intention or purpose of an agent as the basis for organising our taxonomy. One of the main theses of the present work is that the structure of any dialogue between agents is a consequence of its purpose or intention.

2.2 Context; Explicit and Implicit Communication

One of the most striking features of human verbal communication is the seemingly vast distance between what is explicitly said (i.e. the sentence semantics) and what is actually meant. Utterance meaning can basically be a function of two different components.

- Sentence or linguistic meaning. That is, the meaning of the sentence as it stands by itself, the semantics of the syntax.
- Context. There are many contextual factors that affect the meaning of an utterance, non-linguistic devices (tone, delivery, stress, pauses), the immediate cognitive environment, what has been said recently, what the relationship between hearer and listener is like, memory, prejudice (and ignorance). These all contribute to the meaning of an utterance (or as Searle calls it, a speech act). For any given sentence, any infinity of meanings can be given to that sentence depending on who said it, when, where and with whom. All it seems that the rules of grammar provide is merely a clue as to how to interpret a given sentence.

In most of the cases that concern us, context has the dominant role. Elucidating context is what causes unconstrained computations that involve dialogue (e.g. for cooperative planning) in AI to be so inefficient: unless the exchanges are constrained, the communication, that is about exploring a context swamps the useful communication about what can be called "getting on with the job".

In many tasks that involve cooperation between agents, it is possible to constrain the former kind of communication by requiring all dialogues to be conducted in accordance with protocols. The contextual negotiation that is mentioned above then reduces to a negotiation (which can be brief) about the protocol to be used.

In this article we describe some of the features of protocols and how they can be built. Questions such as negotiation will be treated in a future article.

We begin by considering what reasoning devices an intelligent agent should be capable of using, with the basic motive being for each agent to update its knowledge of the world.

3 A Taxonomy of 'tones' of communication

Given here is a list of possible 'tones' of communication that it would seem beneficial to explore. For each, we should try to invent protocols to aid in their fulfilment. The idea, then, is that an agent (e.g a robot) who wanted to initiate communication would select a particular protocol. He would then communicate that he was using this protocol by stating an appropriate header code. This would then allow the intended audience to select the corresponding protocol to enable successful communication or to ignore irrelevant communications. From this point the protocol limits the possibilities of communication between the agents.

1. Action requesting
2. Information seeking
3. Information probing
4. Information checking
5. Instructing
6. Informing
7. Understanding an unexpected event
8. Warning
9. Advising
10. Persuading
11. Promising
12. Bargaining
13. Impressing
14. Intimidating
15. Threatening

16. Commanding
17. Encouraging
18. Expressing (i.e. of one's own state)
19. Offending
20. Misleading
21. Amusing

There is a general idea of decreasing level of importance as one reads down the list. This is not in any way an analytic list. Many of the tones will be subsets of other tones, many tones will be used as methods of realising larger tones. For example, promising, bargaining, impressing and intimidating can all be used to fulfil a 'persuade' motive. As we shall see later, bargaining essentially consists of an action-seeking dialogue and a promise. Let us elaborate a little and give a short dialogue for each example. Let us introduce two robots A and B collecting garbage on the planet Mars. Robot B sweeps up garbage into a wheelbarrow, then takes it to A, who is situated at an incinerator. B unloads the rubbish and A shovels the garbage into the incinerator.

1. Action requesting
   - A : Would you unload the rubbish over there please?
2. Information seeking
   - B : Which area should I clear next?
3. Information probing
   - A : Do you know anything about wheelbarrows.?
   - B : I know their history
   - A : No, about how to use them ?
   - B : Sure...
4. Information checking
   - A : We aren't here to look for Martians are we ?
   - B : No
5. Instructing
   - A : Then you place one hand on each of the two handles, OK?
   - B : What, like this ?
   - A : No, they're called wheels, they always touch the ground, these are the handles, now lift.

- B : Put me down you fool, lift the handles up, vertically thats it, now push - ow - not into me you fool.

6. Informing
   - B : This will be my last trip for today.
7. Warning
   - A : You're too close to the incinerator.
   - B : What?
   - A : You'll melt if you go near hot things.
8. Advising
   - A : If I were you I would pick up lighter rocks.
   - B : Why?
   - A : Because your life expectancy would increase.
9. Understanding an unexpected event.
   - A : Why are you unloading the rubbish back onto the ground ?
   - B : We've been told that these are rocks. There isn't any garbage on Mars.
10. Persuading
    - A : Look, I'd do the same thing for you, remember all I've done for you.
11. Promising
    - B : I will fetch another shovel for you.
12. Bargaining
    - A : If you place the garbage closer to me then I'll give you a hand collecting garbage tomorrow.
13. Impressing
    - A : I have been a garbage incinerator all my life.
14. Intimidating
    - A : I really think I could do that better than you, you know.
15. Threatening
    - A : If you don't stop unloading the rubbish on me, I will spread all the rubbish back on the ground.
16. Commanding

- A : I order you to pick up that garbage.
- B : Who are you to order me ?
- A : Check out this badge sonny.

17. Encouraging

    - A : You'll be great, the last time you did it it was fantastic.

18. Expressing

    - A : I'm not very happy with the way you are doing your job.
    - B : Why's that then?

19. Offending

    - A : You have the intelligence of a soiled piece of Martian clay.
    - B : Why are you getting so upset ?
    - A : Because you keep bringing back the heaviest pieces of garbage.

20. Misleading

    - A : It's best to bring me the smallest pieces of Garbage, because they burn more easily.

21. Amusing

    - A : Did you hear the one about the Venusian road builder ?

We now look at a few cases in more detail and generality.

4 Methods with Examples

4.1 Warning

How then do we go about writing down these scripts? To avoid re-inventing various wheels, the first thing to do is to look at some examples of some of these tones of communication in the human world. Let us consider warning, as an example. Notice first that it fits nicely into Searle's classification of an illocutionary act, since as it is performative it actually describes the action that it is performing. However a warning can either be directive, in the sense of "perform this action to avert the danger", or it can be assertive i.e. the speaker gives the hearer some information about the danger (often spatial location data) and the listener can then in his increased knowledge take the necessary avoiding action. We consider the tone to be 'warning' when used to describe immediate danger, which we assume to be out of the control of the speaker.

To avoid being more original than we have been in the previous sections, let us call out two communicating agents A, and B. Then the paradigmatic, or at least, most typical case of warning occurs when the speaker declares a danger (as in "watch out"), the hearer looks to the speaker and the speaker than points or looks to where the danger is manifesting itself. All these elements can be laid out, in that order, in a typical warning protocol.

What is happening here? A perceives a possible expected event, likely to be harmful to B. Merely by A shouting "watch out" , B is now aware of the fact that A considers B to be in danger. B, prompted by A, is then guided to the location of the danger and perceives it for himself. The information being transferred then is solely that the speaker considers there to be a danger manifesting itself at a specific physical location.

Notice firstly that the manifestation of danger in this type of warning is physical. Now, what in general are the kinds of things that A should be considering before deciding what method to use in warning B?

- The severity and imminence of the danger. For instance B may only have time to say one thing, in which case he should make it count. (e.g. stop, duck)
- Whether B has perceived the danger and, if he hasn't could he ? In the human world warning is very often about getting the hearer to perceive the danger for himself. However there may be spatial or biological restrictions preventing this. The most common one is if the danger can only be seen from A's position and not B's.
- Whether once perceived B would know why the predicted event was dangerous. Of course it is not enough to get B to see the danger, there is no reason to suggest that B will necessarily perceive the possible occurrence of this event to be dangerous. For example, someone not being aware that a snake is poisonous will not be aware of any possible danger.

The suggestion, then, is to have four types of strategy available to the potential warner. This is an instance of identifying sub-structure in a particular class of protocol.

1. Perform a danger-preventing action.
2. Perform a danger-perceiving action.
3. Assuming the physical manifestation of the danger has been perceived, and (though the hearer is unable to realise why this event is dangerous) then give information about the danger.
4. Assuming the physical manifestation of the danger has not been perceived, give information about the danger.

Notice that the first two strategies are directive, and the second two are assertive in nature. It is important to allow A to be able to skip between the strategies. For example if he gets B to perceive the danger using strategy (2) and B does not respond because he doesn't have the necessary knowledge about the danger, he might try using strategy (3).

When protocols are not simple and linear, a linear presentation or development (as in written text) is not the clearest way to organise the relevant information. We have found that a diagram notation that has much in common with state transition diagrams, as in figure 1, is helpful. Nodes in a diagram represent the agents (a circle for A, and a rectangle for B) and their reasoning at a given stage in the protocol. On the arcs are the exchanged communications.

At each node the agent's possible reasoning is stated. For each piece of possible reasoning, an arc is drawn, and the communication type is stated. These arrows may have a counter to prevent loops in our communication. Figure 1 shows part of a simplified warning protocol.

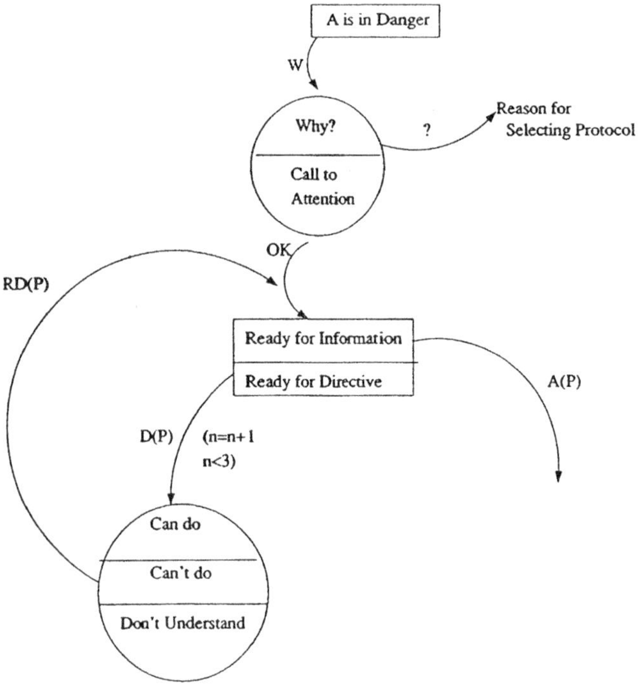

Figure 1: Part of a possible warning protocol

B considers A to be in danger, and sends the communication *W*. This is a protocol heading, and informs A not only of the fact that B considers A to be in danger, but also what Protocol should be selected by A, to engage in a dialogue with B. At this stage (as with any protocol) the reasons for the choice of protocol can be sought. If however A accepts the idea that B's warning should be taken seriously on the face of it, he will respond with an *OK* message, which informs B that A has her message, and has selected the necessary protocol. At this point the protocol allows B to either make an assertive proposition about the danger, or give a directive proposition, depending on the circumstance. Suppose B gives a directive, but A is unable to perform this (represented by *Can't do* in the diagram). A replies with a reason stating why he couldn't perform the suggested action. B has to choose again whether to give a directive or an assertive. Counters and conditions are placed on the arcs to make sure that an agent is forced into changing tactics in fulfilling the purpose of the dialogue, thus avoiding repetitious and useless dialogues.

4.2 Using logic to represent initial situations thus giving rise to variations within a tone of dialogue

The use of a logic's expressive power will help us guide our thoughts in deciding on protocols. As we go through, we shall try to impose axioms on our logics, with the hope in mind of being able to find an existing logic from the stock of past AI-related work on planning belief, intentions etc., which will meet our specific requirements. We try to represent the basic mental state of the speaker, and then see how capturing this knowledge can help us reason about the creation of scripts.

It is important that wherever possible the speaker only passes knowledge that the hearer would otherwise be unable to gain from the environment. Initially we introduce a motivational operator, desire.

- DESIRE

then given an agent A, and an event X we can write

- A DESIRE X

meaning that A would like the event X to occur.
Let us next introduce two epistemic operators

- KNOW
- ASSUME

So, assuming we have some set of propositions I, or any other formally well-defined material I, we could have an expression of the form

- A DESIRE (B KNOW I)

which would mean that A wishes that B have the knowledge I.
Next we need an intentional operator, so that assuming that there is some action X,

- A INTEND X

means that A has every intention of 'doing' the action X.
Now we are in a position to see how it helps us to describe some pre-conditions for particular tones of dialogue, and see how this leads to discussion about possible protocols.

4.3 Action seeking

This category fits neatly within the directive category of Searle, by virtue of it being an attempt by the hearer to get the speaker to perform some action. We have the situation where A desires an action X to be performed in the world by B. Let us then write down the mental state of the speaker.

1. A DESIRE X
2. A ASSUME (B ABLE-TO-PERFORM X)
3. A INTEND C where R(C) $\rightarrow$ B INTEND X
4. A DESIRE (B INTEND X)
5. A ASSUME (B (NOT INTEND) X)
6. A ASSUME
   (a) B DESIRE X
   (b) B (NOT DESIRE) X

Notice firstly that the logic may serve as a means of selecting the appropriate protocol by an agent wishing to initiate a conversation. He matches the pre-conditions of each protocol against his own current mental state, and is then able to select the most suitable protocol.

Thus what we have for the tone of 'action-seeking' to be initiated is that A desires the action X, and assuming that B is in a position to do this, wants B to perform this action X. He does this by communicating C, where the result of C, given by R(C), leads to B intending to perform the action A.

Let us consider some of the cases

1. B is not in a position to perform X. The reply from B would then be a clear description of the reason why B feels he is in such a position. A would then either negate his original assumption or continue by trying to convince B that the action X is possible.

2. Where the communication is unsuccessful. It might be that not enough information has been received (this may include knowledge about how to go about performing the task, or to aid B to decide on his willingness to perform the task), or that the meaning was ambiguous, or that there was a noise in the communicating channel. Often B might ask A to repeat the request, or clarify some point.

3. If A assumes (correctly) that B also desires X, then the dialogue would normally not involve anything more than the actual request.

4. If A assumes (correctly) that B does not desire A, then he will have to supply some reason along with the request, typically stressing how important the task is for a particular goal, or for the speaker, or possibly reminding him of their

friendship, favours done in the past, and so on. If these are unsuccessful then B might try other tones of dialogue, for example bargaining, threatening or by commanding if A stood in the necessary position to be able to do this to B.

5. If A assumes incorrectly the desirability of X to B, B should firstly inform A of his true wishes. A would then be able to reconsider the situation with a better knowledge of the world.

One thing that is worth noting is that A may request of B not to do something. If he had sufficient authority, this would become an example of prohibiting.

A very similar account can be given of information seeking.

4.4 Dialogues expressing intention about future actions

We now take a look at the world of what Searle calls the commissives, namely the speaker informing the hearer of a intention about a future action. Let us first consider some necessary preconditions for the act of promising. For ease of exposition we introduce a new predicate

- EXPECT

which is merely in fact, a subset of assume where the assumed action is in the future. There are axioms.

- A INTEND X $\rightarrow$ A EXPECT X
- A ASSUME (B INTEND X) $\rightarrow$ A EXPECT X

The most straightforward example is when A informs B of his intention to do something. The verb commit is used to describe this action. This dialogue is a subset of informing.

1. A DESIRE (B KNOW (A INTEND X))
2. A INTEND C where R(C) $\rightarrow$ B KNOW (A INTEND X)
3. A INTEND X
4. A ASSUME (A ABLE-TO-PERFORM X)

   A, then, merely informs B of his intention to perform some action, presumably so that B can make plans accordingly, or give B a chance to air his views on the subject (including the possibility of pointing out flaws in the fourth predicate). The next act is that of promising. This has two extra conditions, namely, that A assumes that B desires the situation resulting from the action X, and that A doesn't expect the action X to occur in the normal course of events.

   These can be written

5. A ASSUME (B EXPECT (NOT X))

6. A ASSUME (B DESIRE X)

After all of this, we can see where the conversation may differ from the original example of informing. B may be expecting the event X to happen anyway and thus explains why he thinks his expected model of the world is perhaps different from A's. Perhaps B does not desire X, and this would then be communicated, optionally with reasons explaining why he did not desire such an event.

Notice also that if predicate 6 were reversed, then we would have necessary pre-conditions for threatening in the sense of the verb 'threatening' (let us for the sake of argument call this tone threatening2.) However this 'tone of dialogue' is seldom used alone, it is used as a way of getting the hearer to perform (or equivalently not perform) some action A. Let us go on finally to discuss this tone (threatening1) along with the tone of bargaining (which is very similar in structure).

4.5 Threatening and Bargaining

The basic idea of threatening is that, if the hearer does not perform some action, then the speaker will perform some action that the hearer does not desire. So at this level it has commissive elements and directive elements, although the dialogue may also contain elements from the other categories. Here are some of the mental attitudes the speaker will have.

Suppose that A wants B to perform X and threatens him by communicating that he will perform Y if A does not perform X.

1. A DESIRE (B INTEND X)
2. A ASSUME (B (NOT INTEND) X)
3. A ASSUME (B (NOT DESIRE) X)
4. A ASSUME (B (NOT DESIRE) Y)
5. A ASSUME ((B (NOT DESIRE) X) $\leq$ (B (NOT DESIRE) Y))
6. A DESIRE (B KNOW ((B (NOT INTEND) X) $\rightarrow$ (A INTEND X))

The first thing to notice is how similar this is to action seeking. The only difference is the introduction of an action Y. It then leads us to consider how, if an action-seeking protocol were ineffective, the agent might consider threatening as another strategy. In which case he would have to search for an event Y, which satisfied the above constraints. Such a writing down pre-conditions shows how various strategies are related (how they lead on from one another), and how the agent must reason, to meet the pre-conditions required to initiate a particular protocol.

Now we can consider some of the knowledge that may have to be exchanged. For example a typical reply may involve A's getting assumptions 4 and 5 wrong, respectively, "Go ahead and do X, see if I care" and "I'd much rather you did Y than I did X". Then assuming that A considers that B is being honest he will have to reconsider, for example, by changing Y so as to make it even less desirable for A. In any case maybe B intended to do X anyway.

From the writing down in logic of some of the mental attitudes of the person initiating a particular tone of dialogue, we can see the kinds of knowledge that should be transferred.

Finally, as it is so close to threatening, let us briefly consider bargaining. Some of the mental attitudes of the agent who decides to initiate this tone will be.

1. A DESIRE (B INTEND X)

2. A ASSUME (B (NOT INTEND) X)

3. A ASSUME (B DESIRE (A INTEND Y))

We have two linked acts of promising. A is promising Y, and assuming B enters into the discussion, B is considering promising something close to X. Notice how action-seeking is also an element of bargaining, so we can draw upon our experiences of preceding dialogues. Let us write down a list of the possible responses and reasoning that B might give. She might reason that she

1. is not able to perform X

2. is not prepared to perform X

3. was to perform X anyway

4. does not desire Y

5. considers the bargain fine

6. feels that the bargain is unfair and so adjustments should be made to the actions X and Y.

7. considers that Y would have occurred in the normal course of events.

It can be seen then that types of dialogue are recurring from previous tones of dialogue. We would like to harness this commonality.

4.6 Mislead

The use of logic has also made it fairly clear how one could allow 'mislead' tones of dialogue. Notice that with all commissives (promising, committing, threatening), an intention to perform some action is expressed. But if we had a promise being made by A to B, without B having any intention to perform the action, then we would have a case of 'mislead'. Similarly let us consider the class of assertives (A communicates some statement he believes to be true about the world). In the logic, the mental state of a speaker wishing to communicate a proposition P may contain.

1. A DESIRE (B KNOW P)

2. A INTEND C where R(C) $\rightarrow$ B KNOW P

3. B KNOW I

The point then is that if we reversed the third predicate we could have another example of a case of 'mislead' (more specifically, lying). For the class of directives we could give a false reason for persuading the listener to perform some action. We should entertain the idea that a mislead protocol would have many assets. As an example suppose we have a senior robot and he has to get a junior robot to perform a certain task. However, the senior robot realises that the junior robot will not be able to understand the reasons for the task or will be unable to act on instructions to carry it out if it is specified in a conventional way. What the senior robot can do then is give a false but simple reason for the task which is sufficient to motivate the junior robot.

4.7 Dealing with the Unexpected

Consider an example of this highly relevant (for robotics, AI) dialogue that actually took place recently. Fortunately, the names of the participants were A and B.

- A : I can't eat that.
- B : (gives puzzled look, tries to examine food so as to understand B's sentence)
- A : What are you doing ... oh I see you don't know do you, I've become a vegetarian.
- B : Good God why ?
- A : I just think animals are too valuable to be used as fodder.
- B : Oh I see. Well er pass it over here then would you ? (licking lips violently) and the er mustard....ketchup....salt....pepper....vinegar...that should cover it. Oh I'm sorry do you want my onions.

So in essence what happens is that A does something, that B can't understand in the context. A realises that, and reveals a new proposition to B, hoping that this will make B realise why A's actions were reasoned. B accepts the proposition as true about the world, but B is still not satisfied with this latest proposition and asks for reason behind it. After probing, A gives reasons which satisfies the curiosity and search for consistency of B. B then ridicules the reasoning behind it by making a (not very good) joke about it.

It is possible to abstract from particular examples of such an analysis, and make general observations about what a protocol may have to deal with. For example, let us concentrate on the situation where A performs an action that B considers unexpected, and wishes to know the thinking behind it. B might typically begin with

- Why did you just do that?

meaning "Is there some knowledge that I don't have that will help me understand what you just did?"

In humans a common reason is that even though A knows P, and A knows that P implies Q, it does not necessarily follow that A is capable of entertaining a conceptualisation of Q at that time. The proposition Q once pointed out will make sense because

B will realise that Q follows logically from what B considers to be true. Probably more relevant to our purposes, though, is the situation that occurs through a change in the knowledge or thinking of A, or a change in the external environment that A has become aware of, but B has not. It is probably best to distinguish between the knowledge that a robot has about himself and the knowledge that he has about the external world. So A gives out the new knowledge with possible reasons for entertaining this new concept, like "I've been told to do this" backed up if necessary by "I've got a new programmer this week".

Similar detailed treatment can be given to all the protocol types that are listed in section 3. The treatment given here is in a linear and conversational way. However, for a more compact means of reasoning about various alternatives the state transition diagrams seem to offer the best representation. The examples chosen in the present section have been chosen for illustration and to keep the paper short.

4.8 Termination

The protocols must be forced to terminate. Of course there may be many reasons for the termination of a protocol. A promised task may have been completed and reported, an action request may be refused, an accident may terminate a warning protocol. The point is that a dialogue is still 'open' until it is terminated. This does not mean that protocols must run sequentially, indeed, what is envisaged is that protocols run concurrently. For example, if agent A has promised to B that he will perform action X, the protocol could terminate when A reports the successful completion of the task. However both agents will be able to enter into other dialogues whilst this particular promising protocol is still open (i.e. it hasn't terminated). Protocols would be prioritised. For example, a warning protocol which was dealing with an immediate danger should be terminated before other protocols which were open could be continued, or new protocols initiated.

5 Summary

The material reported here is basically for orientation, and to argue that the subject of knowledge interchange protocols belongs within distributed AI because of its usefulness for reducing communication overheads and imposing order on what could otherwise be very unruly computations among autonomous agents.

For each of the forms of protocol mentioned above (and others in the collection given in section 3) there is a general structure in which every line of the conversation or transaction has a specific task of carrying the interchange forward. An agent whose turn it is to contribute to a protocol-controlled communication should be able to add its particular contribution, with minimal effort, from information about its own state and its own view of the world. A scheme based on protocols is therefore a structured means of simplifying communication and its overheads in distributed AI. It has implications for the internal organisation of agents: an agent ought to be 'protocol oriented', in the sense that it recognises the range of protocols that exist, can select the right one for any exchange that it wishes to initiate, and can derive appropriate slot-filling material from its own environment efficiently, whenever its turn to fill a slot in a protocol comes up.

We are interested to obtain further suggestions for types of communication that deserve to figure in the taxonomy in section 3, and comments on the possibilities for integration of the protocol-based scheme in other peoples' implementations or designs for multi-agent cooperation.

In order to introduce our particular idea of "protocols" we have not put any emphasis on "knowledge interchange" above. Therefore many of our examples of what is interchanged refer to items of data, information etc. rather than something that can be regarded indisputably as knowledge. Protocols are effective for constraining the interchange of data in order to improve computing efficiency, but in the case of knowledge exchange (where the purposes are a subset of the set given in section 3) an equally strong justification is that they make systematic and finite behaviour possible. The question of knowledge interchange will become increasingly important as cooperation between agents or programs that hold different knowledge and/or different knowledge representations becomes a more commonplace expectation. (One pressure in this direction is that users' views about reusability of conventional software modules are already being expressed with respect to reusability of knowledge in the form of existing expert-system modules. Emphasis on the blackboard architecture for knowledge-based systems is a similar source of pressure). We intend to cover examples specifically in the exchange of knowledge in a future publication. A relevant test of the ideas reported here has already been carried out by Pankhurst [7].

References

[1] Grice, H.P. Meaning. *Philosophical Review*, Vol. 66, pp.377-388, 1957.

[2] Schiffer, S.R. *Meaning*. London. Oxford University

[3] Searle, J.R. Expression and Meaning in *Studies in the theory of Speech Acts*. J. R. Searle, editor, Cambridge University Press, 1979.

[4] Sperber, D. and Wilson, D. *Relevance*. Blackwell, Oxford, 1987.

[5] Austin, J.L. *How to do things with words*. Oxford University Press, 1962.

[6] Searle, J.R. *Speech Acts*. Cambridge University Press, 1969.

[7] Pankhurst, G.J. *Knowledge Exchange for Expert Systems*. BSc report project, Dept. of Computer Science, University College London, 1989.

DECENTRALIZED A.I.
Yves DEMAZEAU & Jean-Pierre MÜLLER (Eds.)

DISTRIBUTED AI AND MANUFACTURING CONTROL: SOME ISSUES AND INSIGHTS

H. Van Dyke PARUNAK

Industrial Technology Institute
PO Box 1485
Ann Arbor, MI 48106 USA
(313) 769-4049, van@iti.org

A review of a multi-year research program on applications of DAI to manufacturing illustrates the close relations among several DAI concepts and paradigms and emphasizes the value of practical applications in highlighting important research issues in this field.

1. INTRODUCTION

Classical AI has developed a number of concepts and tools, such as knowledge representation, production systems, possible worlds, truth maintenance, planning, and learning. An academic researcher tends to specialize on one or a few of these topics. Those who engineer AI-based systems face a different challenge: coupling several concepts into a coherent application. Systems that use only a single technique are inherently fragile. Real problems require a judicious selection from the full repertoire.

Distributed AI (DAI) is developing its own set of diverse tools and concepts, including blackboards, contract nets, speech act theory, task decomposition, deferred commitment, formalisms for concurrency, and negotiation. Here, as in classical AI, academic researchers refine and polish individual components, while DAI engineers integrate them into solutions to real-world problems.

This paper illustrates how a number of DAI concepts, some of them quite abstract and academic by themselves, form essential components in addressing the problem of controlling a manufacturing cell in a flexible manufacturing system (FMS), and in turn shows how the problems of this domain lead to some interesting DAI concepts.

We begin by describing the problem domain. Then we follow the history of a research program addressing this problem, which leads us through discussions of negotiating systems, the relation between large- and fine-grained parallelism, an application of speech act theory in framing one aspect of the control problem, and the implications of nonlinear dynamics for ecologies of autonomous agents.

2. THE PROBLEM

ITI's work in DAI is in the context of an upper-level control architecture for an experimental flexible manufacturing cell. The cell includes a turning center, a machining center, an assembly robot, an inspection station, a load/unload station, and an automatic storage and retrieval system (ASRS), interconnected by a switched belt conveyor system. [1, 2] A guiding philosophical commitment in this work is to decentralize control and push it as far down in the control hierarchy as possible. As a result, failure of any single node has reduced impact on the system, and the system can be modified locally without extensive changes. This strategy also takes advantage of the distributed computing resource that already exists in many plants. The controller for a single modern machine tool is a computer with significant capacity, and can interact with other workstations.

3. NEGOTIATION AND YAMS

The first control implementation for this system is YAMS ("Yet Another Manufacturing System"), and draws on the "Contract Net" model of control by negotiation. [3, 4, 5, 6]. This section reviews the model and outlines how it is used in YAMS and more recent applications, then summarizes some important issues from that research. For more details on the YAMS application of contract nets to manufacturing and further discussion of the issues raised here, see [7].

3.1. The Contract Net Model

The contract net models transfer of control in a distributed system as negotiation among autonomous intelligent agents. The net consists of a set of *nodes* that negotiate with one another through a set of *messages*. A manager node announces a task to other nodes, who reply with bids. The manager evaluates the bids and awards the task to the most attractive bidder. Other messages handle status reports, termination of a task, and changes in the population of nodes.

Smith originally applied the contract net to a distributed sensor system, such as one might use in air traffic control. [6] Signal collectors invite bids from sensors, and evaluate them on sensory capabilities as well as geographical location. A node responsible for monitoring a local area solicits bids from nodes that can integrate information from sensors, and evaluates bids on the basis of the geographical location of the bidders. An area manager, confronted with sensory information, invites bids from vehicle managers to find which one is best suited to manage the sensed object.

Negotiation can also distribute tasks across a distributed system of CPU's. [8, 9, 10]. Each node accepts only those tasks whose execution it can guarantee by a specified deadline. If it discovers tasks that it cannot guarantee, it uses either direct negotiation or information retained from previous negotiations to find another node that can guarantee their execution.

3.2. Applications of the Contract Net to Manufacturing

At least four mappings of contract net nodes to entities on the factory floor have been proposed.

3.2.1. Negotiation among Hierarchical Levels

YAMS models a manufacturing enterprise as a hierarchy of workcells, or functional groups of machinery. This model corresponds closely to the traditional manufacturing view of a corporation as a hierarchical system of plants, each containing several manufacturing cells, each in turn made up of several workstations.

For example, assume that the Engine Plant has successfully bid on a "make-engine" task. It broadcasts a task announcement for the first step in "make-engine," which is "make-block," and receives bids from two cells that know how to handle large castings, the Block Cell and the Head Cell. The bid from the Block Cell is more favorable, because that cell is already set up for blocks, so the Engine Plant awards the contract to the Block Cell. Suppose, though, that the Block Cell breaks down. With no changes to the software, the Head Cell will now be the successful bidder, and the plant can continue operating while the damaged line is repaired.

3.2.2. Negotiation among Peer Cells

The architecture of Shaw and Whinston [11, 12] permits negotiations among peer workstations, so that an overloaded workstation can share its work with others. One operating mode also supports YAMS-style bidding between hierarchical levels.

3.2.3. Negotiation between Parts and Workstations

Each part in the CADENCE system [13] carries its process plan along with it, and posts to a blackboard a list of its feasible operations (those operations in its process plan for which all prerequisites have been satisfied). Workstations consult the blackboard to find operations that they can perform, and send bids for executing these operations to the parts. These bids can reflect such parameters as the current load of the workstation and the tooling that it has in place. A part then selects a workstation and goes there for the operation to be performed.

3.2.4. Negotation between Suppliers and Consumers

Baker [14] envisions peer workstations negotiating with one another for parts at different levels of completion. The shipping dock posts a task announcement for the finished product, and assembly workstations bid for the right to produce the product. They in turn post task announcements for the component parts, to which producers of those parts respond. In principle, the currency of negotiation can be the actual dollar value of the part at each stage in its production, so that the net implicitly optimizes the expense of production.

3.3. Issues and Insights

Our experience with YAMS raises a number of issues in the application of negotiation to shop floor control, issues that may be expected to apply to the other models that we have described as well.

First, negotiation requires more communications bandwidth than does a centralized control scheme, though traffic can be reduced through a scheme of audience restriction. [7] From an engineering perspective, negotiation is only justified in a volatile environment, where globally distributed information rapidly becomes out of date. Furthermore, simulations show that negotiation is most effective when the negotiating entities have overlapping but not identical capabilities.

Second, because the contract net replaces global information with the exchange of information between local agents, performance anomalies can arise. *Temporal ignorance* reflects the fact that nodes can only see task announcements and bids that have already arrived, not those that are about to arrive. A node may bid on a task for which it is marginally suited and thus commit resources to the extent that it cannot later bid on a task for which it is much better suited. Or a manager may accept a bid moments before a much more attractive one appears. *Spatial ignorance* arises because nodes have knowledge only of contracts to which they are party, and cannot take advantage of the details of other contracts in making their own decisions. *Loading ignorance* arises because nodes do not know how busy other nodes are.

The contract net requires a broadcast capability for distributing task announcements, and many implementations use a bus for all traffic, including bids and awards. In such a system, nodes can reduce their ignorance of one another by eavesdropping on the net. By monitoring bids, a node can learn who its competitors are for various task classes, and by monitoring awards, it can track their loading. The possible politics of such a system quickly become fascinating, and very complex. One can imagine two competing nodes, each waiting until the last possible moment to submit its bid in the hopes of peeking at the other's bid first, together jeopardizing the timely performance of the entire system.

The third issue that emerges from our work with negotiating systems is the distinction between the control medium (a communications network, operating at digital speeds) and the performance medium (the factory floor, with mechanical constraints). In this respect, the manufacturing problem domain differs significantly from other applications of the contract net, such as sensor nets or task allocation on a multiprocessor, where control and performance are both in a computational context. The need to coordinate these two domains leads to our second major application of DAI to manufacturing, the CASCADE system.

4. COARSE-GRAINED AND FINE-GRAINED PARALLELISM

The need to coordinate the control medium and the performance medium motivates CASCADE, a mechanism for distributed material handling. [15, 16, 17, 18, 19] This section describes the subproblem that CASCADE addresses. It traces the evolution of the contract net model into a neural model, and summarizes some issues and insights that CASCADE raises.

4.1. Material Handling in YAMS

Following the contract net literature, our early experiments with YAMS naively concentrated on the digital communications among agents. We very quickly realized that the actual movement of parts among workstations is as much a part of of the interaction of the agents as is the carefully designed negotiation protocol, and so we focused our attention on modeling that movement of parts. Our experience with the contract net led us to extend this model to material handling. In the control domain, software objects corresponding to workstations negotiate for task assignments. In the performance domain, the corresponding objects are physical workstations, which exchange parts. So we seek to define a negotiation protocol for material handling that will incorporate the parts themselves as a component of the communication.

CASCADE draws much of its inspiration from the Japanese KANBAN system of flow control, [20, 21, 22] in which a set of workstations pass tickets back and forth over a predefined pattern of interconnections. Tickets travel either alone (as requests for parts) or attached to parts (in the delivery cycle, as authorizations for the next workstation to begin work). In our vocabulary, tickets are messages in the control medium and parts are messages in the performance medium, and the two are closely coupled. The tickets authorize the workstations to perform their functions, such as producing parts and transporting them throughout the factory. The focus on material handling permits the negotiation protocol to consist only of these two kinds of messages.

Classic KANBAN is a pure pull system. CASCADE generalizes to provide push as well. Under KANBAN, a workstation whose incoming part inventory falls below a given level can order more parts from its suppliers. CASCADE adds to this a mechanism for a workstation whose finished part inventory exceeds a given level to spill those parts to other workstations. It also generalizes the notion of "workstation" to include not only modules that add value to a part, but also material handling equipment such as ASRS's, conveyors, and automatic guided vehicles (AGV's).

4.2. The CASCADE Model

CASCADE as a generalization of KANBAN consists of a network of processing elements (workstations and material handling equipment) with associated threshholds (maximum and minimum part population levels) that govern the movement of parts and requests among the elements. Described in this way, CASCADE is almost isomorphic to a connectionist network, [23] a parallel that is developed more fully elsewhere. [18]

CASCADE has four kinds of objects that interact through local connections: *containers*, *requests*, *units*, and *aggregates*.

A *container* represents a parcel of material that can be moved and stored as an entity. Containers are strongly typed on the basis of the functional state of their contents, and two containers of the same type are interchangeable as far as the manufacturing process is concerned.

A *request* is a message asking for a container. Requests are characterized by the type of container they are seeking.

A *unit* is a collection of containers that are in the same geographical area and that are related to one another. There are two types of units, corresponding to two types of relations between containers.

1. If all the containers in a unit have the same type, the unit is a *TOMP* (an acronym with an obscure and irrelevant history). No functional processing can take place in such a unit, otherwise incoming containers would differ in type from outgoing ones.

2. If the containers in a unit are participants in the same functional operation, the unit is a *process*. A process consumes containers of zero or more types and produces containers of zero or more types. It differs from a TOMP in two ways. Its behavior is stochastic rather than deterministic (at least from the perspective of the material handling system), and its output can be of a different type than its input.

Every container belongs to exactly one unit at a time, and moves from unit to unit as the system operates.

An *aggregate* is a collection of units that are in the same geographical area. There are two types of aggregates, corresponding to the two types of units.

1. A *mover* is a collection of TOMP's, and models a single geographically limited material handling module, such as a conveyor loop, a zone of an AGV (automatic guided vehicle) system, or an ASRS (automatic storage and retrieval system).

2. A *workstation* is a collection of processes that run on a single geographically local and functionally integrated set of machines (typically, a machine tool with associated transfer and inspection mechanisms).

Units and workstations correspond to the processing units of the PDP model, and containers and requests correspond to the signals that move among them. Each TOMP has an absolute (*ABS*), a maximum (*MAX*), and a minimum (*MIN*) capacity for containers of its type, $ABS \geq MAX \geq MIN \geq 0$, and is connected to one or more other units on adjacent aggregates. Its population (the number of containers it contains) can never exceed *ABS*. If its population exceeds its maximum capacity, it seeks to spill the excess to a neighboring unit. If its population falls below its minimum capacity, it seeks to fill up to the minimum from its neighbors. Thus the units form a network through which containers and requests for containers propagate.

The analog to PDP's activation is a vector recording the TOMP population and number of requests received. The spilling and filling rule corresponds to PDP's propagation rule. Because traffic between nodes is quantized (discrete parts and requests), the probabilities in the connectivity matrix define, not the fraction of its output that a node sends to each neighbor (as in PDP), but the probability that the entire output will be sent to a given neighbor. This matrix in turn changes on the basis of experience, to implement a connectivity learning rule.

4.3. Issues and Insights

The references give more details on the structure of CASCADE and its behavior. For the purposes of this paper, the system illustrates two important points.

First, CASCADE began as an attempt to apply techniques of coarse-grained parallel systems (negotiation) to material handling. What finally emerged was an isomorph of a fine-grained parallel system, a PDP network. This experience suggests that the boundary between these two kinds of systems is not as rigid as one might suppose. The phenomenon is similar to a marching band, in which each agent carries out a wide range of intelligent behavior, but constrains its interactions with other agents in the interests of providing a greater measure of coherence in the whole system.

Second, we have extended the PDP parallel to show that CASCADE is computationally equivalent to an arbitrary Turing machine. [24]. This result implies that most of the interesting properties of a CASCADE system are formally undecidable. In fact, our result is even stronger: any factory with sufficient feedback mechanisms to implement simple KANBAN crosses the brink into undecidability. This conclusion bodes ill for conventional notions of purely predictive general-purpose scheduling mechanisms, and reinforces the research directions currently in vogue to explore real-time, reactive scheduling of complex distributed systems.

5. INTEGRATING MACHINES AND PEOPLE: WHAT IS CONTROL?

As a manufacturing control system becomes more complex and more intelligent, its interface with humans becomes more difficult to manage. In earlier times, humans made all the important decisions, and automation only carried out simple tasks. Now, the kinds of intelligence that we have been discussing give significant capability to the machine. It is more of a peer to human agents, and in some cases may actually be better suited than humans to make critical control decisions.

Conventional control schemes fix the interrelation of agents in advance, [25, 26] but intelligent control requires that the relations among agents can *change* as the system operates. Consider the case when one agent is a human operator and the other is the control program for a nuclear power plant. Most of the time, the control program runs the plant and the operator is effectively a consultant, unable to respond to the mass of data as rapidly as the system requires. Sometimes, though, the operator must take over and the control program serves only as a data gathering tool. The difference between these two states represents a change in the relation between the two agents. More complex systems will require the ability to reason about when control should be transferred, who decides to transfer, and how the details of the exchange are executed, all implying a symbolic formalization of the notion of control.

This section outlines a theoretical framework within which such questions can be formalized. We develop an intuition of control, then formalize it, identify some of the varieties of control to which it leads, and summarize some issues and insights.

5.1. What is Control?

The notion of one agent controlling another is not new to formal analyses of distributed systems, but, as Castelfranchi [27] has observed, it has not previously been explicated. For example, Cohen and Perrault [28] introduce an operator *CAUSE-TO-WANT(AGT1, AGT, ACT)* by which *AGT1* causes *AGT* to want to do *ACT*, but do not delve into just how this takes place, beyond noting the necessary but not sufficient condition that *AGT1* must at least cause *AGT* to know that

AGT1 wants *AGT* to do *ACT*.

Some intuitions that at first glance seem to capture the notion of control are not in fact adequate.

In classical hierarchical control, the controller is the agent with the most global view guiding its actions. It achieves this global view because of its position at the top of the hierarchy, receiving information from agents at lower levels, and uses this privileged perspective to formulate plans and pass them to lower-level agents for execution. Control in such an architecture is a static consequence of the structure of the system rather than a dynamic state that can shift as the system operates.

The ability to give commands does not constitute control, as many a frustrated parent can attest. Nor can one patch this definition by adding the requirement that the command be obeyed. A relation of control exists between a command-giving superior and a subordinate who wants to obey, but is hindered by the environment.

A more promising definition, and the one that we develop, is that agent X controls agent Y when X supplies some resource that Y requires, and can make availability of that resource contingent on Y's behavior. The resource may be material, as is the case in an employment environment where the employer supplies a salary to employees. It may also be information, as in classical hierarchical control schemes.

We will discuss several consequences of this intuition once we have made it more precise. At the outset, though, it is worth noting that according to this intuition, control must be specific to a certain domain. In a marriage with one breadwinner, the spouse working outside of the home is likely to control what region of the country the family lives in, while the other probably controls what's for dinner. Each manipulates some resource that constrains the behavior of the other. Furthermore, these decisions may be interlocking, leading to cooperative or shared control rather than absolute control. Building on this insight, transfer of control may simply be shifting the focus from one domain to another, so that its controlling entity comes to the fore.

5.2. A Formal Sketch of Control

To sharpen our intuition of control, we extend Cohen and Levesque's axiomatization of speech act theory, [29, 30] which is in turn a formalization of Bratman's theory of intention. [31] First we summarize some useful entities and predicates from the existing theory, then introduce extensions culminating in a formal predicate expressing control. These extensions address many of the limitations of current speech act formalisms noted by Castelfranchi [27].

5.2.1. Entities

We assume four sets of entities: Agents (represented by the variables x, y, z), Resources (r, s, t), Propositions (o, p, q, which are either True or False), and events (a,b, c, which either Succeed or Fail).

Agents are sets of individuals, to allow occasions when several individuals act in concert. In most cases, an agent is a set containing only one individual. Similarly, resources are sets.

Events can be built up into more complex events with three operators: choice ($a|b$ is the event consisting of either a or b), sequence ($a;b$ is the event consisting of a followed by b); and iteration (a^* is the event consisting of a repeated zero or more times). We also have a testing function *?* that maps a proposition p to the event $p?$ that Succeeds just when p is True.

5.2.2. Useful Predicates

For further detail on the following expressions and the concepts that underlie them, see Cohen and Levesque. [29, 30]

(BEL x p) p follows from x's beliefs.

(GOAL x p) p follows from x's goals. Goals are chosen from desires to be consistent; $(GOAL\ x\ p) \rightarrow (DESIRE\ x\ p)$, but while $(DESIRE\ x\ p) \wedge (DESIRE\ x\ \neg p)$ is satisfiable, $(GOAL\ x\ p) \wedge (GOAL\ x\ \neg p)$ is not.

(AGT x a) x is the only agent of a.

(HAPPENS a) a is about to happen. For convenience, we define $(HAPPENS\ x\ a) \equiv (AGT\ x\ a) \wedge (HAPPENS\ a)$.

(DONE a) a has just happened. Again for convenience, $(DONE\ x\ a) \equiv (AGT\ x\ a) \wedge (DONE\ a)$.

(FOREVER p) $\forall x\ (HAPPENS\ x) \rightarrow (HAPPENS\ x;p?)$.

(EVENTUALLY p)
$\exists x\ (HAPPENS\ x;p?)$.

(LATER p) $\neg p \wedge (EVENTUALLY\ p)$.

(BEFORE p q) $\forall c\ (HAPPENS\ c;q?) \rightarrow \exists a\ (a \leq c) \wedge (HAPPENS\ a;p?)$. ($\leq$ is the natural time ordering on the completion of events that

terminate.)

(P-R-Goal x p q) Persistent, relativized goal:

$$(GOAL\ x\ (LATER\ p)) \wedge (BEL\ x\ \neg p)$$
$$\wedge\ (BEFORE\ [(BEL\ x\ p) \vee (BEL\ x\ (FOREVER\ \neg p))$$
$$\vee\ (BEL\ x\ \neg q)]\neg(GOAL\ x\ (LATER\ p)))$$

Informally, agent x has a goal to see p, which it thinks is presently false, become true, and it will retain this goal until p becomes true, it is persuaded that p can never be satisfied, or some other proposition q (with respect to which p is "relative") becomes false.

(INTEND1 x a q) Intention relative to an event, $(P\text{–}R\text{–}GOAL\ x\ (DONE\ x\ (BEL\ x\ (HAPPENS\ a))?;a)\ q)$. It is convenient to define a binary form,

$$(INTEND1\ x\ a) \equiv$$
$$(INTEND1\ x\ a\ (EVENTUALLY\ (DONE\ a)))$$

5.2.3. On to Control

To capture our intuition of control, we add several predicates and one event.

(POSSESS x r) Agent x possesses resource r.

(PROVISION x y r)

x can supply y with r. To be more precise, note that *(POSSESS y r)?* is the event of y possessing r. Then

$$(PROVISION\ x\ y\ r) \equiv$$
$$(x \neq y) \wedge \neg(POSSESS\ y\ r)$$
$$\wedge\ (AGT\ x\ (POSSESS\ y\ r)?)$$

Two details are worth noting about provisioning. First, except in a monopoly, x is a compound agent (consisting of more than one individual), and the notion of control that we will derive from *PROVISION* will therefore admit one form of shared control, represented by multiple sources of a single resource. We will shortly see a second form of shared control. Second, we have not required *(POSSESS x r)*. x may merely have some way of gaining possession of r, or even of controlling some third party to give it to y without x ever possessing it.

(REQUIRE a r) Event a requires resource r for its success. If r is a set with more than one member, a requires more than one atomic resource. If these resources are provisioned by different agents, we can have a second form of shared control by the various provisioners of

these resources.

(GIVE x y r) The event of x giving r to y.

Now we can express our intuition about control more formally. A relation of control involves four entities: two agents (the *controller* and the *controllee*), an event (the *target*) in which the controller has an interest, and a resource (the *rope*) that the controller can restrict in order to influence the controlee's agency in the target. Control can be either direct or indirect.

Direct control exists when the rope is required for execution of the target. The controller can prevent the controllee from executing the target simply by withholding the rope: (*DCONTROL* x y a r) $\equiv$ (*REQUIRE* a r) $\wedge$ (*PROVISION* x y r).

Direct control is only negative. The controller can prevent execution of the target, but cannot compel it. (Thus our definition of *DCONTROL* does not need to require *(AGT y a)*). To compel behavior, we apply the rope, not to the target, but to some other event that the controllee *INTEND*s to execute. This indirection of control through a secondary event permits both motivation and inhibition of the target. For example, in an employment paradigm, the rope is salary, which the employee (the controllee) requires for the strongly intended events of eating, being clothed, and being sheltered. The employer (the controller) can either motivate or inhibit a target, by making payment of salary dependent on the performance or nonperformance of the target, respectively.

To adopt a mechanical analogy, direct control is like moving the target with the rope. One can affect execution of the target by pulling the rope (withholding a needed resource) but not by pushing (supplying more of the resource than is needed). But if there were a tensioning spring at the far end of the rope, one could move that far end (and any object attached there) either forward (by pulling) or backward (by paying out rope and allowing the tensioning spring to retract it). Indirect control uses an event that the controller already intends as the tensioning spring.

Indirect control is thus possible when

- the controllee has a preexisting intention for some event (which we mnemonically call the *spring*);
- the controller can exert *DCONTROL* on the spring;
- the controller makes the rope (the resources for the spring) contingent on the controllee executing another of its specified abilities as prerequisites.

Formally,

$(ICONTROL\ x\ y\ a\ r\ b) \equiv$
$(INTEND1\ y\ b)$
$\wedge\ (DCONTROL\ x\ y\ b\ r)$
$\wedge\ (AGT\ y\ a)$
$\wedge\ (BEL\ y\ (INTEND1\ x\ [BEFORE\ (INTEND1\ y\ a)\ (GIVE\ x\ y\ r)?]))$

Clause by clause, this definition asserts:

$(INTEND1\ y\ b)$ There is a spring.

$(DCONTROL\ x\ y\ b\ r)$
The controller holds a rope for the spring.

$(AGT\ y\ a)$ The controllee is the agent of the target (now necessary because *ICONTROL* can be positive as well as negative).

$(BEL\ y\ (INTEND1\ x\ [BEFORE\ (INTEND1\ y\ a)\ (GIVE\ x\ y\ r)?]))$
The controllee believes that the controller intends that the controllee adopt an intention for the target before the controller will release the rope for the spring.

From this point, definition of *CAUSE-TO-WANT* is trivial: $(CAUSE\text{-}TO\text{-}WANT\ x\ y\ a) \equiv \exists r,b\ (ICONTROL\ x\ y\ a\ r\ b)$

5.3. Varieties of Control

This model permits us to discuss several variants of control.

There are three basic requirements of control.

1. A rope, something that the controller has and the controllee wants.

2. A target, something that the controllee can do that the controller wants done.

3. Some knowledge of mutual intentions.

Each of these can be nuanced through the modality of belief, leading to several varieties of (indirect) control. For instance, a paranoid agent x will behave like a controllee if it believes that another agent y holds a rope and intention to restrict that rope contingent on some action of x, even if y actually has neither rope nor intention. In some situations, it is important to distinguish such *de facto* control from a *de jure* relationship of control that asserts the joint intentions of the two agents.

A control deadlock can arise in two ways. First, an agent might be the controllee for multiple *ICONTROL* relations, each leveraged through the same spring (the existentially qualified *b* of our definition), but each relying on a different rope, and having mutually exclusive targets. In this case, the controllee can never satisfy all of its controllers, and so can never execute its spring. Second, the controllee may not be able consistently to intend both the target and the spring. The behavior of *ICONTROL* in both cases results from the fact that it models intention as a variety of *P-R-GOAL*, and a clause in the definition of such goals assures that agents drop them when they come to believe that they are impossible. In the case of conflicting control relationships, a rational controllee that is able to draw all the conclusions of what it knows will recognize that its spring is impossible and will drop it, thus dissolving all of the control relations. But a rational controller with complete knowledge of the situation will know that the control relation is in jeopardy, and will seek a new rope and/or target that does not present this conflict.

The model clearly allows for reciprocal control, where the controller in one relationship is the controllee in another.

The control exercised by the chairperson of a volunteer committee presents an interesting case, since "volunteer" seems to imply the absence of a rope. One possible analysis is that the spring is the controllee's desire to accomplish the committee's goal. (Agents do not commonly volunteer for activities in which they do not have an antecedent interest.) The resource controlled by the chairperson is information, including (but not limited to) details on coordination with other members of the committee that are needed to get the job done.

It is overly simplistic to define control as a predicate in standard binary logic. In human societies, control is a matter of degree. How can the model be extended to provide for this nuance?

- Other predicates in the theory besides *ICONTROL* are probably overly restrictive. Human agents, for example, can define a (partial) order over their goals, which might be modeled with a *PREFER* predicate. Then one could measure degree of control by some combination of the strengths of the controllee's goals for two events: the spring and the target.

- We have made provisioning an "all-or-nothing" affair. If the provisioner of the rope includes more than one individual, our definition assumes that all the individuals in the (compound) provisioner agree on the intention in the last conjunct of the definition of *ICONTROL* (or at least that the controllee believes that they all agree). In reality, different provisioners of the same resource may have different intentions toward the controllee. The strength of control in this case is a measure of the marketplace in which the controllee acquires its resources.

- A similar situation results from the extension of *ICONTROL* to permit multiple ropes for a single spring, or even multiple springs. If a spring has multiple ropes, fewer provisioners for those ropes means stronger control, since there is less chance that the provisioners will disagree about the critical intention in the last clause of *ICONTROL*. Also, the more springs motivate a target, the stronger the resulting relation of control.

- The legendary "old-boy network" reflects a tendency for people to develop densely interconnected networks of reciprocal provisioning relationships. Presumably, a control relation that is part of such a network will reflect stronger intentions on the part of its participants than one that crosses network boundaries. (We are more interested in keeping those we depend on happy than in satisfying strangers.) Building on this insight, one can define a strength of the relationship between two agents based on the number of provisioning relations between them, and use this to calibrate the strength of any control relations that they share.

5.4. Issues and Insights

Engineers who design manufacturing systems are preoccupied with control. A rich body of techniques has been developed to describe and manipulate control at the level of individual devices. Speech act theory permits us to sketch out a comparable set of techniques for multi-agent systems, including those that incorporate both human and artificial agents. The dominant insight emerging from the preliminary work we have described here is that control need not be unilateral or absolute. Agents typically exercise reciprocal control over one another, and this control must be described in terms of degree.

6. THE PROBLEM OF CHAOS

The distributed systems with which we have experimented often exhibit surprising complexity. A malfunctioning application could be both economically and physically dangerous, so the responsible engineering of applications of DAI must include analysis of the overall dynamics of our systems.

This section of the paper reports on a direction of investigation that we believe to be fruitful, but that we are only now developing: the search for formally chaotic behavior in DAI applications. Over the last twenty-five years, interest has steadily grown in formally chaotic systems, nonlinear systems that though deterministic can exhibit surprising complexities in their behavior. This section briefly introduces the concept of formal chaos, explains why it is a potential problem for a DAI application such as factory floor control, and suggests directions that the fact of chaos urges us to pursue in our research.

6.1. Characterizing Chaos

Good technical summaries of chaos theory are available [32, 33], as well as a responsible popular introduction [34]. Here we briefly review the characteristics of formal chaos and the kind of systems that generate it.

If we consider the trajectory of a deterministic system through state space, a chaotic system is distinguished from other dynamic systems by non-periodic recurrence, or what has been described as "folding and stretching." The trajectory stays within a bounded region of phase space, as though it were folded onto itself. Thus the system differs from a formally unstable system whose state parameters can increase without bound. The "stretching" metaphor suggests that this folding does not monotonically shrink the trajectory, and so differentiates a chaotic system from one whose state trajectory evolves into a single point or a repeating cycle.

If one examines the behavior of system parameters through time in the frequency domain, the spectrum of a chaotic system is characterized by white noise rather than the distinctive peaks that typify nonchaotic oscillation.

Perhaps the most salient characterization from an engineering perspective is that arbitrarily small changes in the starting conditions of a chaotic system can lead to widely divergent states as the system evolves. Though a chaotic system is deterministic, our inability to define completely the starting conditions means that we cannot predict its long-term behavior.

Surprisingly simple systems can exhibit chaos. Consider the logistic equation $x(t+1) = Rx(t)[1-x(t)]$, $0 < x < 1$. One model of this equation is an ecological system in which x measures the population density of some organism (say, ducks per square-duck of pond), R represents the reproduction rate, and t is measured in breeding seasons. The $x(t)$ term indicates that when the ducks are too sparse to find one another, the population will die off. The $1\text{-}x(t)$ term indicates that if there are too many ducks, the food supply will not support them, and the population will decline. Some intermediate population will be stable, its exact value depending on the growth rate R. For small values of R, a small change in $x(0)$ (or in R) will lead to a small change in the stable population, but beyond a certain value of R the system is chaotic, and arbitrarily small differences in $x(0)$ (or R) result in widely different stable populations. In a situation in which R itself is changing, the population may never stabilize, but exhibit wide, erratic swings.

Another common generator of chaos is a damped, driven, nonlinear oscillator, such as a rigid pendulum swinging beyond the range in which $\theta \approx sin(\theta)$. Under certain circumstances, chaotic behavior can arise when the driving and resonant frequencies of the oscillator are different from one another.

These simple chaotic systems share some common features. Both are nonlinear; chaos cannot arise in a linear system, though there are nonlinear systems that are not chaotic. Both operate within bounded state spaces; the population of ducks cannot exceed 1 or fall below 0, and the angle of the oscillator will always be between 0 and 2π. For our purposes, it is important to note that both represent coupled interactions: in the first instance between ducks who are either mating or competing for a fixed food supply; in the second, between the resonant frequency of the oscillator and the driving frequency.

6.2. Chaos in DAI Systems

All three of the characteristics that we observe in our simple examples of chaotic systems apply to DAI applications. Our agents, like all heuristic applications, are strongly nonlinear. Their behavior is bounded, if only by the physical constraints of their implementations. The coupling among them is the distinctive contribution of DAI, and the motive for us to consider the effects of chaos in the context of DAI research.

Our argument so far is only a plausibility argument for the existence of chaos in multi-agent systems. In fact, two groups of researchers have reported actual observations of chaos in such systems.

Kephart and his colleagues have studied systems of multiple agents competing for resources. [35, 36] When agents compete for as few as three resources, or try to cooperate in the use of as few as two resources, chaotic regimes can arise. The systems exhibit period doubling and then chaotic behavior as the decision rates of the agents increase. Increasing the uncertainty in the agents' knowledge of the environment, while lowering the overall system efficiency, permits higher decision rates before the phase transitions occur.

Kephart's model offers obvious parallels with modern decentralized FMS architectures, in particular with negotiating architectures such as those discussed above.

The existence of chaotic regimes has also been reported in an asymptotic analytical model of a production line including production workstations and an assembly workstation, separated by buffer inventory replenished with a fixed period policy. [37] As the time delay in the production subsystem increases, the average production rate of the assembly workstation moves from stability to a limit cycle and then to chaos. The separate agents in this case are the production workstations, whose different production cycle times are coupled through the buffer inventory from which the assembly workstation draws parts.

6.3. Issues and Insights

At this point, we have just begun to explore the implications of chaotic behavior in DAI systems in general and in intelligent manufacturing systems in particular. The fundamental insight is that chaos can arise in such systems, and an engineering approach to DAI needs to deal with it. In particular:

- We need to understand the implications for the usefulness of a particular system if it enters a chaotic regime. In some cases, chaos may not interfere with the intended function of the system, and might even be a simple means of exploring a large search space.

- Where chaos is detrimental, we may be able to constrain either the structure or the operating parameters of a system to preclude chaos. A structure that exhibits chaos typically does so only over a portion of its operating range, and useful behavior may be available outside of that range.

- If we intend to control chaos by managing parameters rather than structure, our systems need to be able to recognize when they are getting close to chaotic behavior. Some recent work offers promise in contributing to this approach. [37]

7. CONCLUSION

This paper has described an odyssey through some prominent concepts in DAI: negotiating systems, fine vs. coarse grained parallelism, speech act theory, and the emergence, recognition, and control of chaotic behavior. Our experience shows that real applications are incredibly rich forces to integrate the concepts being developed in the laboratory. The realization of this richness ought to increase the interest of application developers in the full range of techniques that the academy develops, and at the same time challenge more theoretical researchers to investigate the practical constraints that arise when their concepts move into the engineering world.

ACKNOWLEDGEMENTS

I am grateful for the insightful comments of Les Gasser and George Kiss on portions of this paper. Portions of this research are supported in part by CAMRSS, the Center for Autonomous and Man-controlled Robotics and Sensing Systems, a NASA Commercialization Center. The programs of the Industrial Technology Institute are partially supported by the W.K. Kellogg Foundation.

REFERENCES

[1] H.V.D. Parunak; B.W. Irish; J. Kindrick; and P.W. Lozo, "Fractal Actors for Distributed Manufacturing Control," in *Proceedings of the Second IEEE Conference on Artificial Intelligence Applications*, IEEE, 1985, pp. 653-660.

[2] H.V.D. Parunak; J.F. White; P.W. Lozo; R. Judd; B.W. Irish; and J. Kindrick, "An Architecture for Heuristic Factory Control," in *Proceedings of the American Control Conference*, American Automatic Control Council, 1986, pp. 548-558.

[3] R.G. Smith, "A Framework for Problem Solving in a Distributed Processing Environment," technical report HPP-78-28, Stanford University Heuristic Programming Project, 1978, Computer Science Department Report STAN-CS-78-700.

[4] R.G. Smith, "The Contract Net Protocol: High-Level Communication and Control in a Distributed Problem Solver," *IEEE Transactions on Computers*, vol. C-29, no. 12, pp. 1104-1113, December 1980.

[5] R.G. Smith and R. Davis, "Frameworks for Cooperation in Distributed Problem Solving," *IEEE Transactions on Systems, Man, and Cybernetics*, vol. SMC-11, no. 1, pp. 61-70, January 1981.

[6] R. Davis and R.G. Smith, "Negotiation as a Metaphor for Distributed Problem Solving," *Artificial Intelligence*, vol. 20, pp. 63-109, 1983.

[7] H.V.D. Parunak, "Manufacturing Experience with the Contract Net," in *Distributed Artificial Intelligence*, Huhns, M., ed. Pitman, 1987, pp. 285-310, originally presented at the 1985 Workshop on Distributed Artificial Intelligence, Sea Ranch, CA.

[8] K. Ramamritham and J.A. Stankovic, "Dynamic Task Scheduling in Hard Real-Time Distributed Systems," *IEEE Software*, vol. 1, pp. 65-75, July 1984.

[9] J.A. Stankovic and I.S. Sidhu, "An Adaptive Bidding Algorithm For Processes, Clusters and Distributed Groups," in *Proceedings of the Fourth International Conference on Distributed Computing Systems*, IEEE, 1984, pp. 49-59.

[10] W. Zhao; K. Ramamritham; and J.A. Stankovic, "Scheduling Tasks with Resource Requirements in Hard Real-Time Systems", Dept. of Computer and Information Science, University of Massachusetts at Amherst.

[11] M.J. Shaw and A.B. Whinston, "Task Bidding and Distributed Planning in Flexible Manufacturing," in *Proceedings of the Second IEEE Conference on Artificial Intelligence Applications*, IEEE, 1985, pp. 184-189.

[12] M.J.P. Shaw and A.B. Whinston, "Automatic Planning and Flexible Scheduling: A Knowledge-Based Approach," in *Proceedings of the IEEE International Conference on Robotics and Automation*, IEEE, 1985, pp. 890-894.

[13] J.G. Maley, "Managing the Flow of Intelligent Parts," *Robotics & Computer-Integrated Manufacturing*, vol. 4, no. 3/4, pp. 525-530, 1988.

[14] A.D. Baker, "Complete Manufacturing Control Using a Contract Net: A Simulation Study," in *Proceedings of the International Conference on Computer Integrated Manufacturing (CIMIC)*, IEEE, 1988, pp. 100-109.

[15] H.V.D. Parunak; P.W. Lozo; R. Judd; B.W. Irish; and J. Kindrick, "A Distributed Heuristic Strategy for Material Transportation," in *Proceedings of the 1986 Conference on Intelligent Systems and Machines*, Oakland University, 1986.

[16] H.V.D. Parunak; J. Kindrick; and B.W. Irish, "A Connectionist Model for Material Handling," *Robotics and Computer Integrated Manufacturing*, vol. 4, no. 3/4, pp. 643-654, 1988.

[17] H.V.D. Parunak; J. Kindrick; and B.W. Irish, "Material Handling: A Conservative Domain for Neural Connectivity and Propagation," in *Proceedings of the Sixth National Conference on Artificial Intelligence (AAAI'87)*, AAAI, 1987, pp. 307-311.

[18] H.V.D. Parunak; J. Kindrick; and B.W. Irish, "Supplier-Consumer Nets for Material Handling," in *Proceedings of the First IEEE International Conference on Neural Networks*, IEEE, 1987.

[19] H.V.D. Parunak, J.D. Kindrick, and B.W. Irish, "Viewing the Factory as a Computer: A Cognitive Approach to Material Handling," in *Artificial Intelligence: Manufacturing Theory and Practice*, S. Kumara, A. Soyster, and R.L. Kashyap, ed. Institute of Industrial Engineers, 1989, pp. 225-263.

[20] R.W. Hall, *Driving the Productivity Machine: Production Planning and Control in Japan*. American Production and Inventory Control Society, 1981.

[21] R.J. Schonberger, *Japanese Manufacturing Techniques*. The Free Press, 1982.

[22] Y. Sugimori; K. Kusunoki; F. Cho; and S. Uchikawa, "Toyota production system and Kanban system: Materialization of just-in-time and respect-for-human system," *International Journal of Production Research*, vol. 15, no. 6, pp. 553-564, 1977.

[23] D.E. Rumelhart; G.E. Hinton; and J.L. McClelland, "A General Framework for Parallel Distributed Processing," in *Parallel Distributed Processing*, MIT Press, 1986, pp. 45-76.

[24] H.V.D. Parunak, "Why Scheduling is Hard (and How to Do It Anyway)," in *Proceedings of the Material Handling Focus '87*, Material Handling Research Center, Georgia Institute of Technology, 1987.

[25] J.S. Albus; A.J. Barbera; and R.N. Nagel, "Theory and Practice of Hierarchical Control," in *Proceedings of the Twenty-Third IEEE Computer Society International Conference*, IEEE, 1981, pp. 18-35.

[26] H.V.D. Parunak and J.F. White, "A Synthesis of Factory Reference Models," in *Proceedings of the IEEE Workshop on Languages for Automation, August 1987, Vienna*, IEEE, 1987, pp. 109-112.

[27] C. Castelfranchi, "SOCIAL POWER: A Point Missed in Multi-Agent, DAI and HCI," in *Proceedings of the European Workshop on Modelling an Autonomous Agent in a Multi-agent World*, CEE, 1989.

[28] P.R. Cohen and C.R. Perrault, "Elements of a Plan-Based Theory of Speech," *Cognitive Science*, vol. 3, pp. 177-212, 1979.

[29] P.R. Cohen and H.J. Levesque, "Persistence, Intention, and Commitment," in *Proceedings of the 1986 Timberline Workshop on Planning and Practical Reasoning*, AAAI, 1986, pp. 297-340.

[30] P.R. Cohen and H.J. Levesque, " Rational Interaction as the Basis for Communication," Technical Note 433, SRI, 1988.

[31] M. Bratman, *Intentions, Plans, and Practical Reason*. Harvard University Press, 1987.

[32] J.M.T. Thompson and H.B. Stewart, *Nonlinear Dynamics and Chaos*. John Wiley, 1986.

[33] H.G. Schuster, *Deterministic Chaos: An Introduction*. VCH Publications, 1987.

[34] J. Gleick, *Chaos: Making a New Science*. Viking, 1987.

[35] J.O. Kephart, T. Hogg, and B.A. Huberman, "Dynamics of Computational Ecosystems", Presented at the 1988 Workshop on Distributed Artificial Intelligence

[36] B.A. Huberman, editor, *The Ecology of Computation*. North-Holland, 1988.

[37] J.-T. Lim, S.M. Meerkov, and F. Top, "Dynamics in Production-Inventory-Assembly Manufacturing Systems," in *Proceedings of the 28th Conference on Decision and Control*, IEEE, 1987, pp. 644.

Interactions between Reasoning Capabilities

DECENTRALIZED A.I.
Yves DEMAZEAU & Jean-Pierre MÜLLER (Eds.)

INTERACTIONS AMONG AUTONOMOUS PLANNING AGENTS

Frank VON MARTIAL

German National Research Center for Computer Science (GMD)
Institute for Applied Information Technology (F3)
Schloß Birlinghoven, D-5205 Sankt Augustin 1
West Germany

Autonomous planning agents are agents who independently create plans to reach their own goals. If these plans are executed in a common environment, we have to consider *interactions among autonomous planning agents*. This paper will deal with those interactions which appear as relationships between the agents plans. Classification of the possible relationships between the agents' plans is established. The taxonomy presented will comprise both harmful (negative) and favorable (positive) relationships. A system which hopes to perform a meaningful coordination of individually created plans has to cover the whole range of interactions that can occur among intelligent agents; the detection of negative relationships is crucial to prevent conflicts and the detection of positive relationships may help to utilize the favorable potential which may exist among different plans.

1. INTRODUCTION

A *multiagent plan* is a plan which has been generated for several executing agents. If these plans are individually created by autonomous agents and are executed in the same environment, coordination of these plans is essential. Coordination of these plans can be performed based on detailed knowledge of the relationships which occur between these plans. These relationships play an important role for reconciling the plans, before execution, and can be utilized to recognize situations which might lead to negative interferences between plans or involving chances for beneficial combinations. Negative relationships are all those relationships between plans which could prevent one or both of the plans from being executed as intended. Positive relationships are all those relations, between two plans, from which some benefit can be derived for one or both of the agents plans by combining them. It is important to have systems which can deal with both types of relationships.

The relationship taxonomy, which is presented in this paper, can also serve as a means to classify work in multiagent or distributed planning in regards to the relationships between the activities considered there.

Although relationships within a single agent plan have been explored in great detail in traditional planning systems (before 1980), they are not applicable in a multi agent setting due to several reasons: first, the world is assumed to be static and only affected by a single agent's actions, tasks are only carried out by a single agent; second, there is no concept for concurrent activities; third, there is no co-operation and coordination between several agents.

The problem of multiagent plan relationships occurs in the areas of multiagent planning, where a single agent generates plans for multiple agents [3, 9, 16], and distributed planning, where the planning activities are distributed among several planners [5, 6, 11]. Many researchers have only considered either negative or positive interactions between agents.

Some of these papers consider only conflicts among agents: Adler et al. have been investigating negotiation strategies for several agents to resolve their conflicts [1]. Conry et al. have been studying conflicts which arise when agents require limited nonlocal resources for their plans [4]. This same source of conflicts has been investigated by Georgeff who has developed several formal models to combine the plans of independent agents [9, 10]. Stuart's synchronizer receives as input one multiagent plan, which still contains conflicting events [17] and its output is a plan in which synchronizing operations are inserted to sequentialize critical operations. Sycara's planner has as input the conflicting goals of multiple agents and as output a compromise acceptable by the agents [18].

Only a few researchers have considered autonomous planning agents with both negative and positive plan relationships: Genesereth, Ginsberg and Rosenschein have been examining the question of how high-level, autonomous, independently motivated agents should interact with each other so as to achieve their goals [8]. They consider situations in which communication between the agents is impossible. Later, they allow communication between agents to resolve conflicts and use a game theoretic model for agent interaction [15]. Wilensky provides examples of negative and positive relationships between goals of different planners [19]. His distinction of resource caused conflicts is also meaningful for the classification demonstrated in this paper. Coordination does not play a role in his investigations and interactions are considered from a single planner's point of view, one who plans only his own activities (single agent planning).

2. THE UNDERLYING MODEL

2.1. Assumptions

What assumptions concerning cooperation and coordination are my multiagent classification based on ?

Concerning the agents, the assumptions are:

- The agents are intelligent and can be regarded as autonomous problem solvers.

- The agents may incorporate the actions of other agents as part of their plans (multiagent planning).
- There is equal distribution of control and authority.
- Agents may have different skills.
- The agents tell the truth concerning their plans.
- Direct communication between agents is allowed and the agents communicate about planned actions ahead of time.
- Each agent wants to solve his individual problem, i.e. the agents are not originally constrained to cooperate, or at least they do not – a situation which occurs quite often in real world settings.
- The agents have a cordial relationship and are not hostile against each other (benevolent assumption).

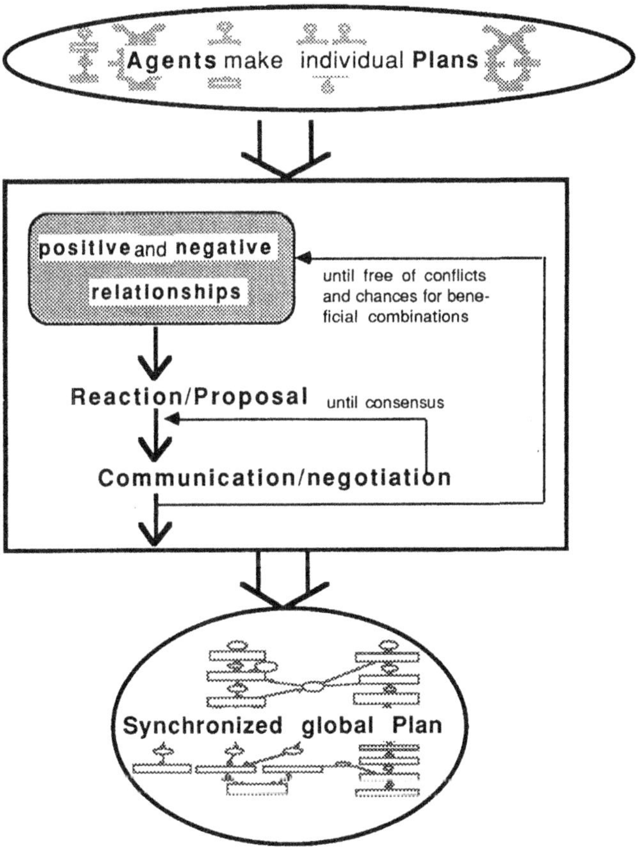

Figure 1: A relationship driven coordination process.

Concerning the plans, the assumptions are:

- There is no overall planning task which has to be solved in close cooperation.
- The actions of plans require resources.
- The plans may contain concurrent activities.
- Individual plans can be constructed for single or multiple agents.
- Plans can be specified at different levels of abstraction.
- The plans have to executed in the same environment.

2.2. The Coordination Process

The process of coordinating the individual plans is illustrated in figure 1. After the agents have developed their plans autonomously, they transfer their individual plans to the other planning agents or a blackboard which can be read by all agents. In order to reconcile these plans several tasks have to be executed:

- recognize and evaluate the possible relationships between the plans,
- work out solutions to deal with these relationships,
- initiate and perform negotiations.

Each agent may utilize subagents to perform these tasks. As a result of the coordination process all the individual plans are integrated into one global plan.

3. CLASSIFYING PLAN RELATIONSHIPS

There are several aspects, each involving opposite features for classifying plan relationships in a multiagent setting:

- single agent vs. multi agent plan relationships (the number of agents involved in execution). Do the relationships exist among the actions of a plan which will be carried out by one single agent or among actions of different agents?
- negative vs. positive relationships (relationship character)
  The relationships can be either harmful or beneficial.
- explicit vs. implicit relationships (ways of detecting the presence of a relationship).
  Relations are explicit when their presence is obvious. Often there is a direct physical connection between several actions, e.g. two actions requiring the same resource. Relations are implicit if they can only be recognized after a "certain amount" of reasoning on the plans involved.
- resource vs. non-resource driven conflicts (conflict source)
  Is a conflict due to excessive access to a limited resource or for some other reason?
- actor vs. action request (request object)
  In case support is desired: Is the action or both action and actor specified?

- direct vs. indirect nonrequested benefit
  Is a positive effect ensured when agents carry out their plans as intended (direct, explicit) or can it be reached by modification of both plans involved in the relationships (indirect, implicit)?

These dimensions may contain further subdimensions.

4. NEGATIVE MULTIAGENT PLAN RELATIONSHIPS

Negative multiagent plan relationships are all those relationships between plans, which may prevent one or both of the plans from being executed as intended. They may involve an incompatible step order, or incompatible resource use, which may lead to conflicts during the plan execution. The detection of negative relationships is crucial for successful plan execution. Negative relationships can be distinguished whether their origin is a resource (physical) or an incompatible situation (logical), also see Figure 2.

4.1. Resource Induced Conflicts

Two plans are in a resource driven negative relationship if both plans require more from the same resource than is available at the required time. A resource can be any object which is needed to perform a plan. The prerequesites for a resource to be involved in a conflict are that it must be limited and sharable. Resource conflicts between multiagent plans can occur only if a restricted resource is needed by several agents at the same time. Thus, it is important to reason about the time requirements of a resource to ascertain whether there is a potential resource conflict. For instance access to a nonconsumable resource means no conflict occurs if the time periods for utilizing this resource do not overlap.

Two classes of resources are recognized:

- *Consumable resources.*
  A resource is consumable if its usability decreases after it has been used in a plan. Requirements for consumable resources are likely to cause a conflict when the amount of the resource, needed by the agents, exceeds the amount available to the agents. Of course the time period requirements have to be considered.
- *Nonconsumable resources.*
  A resource is nonconsumable if its availability does not change after it has been used in a plan. The usability of a nonconsumable resource to the agents is limited through its capacity. A nonconsumable resource is likely to cause a conflict if it is required beyond its availability over a fixed period of time.

4.2. Incompatibility

Two different plans might have goals that require exclusive states to exist (*mutually exclusive states*); the states involved are incompatible with each other. Whereas in the resource driven case the reason for conflicts is physical, here the nature of the reason is logical. The detection of mutually exclusive states or incompatible actions can be very hard. It is not possible to rely on general detection strategies for recognizing an incompatibility relationship. Domain specific heuristics are required and the detection of incompatible activities must be based on prespecified axioms. This axioms state which events should not occur simultaneously. In real world domains there is a large number of actions that can interfere with one another and which could cause severe combinatorial difficulties if for each of them a different axiom would have to be specified.

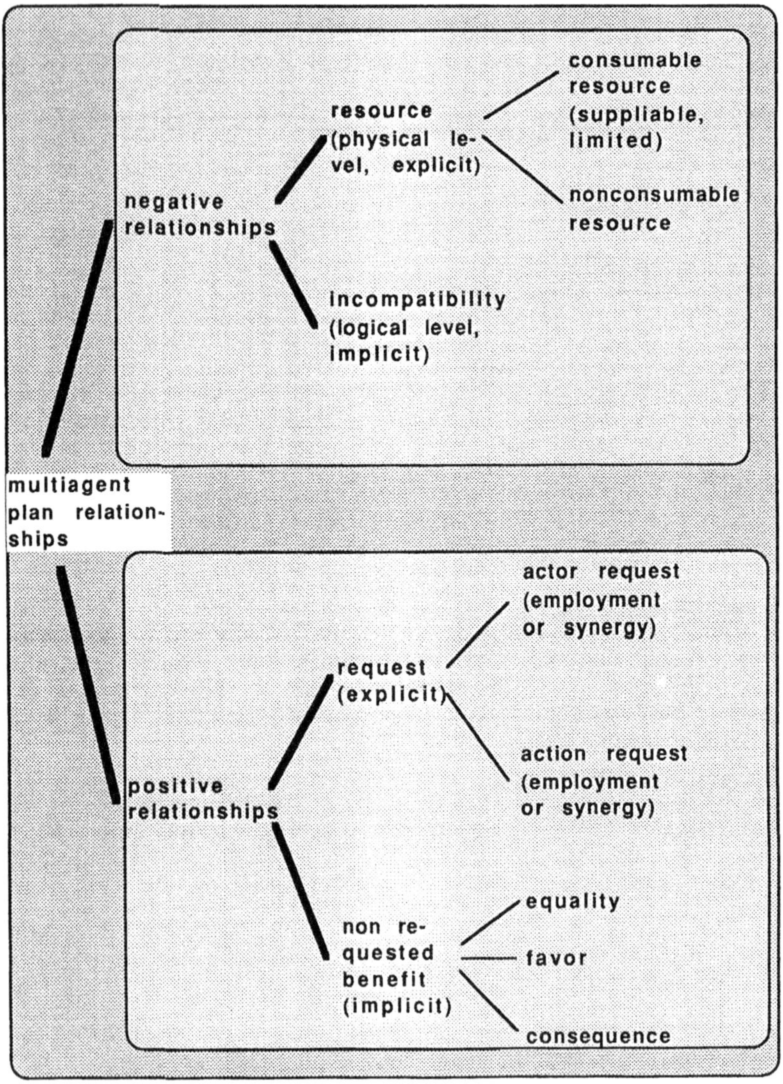

Figure 2: A taxonomy of multiagent plan relationships

5. POSITIVE MULTIAGENT PLAN RELATIONSHIPS

Positive multiagent relationships are all those relations between two plans from which some benefit can be derived, for one or both of the agents' plans, by combining them. They allow for the production of a more efficient overall plan. There could be an action in one agent's plan which supports another agent's subgoal or an action might even accomplish this goal. In these cases the plans, of the involved agents, can be changed to employ this beneficial relationship. In contrast to the detection and prevention of negative interactions the detection and utilization of positive interactions among plans may not be necessary, but can contribute greatly to the efficiency and output of the overall system behavior. The utilization of positive interactions can be seen as optimizing the plans in regard to their combined cost and efficiency. Strategies for the utilization of beneficial relationships depend on the degree of benevolence of the agents towards each other. If the agents are adversaries utilization is hard to achieve.

5.1. Requests

In the case of a request driven positive relationship the planner asks for support concerning the execution of its plan. We will differentiate whether the request is for the execution of activities or for a dedicated actor.

- *Request for an actor.*
  An agent asks for the assistance or participation of another dedicated agent in its plan, i.e. the support of another agent is explicitly mentioned in the agent's plan (multiagent planning). Since the agents are autonomous the "requested" agent must be asked whether it agrees to this request and is willing to carry out the requested activity.
  Two cases of actor requests can be considered: First, the employment case, in which another agent is requested because the planning agent's workload is to high or it does not have the ability or skill to handle the task which is going to be contracted out. The planner has some limitations imposed by its time and abilities. Second, the synergy case, in which one agent needs the aid of another agent for one task, jointly lifting a heavy table for example. Time dependent coordination is necessary because both agents have to act at the same time.
- *Request for a task.*
  The agent wants a task or action to be executed by another unspecified agent. The task of the central agent is to find a particular agent who accepts executing this part; it can suggest an actor using knowledge about the organization or it can offer the job as vacant. As in the case of an actor request we can discriminate between the employment and the synergy case.

5.2. Nonrequested Beneficial Relationship

Sometimes, there is no explicit task to be contracted out or no external agent for support mentioned in one plan. The beneficial relationship is contained implicitly in the plans and a beneficial effect can be achieved by combining two plans. By chance, a single plan can simultaneously fulfill the goals of several plans or does it after a slight adjustment. We will distinguish between three types of nonrequested beneficial relationships:

- *Equality Relationship.*
  Two agents happen to have planned the same action in their individual plans which fulfills the same (sub-)goal. In order to determine whether the actions are equal, they need to be matched against each other. Two actions can also be instantiations of the same higher action. If the same action appears in two plans, only one agent has to carry out the action. Time constraints may play a role, too.

- *Consequence Relationship.*
  The actions of an individual plan implies the accomplishment of another individual plan's goal. Or one action can be seen as an instance of a more abstract higher level action. This kind of relationship can be determined using an action/goal hierarchy. Domain specific heuristics are required for their detection. If one action is implied by another action, just the pursuing action has to be executed.

- *Favor Relationship.*
  Even if an action of one individual plan may not accomplish a goal of another plan as in the consequence- or equality relationship, it may easily contribute to the fulfillment of another agent's goal. An action of an individual plan may be potentially beneficial for the goal of another plan. Sometimes a part of the involved plans (a goal or a sequence of actions) shows some similarity. This potential can be exploited by combining both plans. In this case one agent can benefit by combining both plans. Usually the other agent has to modify his plan slightly to be beneficial to the profiting agent. This kind of plan modification can be termed as 'doing a favor'. The relative benefit has to be considered: How much additional effort is necessary for one agent to help the other (modify his plan/ do the favor) and how much effort is saved for the supported agent?
  Example: Two agents plan to go to the post office during the same time period. One agent wants to buy stamps, the other agent wants to deliver a package. A combined plan in which only one agent goes to the post office and performs both tasks is much more effective concerning the overall effort required.

6. EXAMPLE

An example should illustrate some of the relationships. This example is taken from an office environment.

We assume that the individual plans are modelled by modified Petri nets which have been used in similar way for our multiagent planner VIPS [12]. A Petri net is a formal model used to describe and analyze systems with several components which interact concurrently [2, 14]. The Petri net formalism is very appropriate for representing multiagent plans because it has the basic concepts necessary for modeling a distributed system. A Petri net is visualized as a directed graph having two node types: places (circles) and transitions (rectangles). Only nodes of different types can be connected.

We will designate Petri nets in the following way to denote multiagent plans:

- Transitions model system activities. A role can be attached to a transition which stands for a class of actors who can carry out the modeled activity. A transition can describe an action at different levels of abstraction. A high level transition can be expanded into a subnet which describes the modeled action in more detail. At the highest abstraction level a transition can denote a goal. Time constraints for executing the activity can appear as transition inscriptions.
- Places model resources, conditions and synchronizing states.
- Arcs describe precedence and causal relationships between objects and activities.

In our example there are the two agents Art and Bert. Both have created their individual plans and want to execute them on September 25, 1988. The individual plans are transferred to a blackboard.

Art's plan contains the following actions (Fig. 3 a):

- Pick up: Actor is Art. Pick up Mr. Smith (guest) from the main station (and give him a lift to the office). Time: 8:30 a.m., September 25.
- Produce video: Actor is Art. Make a demonstration video (using the only video camera in the office) of a program running on Symbolics LM7. Time: Morning, September 25.
- Make phone call: Actor is Art. Make a phone call to Mr. Blund. Time: Between 10:00 a.m. and 11:00 a.m, Sept. 25.
- Answer mail: Actor is Art. Answer the received mail which is in the mail box. Time: Any time on Sept. 25 after having finished the video film.
- Buy stamps: Actor is Art. Buy some commemorative stamps at the post office. Time: During lunch break, Sept. 25.
- Give comment: Actor is Bert. Make comments on Art's demonstration video. Time: Sept 25 and Sept 26. Thus, Art's plan is a multiagent plan.
- Copy papers: Actor is Art. Make a copy of some papers in the library. Time: Afternoon of Sept. 25 or morning Sept. 26 after answering the mail.

This is Bert's plan (Fig. 3 b):

- Pick up: Actor is Bert. Pick up Mr. Smith (guest) from the main station. Time: At 8:30 a.m..
- Give demo: Actor is Bert. Give a demonstration to Mr. Smith on Symbolics LM7. Time: 9:00 - 10:30 a.m.
- Discuss: Actor is Bert. Discuss with Mr. Smith the software which has just been demonstrated. Time: Until lunch.
- Bring package: Actor is Bert. Bring a package to the post office. Time: during lunch break, Sept. 25.
- Read book: Actor is Bert. Read a book. Time: Afternoon, Sept. 25.

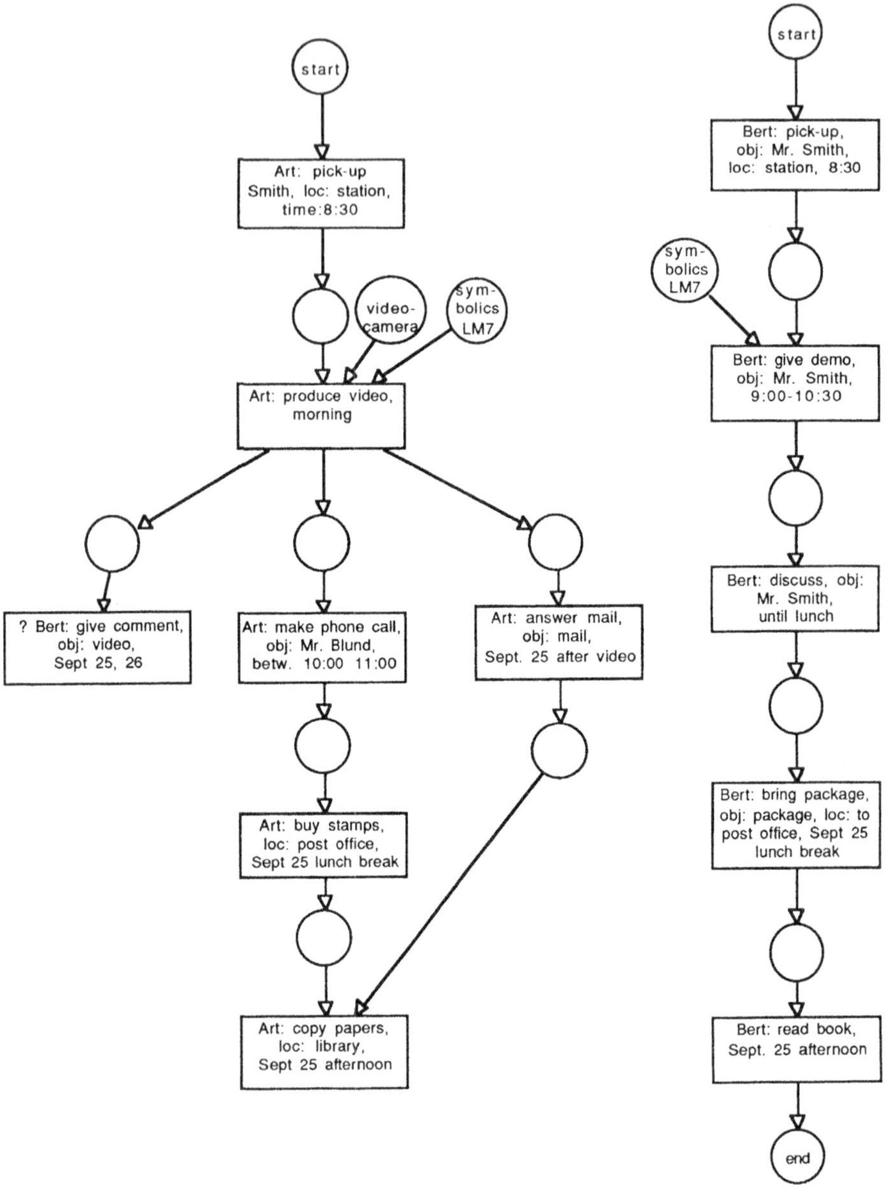

a. Art's Plan b. Bert's Plan

Figure 3: The individual plans

These are the relationships between the two plans (Fig.4):

- Relation-a (equality): Between Art's "pick up" and Bert's "pick up": the same result is produced by the same action.
- Relation-b (non consumable resource conflict): Between Art's "produce video" and Bert's "give demo" there is a resource conflict because of a request for the same nonconsumable resource at the same time period. The same resource, namely the Symbolics LM7, is required.
- Relation-c (favor): Between Art's "buy stamps" and Bert's "bring package": A beneficial effect can be achieved.
- Relation-d (actor request): Between Art's "give comment" and Bert('s plan): Art requires another actor (Bert) for the execution of this action.

Positive relationships in this case are relation-a, relation-c and relation-d. A negative relationship is relation-b. It is the agents' task to detect the various relationships described above. After detection they will propose resolutions for negative interactions or to take advantage of positive interactions.

What are the measures that will be taken to deal with the relationships?

Relation-a: As both workers want to do the same action to achieve the same result, i.e. have the same goals, one person can erase this action from his plan because it is redundant. Which agent erases the action can be dependent on when the agents wants to do this action, at what time the result of the action is needed, or which agent has the most workload and wants to be relieved of some of his work. The agents negotiate on the basis of this factors and agree that Art will do the action and Bert is relieved from it.

Relation-b: Both plans require the same resource at the same time period. During compile time there is no decision made which agent has priority over the resource. As it is a non consumable resource, a critical region construct is inserted to resolve the conflict during plan execution. In this situation other measurements are possible, e.g. looking for another equivalent resource or asking an agent to modify his plan.

Relation-c: In this case a beneficial effect can be achieved for Art or Bert as both have a job to do at the post office at the same time. Thus, it is sufficient for only one person to go to the post office. The agents recognize this. To handle a package is physically more expensive than to get stamps. In this case, Art proposes plan modifications which are for his benefit. Finally Bert's action "bring package" is replaced by the following sequence of more detailed activities:
- "go to the post office"
- "deliver package". He delivers the package at the proper counter.
- "buy stamps". He buys stamps for Art.
- "go to work". He goes back to his office.
- "give stamps". He gives the stamps to Art.

On the other hand, Art has to modify his plan only slightly. Instead of going to the post office and buying the stamps he only has to "receive stamps" from Bert. Art and Bert utilize the beneficial potential between their intentions and agree to the proposed plan modifications.

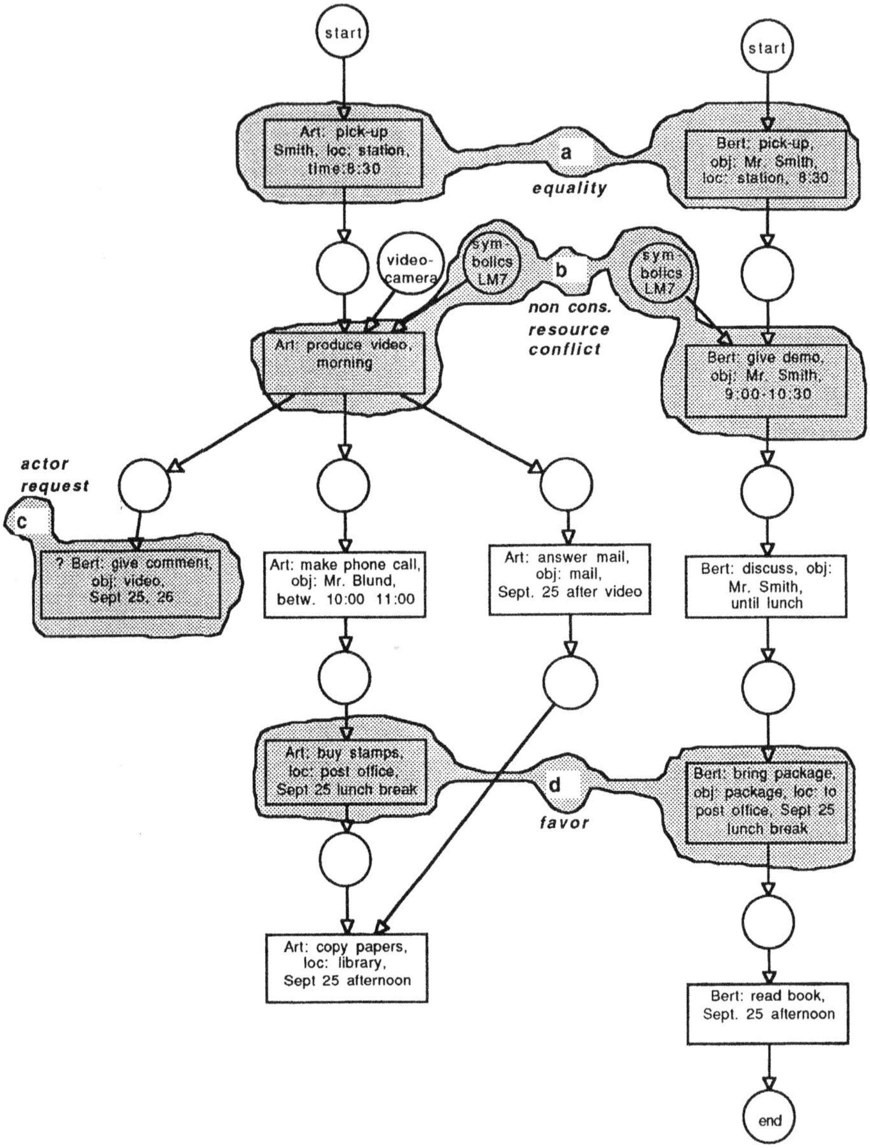

Figure 4: The relationships between the individual plans

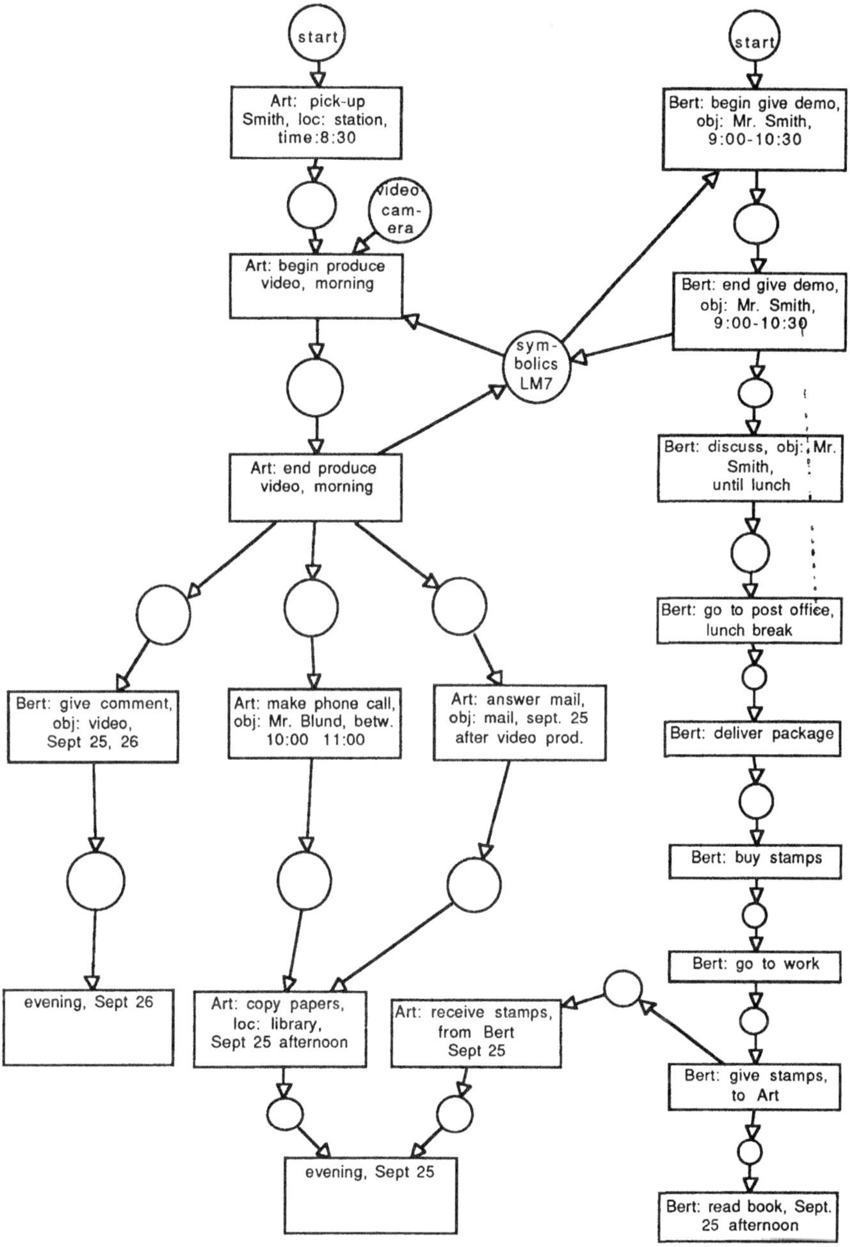

Figure 5: The resulting global plan.

Relation-d: Active cooperation is directly requested. It is necessary that Bert agrees to do the action during the time at which Art would like it to be carried out. Art asks Bert whether this is agreeable for him. Bert agrees and thus makes a commitment to support Art's plan.

The global plan resulting from the coordination process is illustrated in Fig. 5.

7. CONCLUSIONS

We have shown which plan relationships are likely to arise when autonomous agents want to execute multiagent plans in a common environment. Systems which fail to detect these relationships and draw the appropriate conclusions cannot achieve a reasonable coordination of individual plans. Appropriate handling of these relationships plays a crucial role for the prevention of conflicts and the promotion of beneficial actions among the agents. The effects of these relationships for modifying the individual plans in order to integrate them into one consistent global plan structure were illustrated by the example.

Another important class of relationships which has not been made explicit in this paper are temporal relationships. Temporal relationships can be considered between the time intervals which are associated with the actions of plans. In [13] we focus on the role of temporal relationships for the reconciliation of distributed plans with regard to negative plan relationships.

In the future, we want to develop a coordination system which is based on the relationship taxonomy presented in this paper. As an application domain we have selected the office environment. We want to establish domain dependent axioms and heuristics for relationship detection and utilization.

Our implementation will extend the already implemented system VIPS [12]. VIPS ("Visual Interactive Planning System") creates multiagent plans in an interactive process in cooperation with its user. It has been implemented on a SYMBOLICS LISP machine using LISP and PROLOG.

REFERENCES

[1] M. R. Adler, A. B. Davis, R. Weihmeyer, R. W. Worrest, "Conflict-resolution strategies for non-hierarchical distributed agents," in [7], 1989

[2] E. Best, C. Fernandez, "Notations and terminology on Petri net theory," GMD-Technical Report No. 195, March 1987

[3] A. H. Bond, L. G. Gasser, "Readings in Distributed Artificial Intelligence," Morgan Kaufmann Publishers, San Mateo California, 1988

[4] S.E. Conry, R.A. Meyer, V.R. Lesser, "Multistage negotiation in distributed planning," Technical-Report 86-67, Stanford University, CA, March 1986

[5] D. D. Corkhill, "Hierarchical planning in a distributed environment," Proceedings of the Sixth International Joint Conference on Artificial Intelligence, Vols. I and II, Tokyo, 1979. Los Altos, CA: Morgan Kaufmann, pages 168-175, 1979

[6] E. H. Durfee, V. R. Lesser, "Using partial global plans to coordinate distributed problem solvers," Proceedings of the Tenth International Joint Conference on Artificial Intelligence, Vols. I and II, Milano, Italy, 1987. Los Altos, CA: Morgan Kaufmann, pages 875-883, 1987

[7] L. Gasser, M. Huhns, "Distributed Artificial Intelligence", Vol.II, Pitman, London, 1989

[8] M. Genesereth, M.L. Ginsberg, J.S. Rosenschein, "Cooperation without communication," Technical Report HPP-84-36, Stanford University, September 1984

[9] M. Georgeff, "Communication and interaction in multi-agent planning," Proceedings of the National Conference on Artificial Intelligence, Washington, DC, 1983. Los Altos, CA: Morgan Kaufmann, pages 125-129, 1983

[10] M. Georgeff, "A theory of action for multi-agent planning," Proceedings of the National Conference on Artificial Intelligence, University of Texas at Austin, 1984. Los Altos, CA: Morgan Kaufmann, pages 121-125, 1984

[11] B. Hayes-Roth, "A blackboard architecture for control," Artificial Intelligence, Vol. 26, pages 251-321, October 1985

[12] F. v. Martial, F. Victor, "An interactive planner for open systems", Proceedings of the Fourth IEEE Conference on Artificial Intelligence Applications, San Diego, Calif., March 1988

[13] F. v. Martial, "A Conversation model for resolving conflicts among distributed office activities," Proc. of the 5th Conference on Office Information Systems, Cambridge, MA, ACM, New York, April 1990

[14] J. L. Peterson, "Petri net theory and the modeling of systems," Prentice-Hall, Englewood Cliffs, N.J., 1981

[15] J. S. Rosenschein, M. R. Genesereth, "Deals among rational agents," Proceedings of the Ninth International Joint Conference on Artificial Intelligence, Vols. I and II, Los Angeles, 1985. Los Altos, CA: Morgan Kaufmann, pages 91-99, 1985

[16] R. Steeb, S. Cammarata, F.A. Hayes-Roth, P.W. Thorndyke, R.B. Wesson, "Distributed intelligence for air fleet control," Technical Report R-2728-ARPA, Rand Corporation, 1981

[17] C. Stuart, "An implementation of a multi-agent plan synchronizer", Proceedings of the Ninth International Joint Conference on Artificial Intelligence, Vols. I and II, Los Angeles, 1985. Los Altos, CA: Morgan Kaufmann, pages 1031-1033, 1985

[18] K. Sycara, "Resolving goal conflicts via negotiation," Proceedings of the Seventh National Conference on Artificial Intelligence,1988. Los Altos, CA: Morgan Kaufmann, 1988

[19] R. Wilensky, "Planning and understanding," Addison-Wesley, Reading, Massachusetts, 1983

DECENTRALIZED A.I.
Yves DEMAZEAU & Jean-Pierre MÜLLER (Eds.)

A TEMPORAL PLANNER FOR MODELLING AUTONOMOUS AGENTS

Michel LIZOTTE et Bernard MOULIN

Département d'informatique
Université Laval
Ste-Foy, Québec G1K 7P4, Canada

A multi-agent world can be defined as a system in which several agents interact. We define a scene as the result of the interactions taking place between a set of autonomous actors within a given spatio-temporal framework.
To specify an actor we have introduced the concept of "ACTEM" ("ACTing systEM") that is characterized by :

- planning and decision making capabilities (selection, creation, adaptation, and execution of action plans);
- behavioural knowledge (rules and pre-defined activities that can be used by an actem to elaborate an appropriate behaviour in a given situation);
- structural knowledge (conceptual structures that organize knowledge related to the world with which an actem interacts);
- communication capabilities (messages exchanged with other actems).

In this paper we present the main characteristics of SAIRVO, a temporal planning system which implements the actem model and combines various characteristics of both expert systems and planners, as well as an interaction mode between actems in the form of message exchanges.

1. Introduction

A multi-agent world can be defined as a system in which several agents interact [10]. An agent is considered as a physical or abstract entity which is able to act on itself and on its environment, to manipulate a partial representation of its environment, to communicate with other agents. The agent's behaviour is a consequence of its perception, of its knowledge and of its interactions with other agents.

Two main directions have emerged in the research field related to the study of multi-agent worlds [9] :

- Agents can be considered as specialized modules interacting together according to a specific architecture. Each agent can be represented by a knowledge base or a specialized procedure. This approach corresponds to the "multi-expert system" paradigm or Distributed Artificial Intelligence (DAI).
- Agents can be considered as autonomous entities which have perception and communication capabilities, as well as decision abilities. They can act on their environment in an autonomous way. This approach corresponds to the paradigm of "a robot acting in a multi-robot environment".

Our research relates to the second approach. We define a scene as the result of the interactions taking place between a set of autonomous systems within a given spatio-temporal framework. In the LUDUS Project (Laval University Design and Use of Scenes) we are interested in developing a scene management system which will enable us to specify the knowledge of several autonomous actors and to simulate their behaviour and interactions within the context of a given scenario [19].

In our model the actors' autonomy stems from the possibility of modelling decision and planning knowledge in appropriate knowledge bases. To specify an actor we have introduced the concept of "ACTEM" ("ACTing systEM") that is characterized by [21]:

- planning and decision making capabilities (selection, creation, adaptation, and execution of action plans);
- behavioural knowledge (rules and pre-defined activities that can be used by an actem to elaborate an appropriate behaviour in a given situation);
- structural knowledge (conceptual structures that organize knowledge related to the world with which an actem interacts);
- communication capabilities (messages exchanged with other actems).

In this paper we present the main characteristics of SAIRVO ("Simulateur d'un Agent Intelligent qui Réagit en Visant des Objectifs), a planning system which implements the actem model and combines various characteristics of both expert systems and planners, as well as an interaction mode between actems in the form of message exchanges [13]

[15, 16].
In section 2 we present the main principles which led us during SAIRVO's design. In section 3 we give an overview of the planner's main knowledge structures and describe its architecture in section 4.

2. Principles underlying SAIRVO's planning model

A planner can be considered as a system which has the ability to program its own behaviour when establishing an action plan that will enable it to evolve from an initial state to a final state (or goal). When the planner builds its plan, it must combine various primitive actions while avoiding conflicts which may appear when these actions will be applied.
Our approach of planning is based on several principles dealing with time management and the planner's world modelling, the representation of its motivations and behavioural knowledge, the dynamic construction of its planning knowledge, as well as the use of metaplanning techniques to coordinate the planner's reasoning activities [14].

Principle of knowledge separation

This principle goes beyond Wilkin's proposal of separating knowledge about causality from knowledge about actions [27]. In our model, the main knowledge categories are conceptually separated in distinct knowledge bases :
- Structural knowledge : the actem's beliefs which are related to the description of the world, as well as its knowledge of the evolutionary laws which apply on this world.
- Decision-making knowledge : the potential states (goals and sub-goals) that the actem can try to achieve, as well as motivation rules which enable the planner to select or abandon goals according to its structural beliefs' evolution.
- previsional knowledge which describes the actem's beliefs related to the possible world evolution as a consequence of the planning process : temporal constraint network, protections, conflicts, coincidences.
- behavioural knowledge describing the primitive or composed activities that the actem knows : activation conditions related to the actem's structural beliefs (preconditions); selection rules enabling the planner to select activities in order to achieve potential states; temporal constraints which are used to relate actions and the actem's previsional knowledge in a coherent way; previsions which indicate the consequences of a given activity; ways of interacting with the environment (procedures and messages).

Principle of using an explicit temporal model

The actem manipulates time in an explicit way. Time is considered as a continuous linear function which can be used to generate dates (points in time). The actem perceives the world as a collection of facts which are states associated with a time interval that indicates the validity period of the fact. Our approach is similar to FORBIN's temporal model [5] [6] which uses a temporal notation based loosely on Mc Dermott's temporal logic [17].

Principle of autonomy and openness

The actem takes its decisions and creates its plans in an autonomous way. It depends on its environment only for learning information describing the world and its evolution (structural knowledge).

The actem communicates with other actems in its environment by exchanging messages with them. Our approach applies the concept of "open system" [11] to the planning domain.

The actem can act on its environment by executing specialized procedures related to the activities which are part of the plan currently applied.

Principle of intension persistence

We are meeting the main requirements of an "intention theory" [3] with the four main knowledge categories that are manipulated by the actem : structural knowledge (or beliefs), decision-making knowledge (goals), temporal knowledge (previsional beliefs), behavioural knowledge, as well as the interelationships between these categories. The actem implements the principle of intension persistence [3] : the creation of a plan related to a given goal can only be canceled if the actem receives from its environment a message which generates a new fact (structural belief) that invalidates the goal through a motivation rule.

Principle of stereotyped knowledge precedence

As human planners, the actem will not always build new plans from primitive activities (or operators), but it will try to use in first place stereotyped plans that it knows to be appliable to the given situation. This principle is motivated by the fact that the process of constructing new plans is the activity which consumes most of a planner's ressources (mainly time) : trying to use stereotyped plans can help increase the overall efficiency of the planning process.

SAIRVO uses primitive and composed plan schemas and gives priority to the stereotyped plans associated with its goals, whenever it is possible.

This principle leads to the idea of learning and memorizing new stereotyped plans, after they have been constructed by the planner for the first time (this learning process is not implemented in SAIRVO's current version).

The principle of dealing with goal interactions

Dealing with goal interactions is a very important issue when it comes to planning systems. NOAH [22] and NONLIN [24] used "critics" as special procedures which are able to identify positive or negative goal interactions. The notion of constraint concept has been implemented in SIPE by means of a constraint language [27] . Wilenski [26] has proposed a theory for dealing with interactions.

In our model the actem must deal with negative interactions (goal conflicts) and positive interactions (goal coincidences).

Principle of using metarules to control the planning process

It is well accepted that a planner should be able to alternate planning and execution phases according to the evolution of its environment and of its reasoning process.

The actem model implements a dynamic planning strategy which is based on the use of metarules [26]. These metarules activate the appropriate planner's functions according to the evolution of the planning process and to the reactions of the environment.

3. An overview of the planner's main knowledge structures

In this section we describe the main knowledge structures which have been implemented in SAIRVO as a consequence of the application of the principles presented in the previous section.

Our examples will be related to the following short story which describes a scene involving actem Mary.

Mary wants to announce John her departure. She goes to the living room. She takes the phone and dials John's number. She does not get any answer. So, she will write him. She goes to her desk, takes a piece of paper and writes John a letter. She takes an envelop and labels it with John's address. She has to go to the post office. Suddenly, the door bell rings. She goes to the door and opens it. That's John. Mary will not go to the post office.

3.1 The actem's structural knowledge

The structural knowledge represents the world in which the actem evolves. We distinguish the intensional and extensional components of the structural knowledge base, as well as the rules describing the evolutionary laws which apply on the world.

The world is supposed to be composed of (physical or abstract) objects which can be definite or not. For instance Mary, John, phone, envelop, paper are some objects of actem Mary's world.

In our model the world is represented by elementary states. **The intensional component of the structural knowledge base** is described with elementary state patterns, which we represent as simplified conceptual graphs [23]. For instance, "Mary goes to the post office" may be represented by Go(AGNT(Mary),<LOC(Post.office)>), where Go, Mary, Post.office are concepts and AGNT and LOC are conceptual relations.
Some aspects of intensional logic may be dealt with, when introducing the PROP predicate (embedded conceptual graph in Sowa's theory) : " it is necessary that John knows about Mary's plans" is represented by Necessary (PROP (Know (AGNT(John), <OBJ(Mary's.plans)>)))

Time management has been considered quite recently by researchers [17] [1] [25] [12] and corresponds to a fundamental characteristic of our model. We may notice that in everyday life we often refer to a given instant without knowing its exact value : usually we plan actions using unknown execution durations. In our model a time stamp is an identifier T that represents an instant, the value of which is known (its value T is an integer), or unknown (T corresponds to a variable). The present time is the identifier "prt".

The intensional component of the structural knowledge base is described with facts ; we will call it the "fact base".
A fact (or structural belief) is a state associated with a time interval which indicates the period of time during which the actem believes that the fact is valid. The limits of the time interval can be known or not. For instance "Mary is situated in the bedroom between instants 5 and 10" is represented by

<Situated (PAT(Mary),<LOC(Bedroom)>, <5, 10>>.

In addition to the facts that describe the world, the actem knows some evolutionary laws of the world [20] which are specified as deduction or inference rules : IF P1 AND P2 AND ... AND Pn THEN C1, where each Pi is a state pattern or any predicate symbolizing a premise and C is a state pattern indicating a unique conclusion.
For instance "IF the door bell rings THEN somebody is waiting at the frontdoor" is represented by rd4(Wait(PAT(x), <LOC(Front.door)>) ->
KNOWN-FACT(Ring(PAT(Door.bell))));

When SAIRVO learns some new facts from its environment, it can use these rules to

deduce facts (beliefs) which were not explicitly mentioned by the environment. The inference rules and the deduction rules are fired by an inference mechanism according to respectively a backward-chaining strategy and a forward-chaining strategy.
This approach is in some ways similar to the "domain rules" of SIPE [28] and to Dean's causal theory [6].

3.2 Decision-making knowledge

A **goal** is considered as a potential state that can be activated during a specific time interval (called activation interval). During that activation interval, the planner will try to achieve the goal. Several goals can be considered simultaneously : it is sufficient that their activation intervals have a common intersection.

The decision space is used to structure the actem's decision-making knowledge : it may be considered as an "augmented inference network" [19][21]. Its nodes represent potential states (ovals) or effective states (rectangles with round corners) and its edges indicate motivation, coconditions, preconditions or activation relations.
Figure 1 presents a portion of Mary's decision space : note that we have simplified the notation of conceptual graphs in this figure by dropping the name of the conceptual relations from the predicates. The activation relations (labelled a in figure 1) organize the potential states in a classical hierarchy of goals and sub-goals.

The "**protections**" of a goal are states which must be verified by the fact-base either when the goal is activated ("preconditions" labelled pr in figure 1) or during the activation period (concurrent conditions or "coconditions" labeled co in figure 1). If the corresponding facts are not present in the fact base, the goal cannot be activated.

The actem selects its goals according to **motivation rules** specified by : IF P1 AND P2 AND ... Pn THEN <C, i>, where Pi are state patterns or any predicate symbolizing a premise, C is a state pattern which will become a goal, i is a priority weight which will be associated with the candidate goal.
For instance the motivation rule rm1 indicates that "Mary will be motivated to announce John some news (priority weight), IF it is necessary that John knows Mary's plans AND if John does not know Mary's plans" : rm1(Announce(AGNT(Mary), <RCPT(John), OBJ(News)>),3) ->

KNOWN-FACT (Necessary(Know(AGNT(John),<OBJ(Mary's plans)>)))
KNOWN-FACT (NOT(Know(AGNT(John),<OBJ(Mary's plans)>)));

Figure 1 : **A portion of actem Mary's decision space**

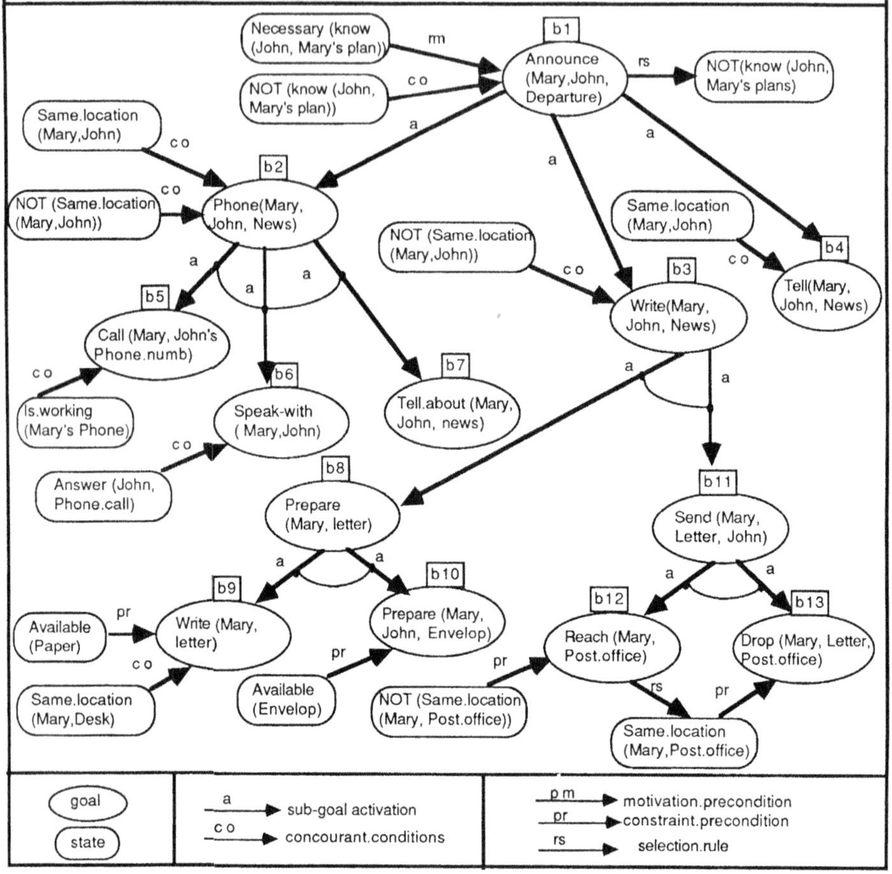

A goal detection mechanism fires the motivation rules according to a forward-chaining strategy. Motivation rules associate the facts (structural beliefs) and potential goals and enable SAIRVO to reason about the actem's intentions [2]. They enable the planner to select goals, but they can also motivate the goal withdrawal if the motivation disappears (problem of intension persistence [3]).

3.3 Temporal knowledge

The actem's previsional beliefs compose a temporal data base which is structured as a **network of temporal constraints**, equivalent to a "time map" [7]: "time maps capture a planner's beliefs concerning the past, present and expected future" [4].
When it creates a new plan, SAIRVO may activate new goals, set protections (preconditions or coconditions), schedule actions etc. Each instance of these knowledge structures is associated with a previsional time interval : a lower bound and an upper bound represented by temporal variables which will be instantiated later on during the planning process.
The planner must calculate and order these previsional time intervals in a coherent way. So, it builds a temporal network which is a graph whose nodes represent the temporal variables and, whose arcs represent temporal constraints (=, ≤ and < relations) holding between the temporal variables. The temporal network represents the chaining of events as the planner anticipates them when it builds its plan. The temporal network supports various complex activities : the goal protection, the scheduling of actions which should be executed simultaneously, the detection of goal coincidences, the resolution of potential goal conflicts.

Figure 3 gives an example of the temporal network when the planner has activated the plan pl1502 which is associated with goal b2.

3.4 Dealing with goal interactions

We distinguish two main interaction categories : facts provided by an unanticipated evolution of the environment; goal conflicts or coincidences appearing during the planning process.

Unanticipated facts are provided by the environment and contradict the actem's previsions : a new fact or an inferred fact may violate a protection or realize an active goal. In either case the planner must update its plan.

When it tries to integrate in the temporal network a new protection, the planner can detect a **potential conflict** (negative interaction), if this protection is not compatible with an anticipated state associated with a time interval which includes the time interval of the protection. In order to recognize these potential conflicts, we use "conflict rules". These rules enable SAIRVO to conclude that two states are mutually exclusive if some object constraints are violated.

Object constraints enable us to specify equality or inequality relations between object couples. These constraints may be created when a new plan is activated, or when positive or negative interactions have been detected.
This approach extends the notion of "resource" [27] used to recognize if actions cannot be executed simultaneously : in Wilkins' approach, an operation description includes a list of variables which specify the objects that are used as resources by this operation; a conflict is detected when simultaneous operations need to use non-compatible resources.

In our model a **coincidence** corresponds to a positive interaction between a goal and a prevision, or between a goal and a fact. Positive interactions are detected when a new goal is activated : the planner compares the new goal with the previsions and with the known or infered facts. If such a coincidence is detected, the goal is achieved and usually some new constraints are added to protect this coincidence.

3.5 Modelling the actem's behaviour

Plan schemas are generic knowledge structures that enable us to specify at once the actem's decision space and its behavioural knowledge. During the planning process, SAIRVO creates plans while instantiating the chosen plan schemas [14].
A plan schema is said to be **"primitive"** if it corresponds to a primitive activity that can be executed directly by the planner, and to be **"composed"** if the corresponding behaviour may be decomposed in more detailed behaviours.
When a plan schema is selected, each sub-goal in it will become a goal that the planner will try to achieve, just as it tries to achieve those that have been recognized by motivation rules. The realization time interval of sub-goals depends on the time interval of the corresponding plan. For instance, the three sub-goals b5, b6 and b7 (figure 1) must be executed sequentially. They are associated with the time intervals <v-td,t4> ,<t4,t5> and <t5,vt-f>.

It is quite usual to describe behaviours for which some states of the actem's fact base must be necessarily verified either when the corresponding activity begins (we call these states **preconditions** in the corresponding plan), or during its execution (we call these states concurrent conditions or "**coconditions**"). For instance, to move from an origin point X towards a destination point Y, we must be in X when the action begins (precondition) and we must be "movable" until the end of the execution (cocondition). FORBIN implements a similar approach with its "assumptions" [6].

A precondition or a cocondition will be considered as a **protection** when the actem can only verify its validity according to the contents of the fact base. A protection corresponds to a time interval which may be used either to protect a current fact until the beginning (precondition) or the end of an action (cocondition), or to verify an execution condition only at the beginning of an action (precondition) or during its execution (cocondition). This kind of protection may delay the implementation of a plan until all preconditions and coconditions are verified.

In some cases, preconditions or coconditions associated with a given behaviour may be considered by the actem as sub-goals it should achieve. The actem must be able to control in the world the state of the objects that are involved by these conditions. Selection rules enable us to associate state patterns with the plan schemas that are required to plan the corresponding goals.

Rather than establishing execution sequences between action couples as classical planifiers do, we use **time constraints** which are relations between unknown times. This kind of representation is interesting because it enables us to reason on times that are not yet linked to a particular action. For instance, a protection which preserves an unplanned goal may refer to the time when the execution of an unknown action will end.

In order to execute primitive operations or to simulate them, a plan schema may include **procedure calls** (Prolog procedures right now).

Thanks to the introduction of time in our model, we can consider, in a new way, the consequences that an operation may induce on the states of the actem's fact base.

We introduce **previsions** to anticipate the **beginning** and the **end** of a state. They correspond respectively to the "add-list" and "delete-list" conditions in STRIPS and NOAH. But there is one main difference : when an end-prevision is set, no information is deleted from the fact base. The system only updates the end-time of the corresponding fact.

In some cases, the result of executing an actem action depends on the answer of its environment. For instance, SAIRVO's user will give it this kind of feedback. It is for that purpose that we specify in the plan schema **uncertain previsions**.

4. General presentation of SAIRVO's architecture

We present here SAIRVO's general architecture with an EPAS diagram [18]. Figure 2 illustrates a global model of the planner that is composed of seven autonomous processes. A rectangle represents a system process, a rectangle with round corners corresponds to information or knowledge accumulation within the system, double squares represent system environment.
Metarules are associated with these various processes. According to their priority levels, the planner activates the metarules in a cyclic way.
Learning new facts (through perception, deduction, protection and goal verification) has the priority on the decision-making function (recognize a goal). This latter function has the priority on the planning function (plan a goal) which is activated prior to the execution function.

The first process, **PERCEIVE A FACT**, receives messages from the **environment**. When a message is recognized, the planner updates its **fact base** and **the clock** indicates the current time of the simulation.

The process **CONCLUDE A FACT** enables the planner to infer new facts by applying its **deduction** or **inference rules** on the fact base.
This process can activate deduction rules in forward chaining or inference rules in backward chaining. When a fact is deduced by a deduction rule, it is added directly to the fact base. A **fact to be inferred** is obtained from an inference rule and stored temporarily.

A protection enables the planner to recall that a given condition in the micro-world must not be violated. The process **VERIFY A PROTECTION** must correct a **plan** when **protections** are violated by a new fact learned from the environment (negative interactions).

There is also a process **VERIFY A GOAL** that examines the contents of the accumulations **facts** and **fact to be inferred** to find new facts (positive interactions) that will enable some of its **goals**. For instance, if Mary has aimed at giving a phone call to John and suddenly, John phones her, she would take advantage of this situation. When a goal is reached in that way, the planner has only to protect the favourable condition by updating the accumulation **protections**. Mary must be sure that nobody will otherwise cut off the phone communication.

Figure 2 : Global architecture of the planner

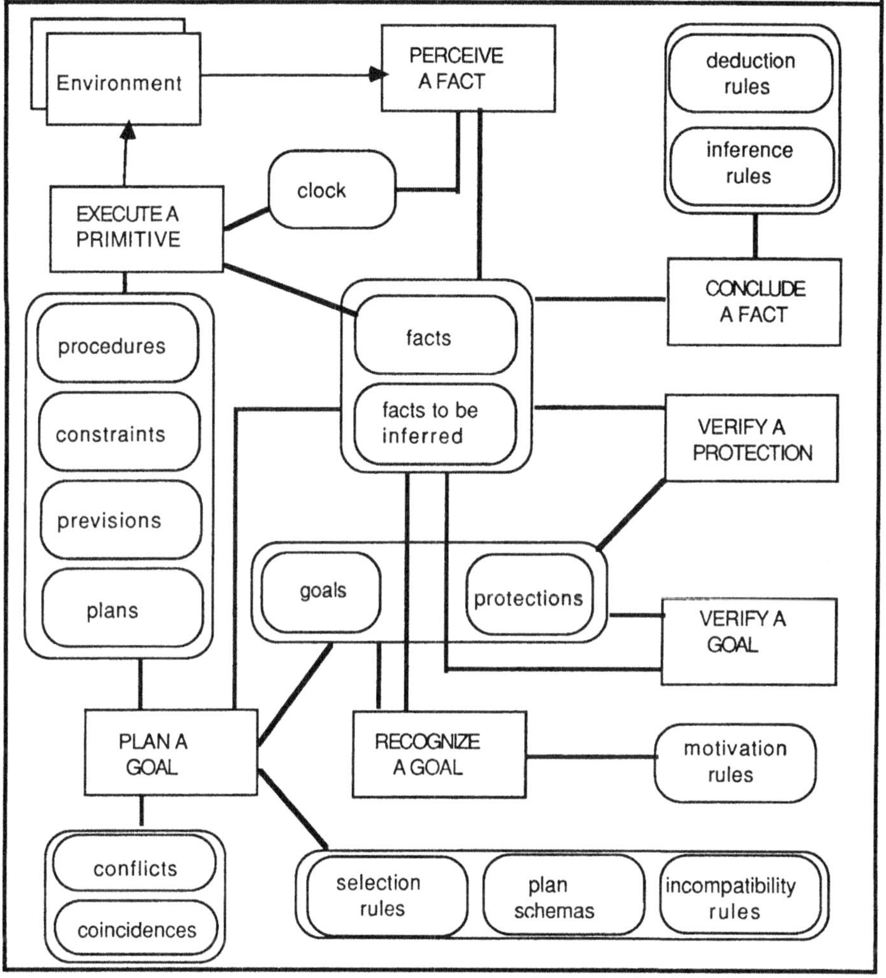

The process **RECOGNIZE A GOAL** selects the planner's goals. The **motivation rules** are applied on all information contained in the accumulations **facts, facts to be inferred** and **goals**.

To build its plans, SAIRVO uses a **temporal network** which is a graph of time constraints that have been selected in the plan schemas during the planning process. Figure 3 illustrates the temporal network after the creation of goals b5, b6 and b7 (coded as bt302, bt303, bt304).

The process **PLAN A GOAL** determines the **plans** that the planner will have to execute in order to reach its goals : it is activated for each goal. First of all it verifies in accumulations **facts, facts to be inferred** and **previsions,** to ensure that the goal has already been reached or that it will be reached as a consequence of the execution of a plan already activated. In that case, we deal with a positive interaction which will be memorized in the accumulation **coincidences**. Otherwise, by using **plan selection rules,** the process tries to identify a plan whose execution can help reach the active goal. After a plan has been identified, the planner tries to activate it using the appropriate action types in the form of protections, constraints, sub-goals, procedures and previsions. The activation of a plan consists in adding the instantiated elements in accumulations **protections, constraints, goals, procedures** and **previsions.**

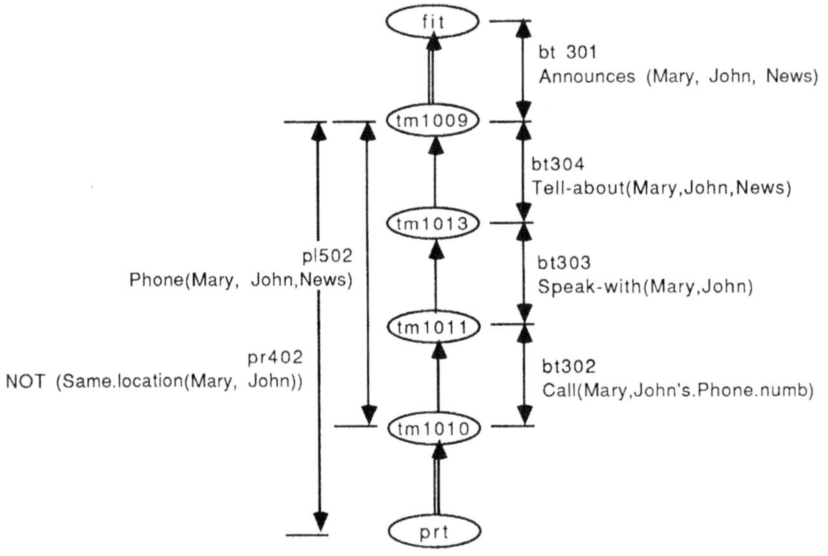

Figure 3 : A temporal network

The process **EXECUTE A PRIMITIVE** executes the set of primitive actions as it has been determined by the process of planning. The order of their execution is specified by the **constraints**. The actions and their effects are described in the accumulation **previsions**. The execution of a primitive is simulated by sending a message to the

environment and some **procedures** may have been eventually executed previously. **The clock** is incremented when a primitive is executed.

4. Conclusion

In this paper we have presented an overview of SAIRVO, a temporal planning system which can be used to implement autonomous agents in a multi-agent world. This system has been implemented in Prolog, and tested on various small applications. The current development directions of LUDUS project correspond to the implementation of a more efficient version of the planning system and the development of a special actem called "game manager" [20] which will have to coordinate the activities of the other actems within the context of a given scenario.

ACKNOWLEDGMENTS

This research is supported by the Natural Sciences and Engineering Research Council of Canada (grant A2218).

REFERENCES

(1) Allen, J., Maintaining Knowledge about Temporal Intervals, in *Communication of the ACM*, vol 26, nb 11, November 1983.

(2) Bratman, M., Two faces of intention, *The Philosophical Review*, XCIII (3), 1984.

(3) Cohen P. R., Levesque H. J., Persistence, intention and commitment, in (G-L 87).

(4) Charniak, E., et McDermott, D., *Introduction to Artificial Intelligence*, Mass.: Addison-Wesley, 1985.

(5) Dean, T. L., Intractability and time-dependent planning, in (G-L 87).

(6) Dean, T. L., Firby, R. J., Miller, D., Hierarchical planning involving deadlines, travel time and ressources, *Computational Intelligence Journal*, vol 4 n 4, November 88.

(7) Dean, T. L., McDermott, D.V., Temporal Data Base Management, *Artificial Intelligence*, vol32, nb 1, April 1987.

(8) Drummond, M. E., A representation of action and belief for automatic planning systems, in (G-L 87).

(9) Ferber, J., Ghallab, M., Problématique des univers multi-agents intelligents, dans les actes des journées nationales *Intelligence Artificielle*, édité par Teknea , Toulouse mars 1988.

(10) Georgeff, M. P., Lansky, A. L. editors, *Reasoning about actions and plans*, Morgan Kaufman pub. 1987.

(11) Hewitt, C., De Jong, P, Open Systems, in *On Conceptual Modelling, Perspectives from Artificial Intelligence, Databases and Programming Languages*, Brodie, Mylopoulos, Schmidt editors, Springer Verlag Pub. Comp. 1984.

(12) Kowalski R., A Logic-based Calculus of Events, *New Generation Computing,* vol 4, pp 67-95, 1986.

(13) Lizotte, M., Système de planification et simulation de comportements, mémoire de maîtrise en intelligence artificielle, Département d'informatique, Université Laval, mars 1988.

(14) Lizotte, M., Moulin, B. , SAIRVO : un planificateur mettant en oeuvre le modèle d'actem, soumis à la revue TSI en septembre 88, révisé en mars 89.

(15) Lizotte, M., Moulin, B. , SAIRVO : a Temporal Planning System, in proceedings of the Second International Conference on Industrial and Engineering Applications of Artificial Intelligence and Expert Systems, Tullahoma, Tennessee USA, June 1989.

(16) Lizotte M., Moulin B., SAIRVO : A Planning System which Implements the Actem Concept, submitted to the journal *Knowledge-Based Systems*, November 1988, accepted for publication July 1989.

(17) McDermott, D., A Temporal Logic for Reasoning About Processes and Plans, *Cognitive Science*, vol. 6, pp. 101-155, 1982.

(18) Moulin, B., La méthode E.P.A.S. pour la modélisation et la conception de systèmes, rapports de recherche DIUL-RR-85-07, 08 et 09, Université Laval,septembre 1985.

(19) Moulin, B., Projet LUDUS (Laval University Design and Use of Scenes), rapport technique DIUL-RT-8605, Université Laval, Département d'informatique (27 pages), mars 1986.

(20) Moulin, B., Le concept d'actem pour la gestion de scènes, dans les actes du colloque GIRICO'87, L'intelligence artificielle au service des organisations, Montréal juin 1987.

(21) Moulin, B.,The Actem Model for Decision Modelling in a Scene Management System, in proceedings of the First International Conference on Industrial and Engineering Applications of Artificial Intelligence and Expert Systems, Tullahoma, Tennessee USA, June 1988.

(22) Sacerdoti, E. D., A Structure for Plans and Behavior, New York: Elsevier North-Holland, 1977.

(23) Sowa, J.F., " Conceptual Structures : Information Processing in Mind and Machine", Addison Wesley 1984.

(24) Tate, A., Generating project networks, Proceedings of the Fifth International Joint Conference on Artificial Intelligence, pp. 888-893, 1977.

(25) Vere S., Planning in Time: Windows and Durations for Activities and Goals, IEEE Transactions on Pattern Analysis and Machine Intelligence, vol. PAMI-5(3), pp. 246-267, 1983.

(26) Wilenski, R., Planning and Understanding: A computational Approach to Human Reasoning, Mass.: Addison-Wesley, 1983.

(27) Wilkins, D. E., Domain-independent Planning: Representation and Plan Generation, Artificial Intelligence, vol. 22, pp. 269-3012, 1984.

(28) Wilkins, D. E., Casual reasoning in planning, special issue on planning, *Computational Intelligence Journal*, vol 4 n 4, November 88.

DECENTRALIZED A.I.
Yves DEMAZEAU & Jean-Pierre MÜLLER (Eds.)

MOTION PLANNING IN A MULTI-AGENT WORLD

Th. Fraichard and Y. Demazeau

LIFIA-INPG
46, av. Félix Viallet,
38031 Grenoble Cedex, France

This paper explores the problem of the coordination of the movements of several vehicles in a dynamic world. The specific case of car-like vehicles moving within an intersection is studied. We present a way to control a subset of such vehicles (the vehicles of this subset will be referred to as being "coordinated"). A centralized supervisor called "intersection manager" computes a reference trajectory for every coordinated vehicle while each vehicle is concerned with the realization of its predetermined reference trajectory. This paper mostly focuses on the intersection manager. This intersection manager makes use of the very structure of the intersection both to estimate the behaviour of the other vehicles and to plan the motions of the coordinated vehicles. Our approach consists first in assigning priorities to the vehicles and then in planning motions one vehicle at a time. For this purpose, we apply a path/velocity decomposition. In order to deal with the uncertainty introduced by the other vehicles, the intersection manager operates periodically on a given interval of time.

1 STATEMENT OF THE PROBLEM

This paper deals with the following problem: given a set of vehicles moving in a dynamic world, we want to coordinate the motions of a subset of these vehicles. Each vehicle has its own goal and this goal is to be achieved with respect to the two following criteria—*optimality* and *safety*. A vehicle has to reach its goal as quickly as possible (optimality) and without colliding either with the other vehicles or with the obstacles of the world in question (safety). This problem has the following characteristics:

- The vehicles: a vehicle is an entity endowed with motion capability. Every vehicle is subject to various kinematic constraints which restrict the type of trajectory it can execute—e.g. constraints on the velocity or on the shape of the trajectory. The goal of a vehicle is to reach a specific location in the world. We assume that, while moving towards its goal, a vehicle obeys a certain set of rules; this set of rules will be referred to as the "behavioural code"; it partially determines the behaviour of a vehicle. Besides every vehicle is able to perceive its local environment through various means of perception (camera, radar...).

- The world: it is cluttered with static but also dynamic obstacles. The static obstacles constitute the limits of the actual evolution space of the vehicles. The dynamic obstacles consists mainly of the vehicles. The subset of vehicles whose motions are to be computed will be referred to as the "coordinated" vehicles. This world is obviously dynamic but also uncertain since the motions of the dynamic obstacles are not known beforehand.

It is possible to view this problem as a particular instance of the piano mover's problem [12,14]. But this type of approach focuses on the geometric and kinematic aspects of the problem and completely disregards the fact that a vehicle can be considered as an agent with means of perception, decision and action and whose behaviour is partially governed by the behavioural code. Therefore we can tackle this problem in a multi-agent perspective. In this framework, the following points have to be dealt with:

- Plan recognition i.e. reasoning about the future intentions of the other vehicles.
- Levels of interaction between the coordinated vehicles.
- Generation of a plan in a multi-agent world.
- Execution of a plan in a dynamic and uncertain world.

2 POSSIBLE APPROACHES

There are many possible ways to tackle this motion planning problem in a multi-agent perspective. We are going to classify these approaches with respect to the level of autonomy of each coordinated vehicle.

1. "independent" approach: a coordinated vehicle is perfectly able to solve its motion problem on its own. In this situation, one vehicle constitutes one agent.
2. "controlled" approach: a coordinated vehicle has no capability of its own, it is a mere actuator. Therefore a system which is totally in charge of the coordinated vehicles is needed. In this situation, the set of coordinated vehicles turn out to constitute one single agent.
3. "interdependent" approach: we are dealing here with a whole range of approaches in between the two extremes already mentioned. In these situations, a coordinated vehicle has various capabilities but it is not able to solve its motion problem on its own. Therefore it is up to a "supervisor" external to the vehicle to provide this lacking capability.

In this classifying scheme, let us notice first that no hypothesis is made either on what a capability is or on what the supervisor is (it can either be centralized or distributed among the coordinated vehicles). Besides no reference is made upon the way the coordinated vehicles will interact with one another.

3 STUDY OF A SPECIFIC CASE

3.1 The Framework

The purpose of our application[1] is to develop software tools in order to guide car-like vehicles moving on a particular subset of the road network—intersections. Two types of vehicle have to be considered when designing such tools: those whose motions are to be guided by the system—i.e. the coordinated vehicles— and the other vehicles. Our assumption on the existence of a behavioural code is instantiated here by the fact that the vehicles are supposed to respect the highway code. This is important since it enables to reason about the vehicles' behaviour and it provides a structure to the evolution space of the vehicles. Indeed, the roadway turns out to be an organized set of lanes. Besides intersections are designed in order to ease the traffic; thus a vehicle has to follow a particular lane and accordingly is not supposed to overtake. In other words, a vehicle roughly follows a predetermined path and merely adjusts its velocity along this path in order to avoid collision with the other vehicles.

3.2 Outline Of The Approach

The complexity of the problem we are dealing with prevents the use of a controlled approach (see [7,11,14] for complexity issues). Indeed, we are considering many vehicles—i.e. a system with a high number of degrees of freedom—moving in a dynamic and uncertain world. As far as the motion planning is concerned, the few suggested solutions to this problem are impractical in actual situations.

Besides in order to satisfy the optimality criterion—i.e. the fact that each vehicle must reach its goal as quickly as possible—we chose an interdependent approach rather than an independent one.

Within our approach, each coordinated vehicle is concerned with the realization of a predetermined reference trajectory—i.e. plan execution. The capabilities of a such a vehicle are rather low it include trajectory following and local obstacle avoidance; the reference trajectory is provided by an "intersection manager" that is a centralized system which is in charge of the coordinated vehicles within a specific intersection. It provides each coordinated vehicle with a reference trajectory. It is up to the intersection manager to deal with the following points: plan recognition (reasoning about the intentions of the other vehicles) and plan generation in a dynamic world. In the paper, we concentrate on the intersection manager and say a few words about the plan execution aspect.

The Intersection Manager

The intersection manager has to provide each coordinated vehicle with a trajectory. Planning in a multi-vehicle world requires considering the motions of the other vehicles. In particular, we must have an estimation of the other vehicles' behaviour. Since this behaviour cannot be known exactly, it is useless to plan on a large period of time. This is why the intersection manager operates on a *planning horizon*. This horizon represents the duration on which it is considered that the hypotheses made on the evolution of the other vehicles are sound.

[1]The work presented here is part of the european EUREKA-PROMETHEUS project.

Periodically, the intersection manager has to plan the motions of the coordinated vehicles for the next horizon. For this purpose, it makes use of a geometric description of the intersection and an estimation of the position/velocity parameters of the vehicles located at the vicinity of the crossroad at the beginning of the horizon. As the goals of the coordinated vehicles are not correlated, we apply a *prioritization approach* [5] i.e. each coordinated vehicle is assigned a priority and the trajectories are planned in the priority order. The point of this approach is to reduce the complexity of the problem by turning the multi-vehicle planning problem into a sequence of one-vehicle planning problem. Besides we make use of a *path/velocity decomposition* [8]. This method consists first in planning a path avoiding the static obstacles and then in adjusting the velocity so as to avoid collisions with the moving obstacles. Indeed, according to the crossroad design principle, a vehicle has to follow a determined path simply by adjusting its velocity in order to avoid collision or give way to other vehicles.

According to these choices and basic hypotheses, the intersection manager is composed of two main modules:

- A *geometric planner* which generates a geometric trajectory for each coordinated vehicle.
- A *temporal planner* which computes for each coordinated vehicle the velocity to apply along the generated trajectory in order to avoid collisions with the other vehicles.

The geometric planner is described in section 3.4 and the temporal planner in section 3.5. Beforehand, section 3.3 presents the world model our system is based on.

A Coordinated Vehicle

As mentioned earlier, a coordinated vehicle is periodically provided with a plan including both geometric and time constraints. Such a plan is "nominal" in the sense that the vehicle has to adapt its actual trajectory constantly according to both the given reference trajectory and the details of the local environment provided by the sensors of the vehicle (especially when other vehicles are located in this environment). For that purpose, we have developed a method based on the potential field scheme [2,4,10]. The nominal trajectory defines a valley of potential that the vehicle is supposed to track and the detected obstacles generate repulsive potential fields. The actual motion is obtained by combining these potential functions.

3.3 The World Model

3.3.1 The Environment

The road network is a highly structured environment (this structure is provided by the highway code). Therefore an obvious way of modelling it is to represent this structure explicitly through a connected set of regions having their own functionality. According to the planning requirements, we distinguish four types of regions—*lanes, crossing regions, entry* and *exit regions*. Basically, the roadway is an organized set of lanes; each lane has its own associated motion constraints. Because of this characteristic, we make use of a freeway-like representation [3] in which a "spine" denotes the oriented main axis of a lane. According to the non-overtaking hypothesis, vehicles are supposed to follow roughly the main axis of the lanes and to move from one lane to the next at an intersection point. Since such lane intersections share common parts of the roadway, it is necessary to represent them explicitly as crossing regions for the vehicles of the related lanes. As explained above, our system deals with subsets of the road network; therefore we have introduced the concept of entry regions and exit regions to interface the considered environment with the rest of the network. Such regions are located at the external extremities of the lanes which are connected to other parts of the road network. Figure 1 shows an example of decomposition of an intersection into regions.

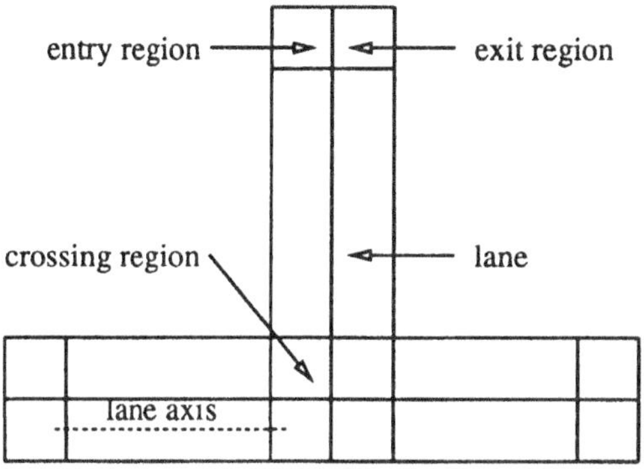

Figure 1: an intersection decomposition

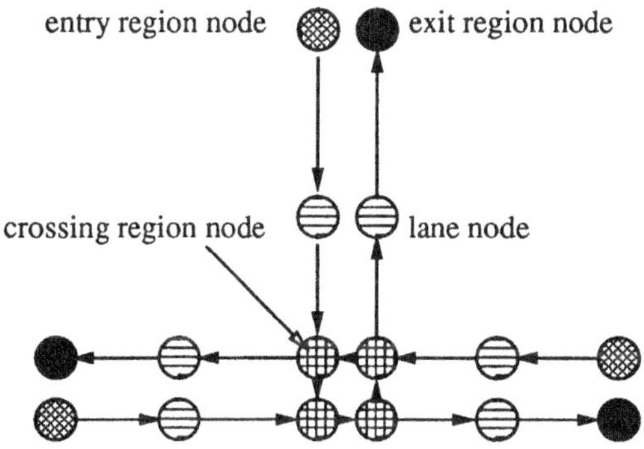

Figure 2: the graph associated to the decomposition of figure 1

Besides in order to represent the connectivity of the road network and the associated motion constraints, the regions obtained are structured using a graph $\mathcal{G}$. A node r_i in $\mathcal{G}$ represents a region. An oriented arc from r_i to r_j indicates that it is possible to move from region r_i to region r_j. Figure 2 shows the graph associated to the decomposition of figure 1.

Whereas it is easy to extract the lanes of a roadway automatically, the definition of the crossing regions is a far more complex task. Indeed, it depends mainly on the topographic structure of the intersection considered. Figure 3 illustrates how complex the decomposition of an intersection can be. Therefore and according to the static nature of the road infrastructure, we make use of an adaptive decomposition mechanism to model these regions.

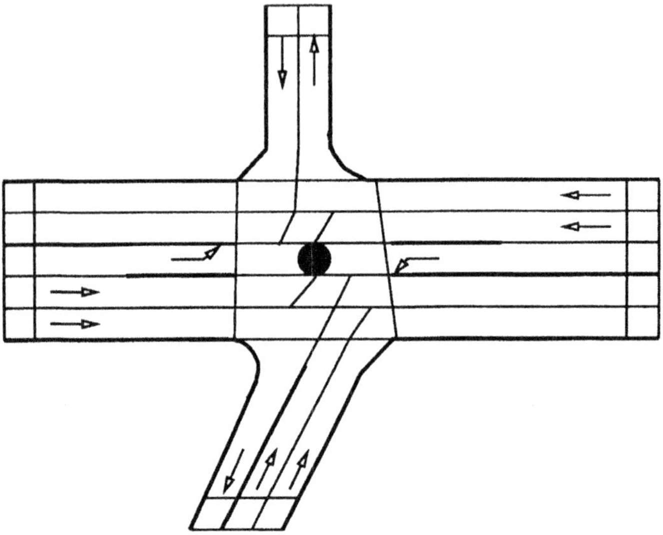

Figure 3: a complex intersection decomposition

3.3.2 The Vehicles

We consider car-like vehicles. Geometrically, they are represented by rectangles. Such a vehicle has two rear-wheels and two directional front-wheels. It is designed so that, during a turn, the axles of the front wheels intersects the rear-wheels axle at a particular point C (see figure 4). It is subject to various kinematic constraints which restrict the type of trajectory it can execute. The three main constraints for such a vehicle are the following: 1) a dependence relation exists between its translational and its rotational degrees of freedom, 2) the curvature radius of its trajectory is lower bounded and 3) its velocity is upper bounded.

3.4 The Geometric Planner

The task of the geometric planner is to compute a nominal geometric trajectory for each coordinated vehicle. This trajectory must enable the vehicle to reach its goal without colliding with the static obstacles and it must be executable by the vehicle according to its own kinematic constraints. In the following, we simply present a sketch of the planning algorithm and refer the reader to [6] for a complete presentation of the geometric planner.

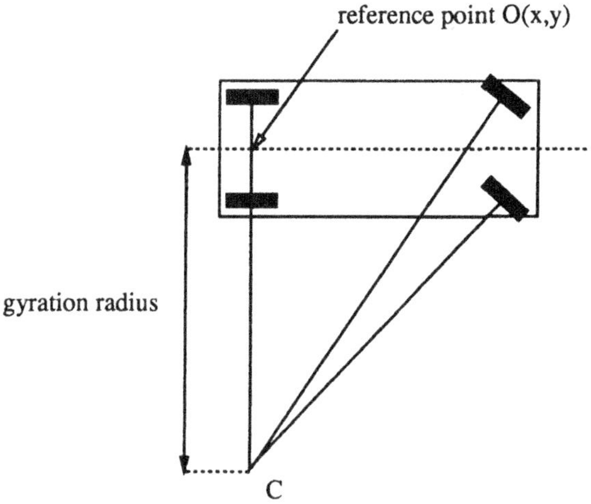

Figure 4: a car-like vehicle

Planning an executable trajectory is performed in two phases consisting first in generating a polygonal line which represents the "skeleton" of the trajectory searched, and then in "smoothing" this polygonal line in order to obtain curved transitions which verifies the vehicle kinematic constraints.

3.4.1 Determining The Skeleton Of The Trajectory

The purpose of this phase is to generate a polygonal line representing a theoretical trajectory avoiding static obstacles but without verifying the kinematic constraints of the vehicle. Such a trajectory is computed in two steps:

1. find a "path": in order to cross an intersection, a vehicle has to go through a specific sequence of regions. According to our world model, this sequence has the following structure:

   entry region, ([lane], crossing region, [lane])*, exit region

   Such a sequence is called a "path". It is easily obtained by searching the graph $\mathcal{G}$ with an A^* algorithm. The heuristic function of the algorithm A^* is the Euclidean distance between the centers of the regions.

2. extract the skeleton: as mentioned above, a vehicle tries to follow the main axis of the regions it goes through. The path provides us with a sequence of regions. In the current implementation, it is assumed that the lane axes are piecewise linear. It is then possible to build a polygonal line whose segments correspond to the axes of the regions crossed by the vehicle.

Figure 5 shows the path and its associated skeleton for a vehicle entering the intersection in the entry region r and aiming at the exit region r'.

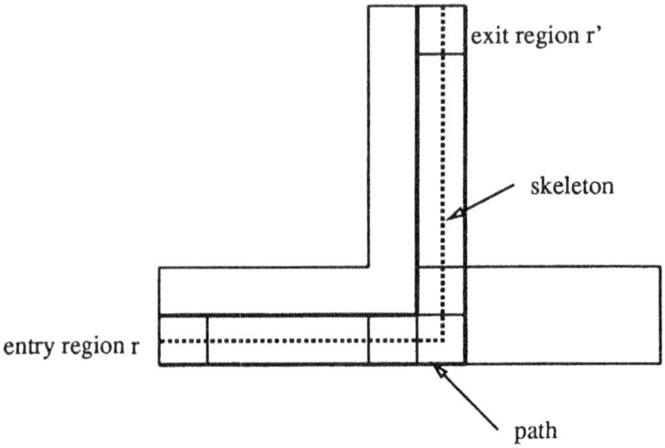

Figure 5: a path and its associated skeleton

3.4.2 Smoothing The Skeleton Of The Trajectory

This phase aims to introduce circular based transitions in the skeleton in order to make the trajectory consistant with the kinematic constraints of the vehicle while avoiding the static obstacles. In the current implementation of the system, the generated trajectories are composed of straight line segments and circular arcs connected so that the resultant trajectory is of class C^1—i.e. the trajectory is differentiable and its derivative is continuous. This smoothing step is based upon the concept of "domain of centers of curvature" introduced in [9]. Figure 6 shows the actual trajectory associated to the skeleton of the figure 5.

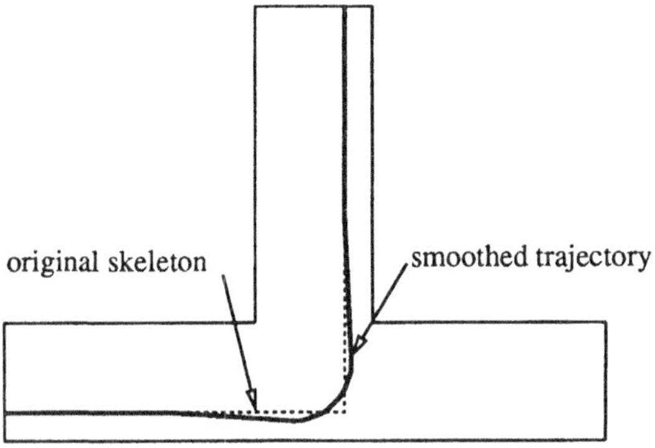

Figure 6: a "smoothed" trajectory

3.5 The Temporal Planner

The task of the temporal planner is to determine the velocity to apply to each coordinated vehicle in order to avoid collisions with the other vehicles. As explained in section 3.2, it operates periodically on the interval of time $[0, horizon]$.For each path generated by the geometric planner, it determines the entrance time to associate to the related regions. This sequence of temporal goals provides us with the average velocity to apply within each region.

3.5.1 Statement Of The Problem

While many vehicles can simultaneously move within a lane, only one vehicle can go through a crossing region at a given time. Since entry and exit regions are narrow areas defined to interface the crossroad considered with the rest of the network, we also consider these regions as unsharable resources at a given time for the vehicles. In the sequel, we call "conflict regions" the regions which cannot be simultaneously occupied by several vehicles—i.e. crossing, entry and exit regions. Then the kinematic behaviour of a vehicle within a given region may be characterized altogether by the occupation constraints associated to the next conflict region on its path. Since our world model warrants that each region is connected to a conflict region (see section 3.3.1), it becomes possible to turn the velocity planning problem into an allocation problem where the conflict regions are resources to be temporally allocated to the vehicles.

Let V be the set of vehicles present in the crossroad and V_C the subset of the coordinated vehicles. We define $OI(v, r)$, the occupation interval of the conflict region r by the vehicle v, as the interval of time during which v is within r. Then the problem to be solved is to find an occupation interval $OI(v, r)$ for each vehicle $v \in V_C$ and for each conflict region r belonging to the path associated to v. These occupation intervals must satisfy the following constraints:

1. monotonicity: the velocity of a vehicle cannot be negative.
2. maximum velocity: a vehicle cannot go beyond a given velocity limit.
3. no collision: if r is a conflict region then

$$\forall v_i, v_j \in V, v_i \neq v_j, OI(v_i, r) \cap OI(v_j, r) = \emptyset.$$

4. no overtaking: a vehicle cannot overtake when moving from one conflict region to the next.

The purpose of the temporal planner is then to find for each vehicle $v \in V_C$ a sequence of occupation intervals which satisfies the four previous constraints and which maximizes the average velocity of v along its trajectory.

3.5.2 Outline Of The Approach

The problem to be solved can be seen as a temporal constraints propagation problem—there is a set of time intervals to determine and a set of associated constraints to be simultaneously satisfied. A thorough survey of the various approaches developed to solve different instances of this problem is made in [13]. Apart from the complexity of the general problem, this survey shows that "strong disjunctive constraints[2]" are still not or inefficiently dealt with. Unfortunately, the no-collision constraint leads to generate strong disjunctive constraints. This means that approaches derived from the work of [1] or [13] cannot be directly applied to solve our problem.

In our system, the planner efficiency is of a major importance because the planning duration must be very short in relation to the planning horizon. Besides it is worthless to try to generate a completely accurate (and therefore costly) temporal plan in as much as this planning relies upon an estimation of the behaviour of the other vehicles. These two reasons led us to apply a prioritization approach consisting in allocating the conflict regions one vehicle at a time. As we will see in section 3.5.4, this approach is not complete—the temporal allocation may fail for a vehicle— but its algorithmic complexity is linear in the number of vehicles. When the planning process fails for some vehicles, it is up to the vehicles (therefore at execution time) to coordinate their motions locally.

3.5.3 The Non Coordinated Vehicles

In order to determine the occupation intervals associated to the non coordinated vehicles, the temporal planner requires an estimation of their behaviour. Since such a vehicle is assumed to respect the highway code, its behaviour is similar to that of a coordinated vehicle. A non coordinated vehicle intending to cross a conflict region is subject to the same temporal constraints than a coordinated vehicle, therefore its kinematic behaviour can be estimated by a conflict region allocation in the same way as for a coordinated vehicle. This means that if the system knows the goal of a non coordinated vehicle then it will be able to determine the sequence of regions this vehicle will go through and their associated temporal intervals. Consequently the system simply has to estimate the goal of each non coordinated vehicle before applying the same planning process to all the vehicles. This estimation is made by taking into account the instantaneous position/velocity parameters of the non coordinated vehicles at the beginning of each planning horizon and possibly symbolic information (e.g. information on the indicators of the vehicle).

3.5.4 The Prioritization

Our prioritization algorithm relies on a "natural" priority order leading first to process a vehicle v moving in a region r at time $t = 0$—i.e. the beginning of the planning horizon— before processing a vehicle v' having r in its path. Figure 7 which represents an intersection at time $t = 0$ illustrates this priority order; the vehicle b occupies the region r on the path of the vehicle a, it is therefore necessary to know when b will leave r before deciding when to "allocate" r to a. In other words, b must be processed before a.

Therefore by using this criterion, we can define a relation *Before* on the set of vehicles V. But this relation can generate cycles of the type "v *Before* v'" and "v' *Before* v". For instance, a cycle exists between the vehicles b and c in figure 7. Such a cycle represents motions to be planned simultaneously. Therefore, it catches the prioritization principle

[2]The constraint "A is either before *or* after B" is an example of a strong disjunctive constraint

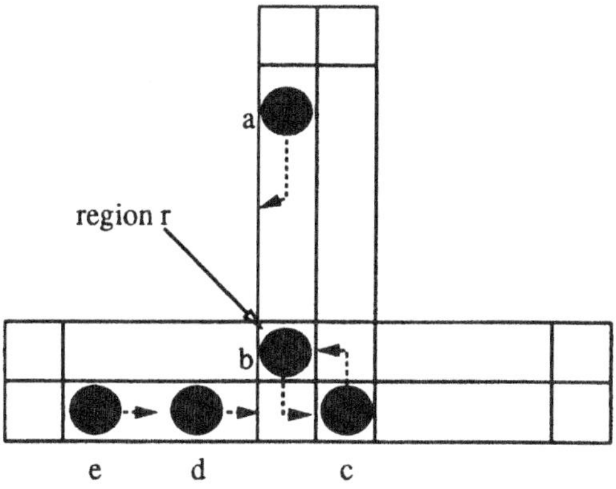

Figure 7: the state of an intersection at time $t = 0$

out. In order to deal with such contradictions and get a total ordering of the vehicles, we apply the following prioritization algorithm:

1. Build the graph associated to the relation *Before*.
2. Turn the relation *Before* in a partial ordering by removing an arbitrary edge in each cycle of this graph.
3. Topologically sort this new graph.

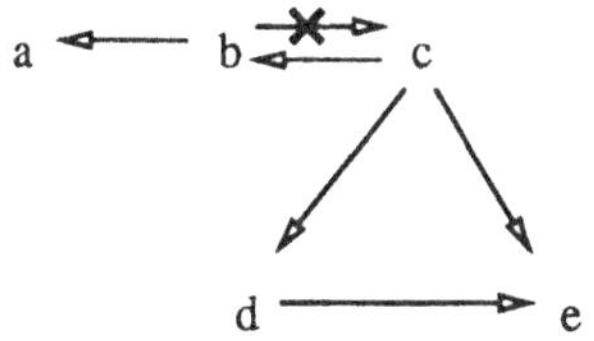

Figure 8: the relation *Before* associated to figure 7

Figure 8 represents the graph of the relation *Before* associated to the intersection of figure 7. An edge starting from the node v and ending to the node v' indicates that vehicle v must be processed before the vehicle v'. *Before* is turned into a partial ordering by removing the edge between the vehicles b and c. The topological sorting of this new relation provides us with the following priority order for the vehicles: c, b, d, e, a.

3.5.5 The Planning Algorithm

Let v_i be the ith vehicle in the prioritization order. According to the prioritization principle, the set of occupation intervals generated by the vehicles $v_1, \ldots, v_{i-1}$ on each conflict region is computed by the system before processing v_i. Then the temporal allocation for v_i is based on an analysis of intervals available associated to the conflict regions belonging to the path of v_i. This analysis is made by sequentially considering the conflict regions of the path of v_i; the set of temporal intervals available for each conflict region is computed according to both the constraints drawn from the vehicles $v_1, \ldots, v_{i-1}$ and the previously analysed conflict region. Since there are several temporal intervals available at each step, the solution space can be represented by a tree. Therefore searching a solution for v_i is achieved using a depth-first search algorithm. This search considers the valid temporal intervals from the earliest to the latest (thus the trajectory will be optimal in terms of velocity) and it terminates when it finds a valid temporal interval either associated to the last conflict region of the path of v_i or ending after *horizon*. For a complete presentation of this algorithm, we refer the reader to [6].

4 EXPERIMENTS

A prototype of the intersection manager is currently developed on a SUN^{TM} Workstation 3/60 in Common Lisp. The geometric planner is still under test. As for the temporal planner, it is implemented and several examples involving up to 20 vehicles in a basic intersection have been successfully processed by the system. We are now testing it with more complex intersections.

The Temporal Planning

In this section, we illustrate the temporal planning process with a small example. The world we consider is a basic intersection. Figure 9 shows the decomposition into regions of the intersection considered. The regions are numbered from 1 to 20.

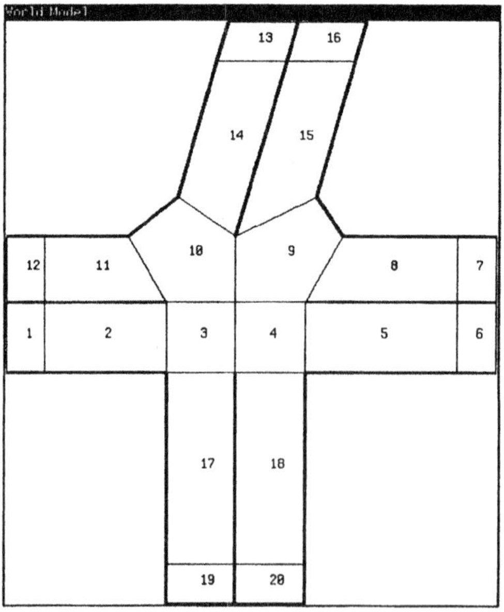

Figure 9: the decomposition of the world

Figure 10 represents the state of the world at the beginning of the planning horizon, say at time $t = 0$. the world contains both coordinated and non coordinated vehicles; they are represented by numbered white disks.

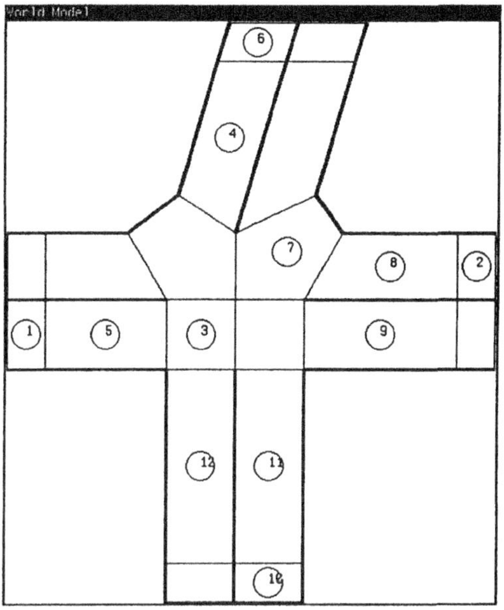

Figure 10: the state of the world at time $t = 0$

The first job of the intersection manager is to estimate the goal—i.e. a particular exit region—of each non coordinated vehicles. In the current implementation, we assume that the system knows the goal of every vehicle. Therefore the intersection manager can determine their path—i.e. a sequence of regions. In the example, the paths of the vehicles are:

```
*** paths of the vehicles ***

vehicle no 12 : (19)
vehicle no 11 : (4 9 10 11 12)
vehicle no 10 : (18 4 5 6)
vehicle no 9 : (6)
vehicle no 8 : (9 10 3 4 5 6)
vehicle no 7 : (15 16)
vehicle no 6 : (14 10 3 4 5 6)
vehicle no 5 : (3 4 9 15 16)
vehicle no 4 : (10 11 12)
vehicle no 3 : (4 5 6)
vehicle no 2 : (8 9 10 3 4 5 6)
vehicle no 1 : (2 3 17 19)
```

The intersection manager is then able to apply the prioritization algorithm. It provides us with the following priority order:

```
*** prioritization ***

No cycle detected
Order = (4 7 9 3 5 6 8 2 11 10 12 1)
```

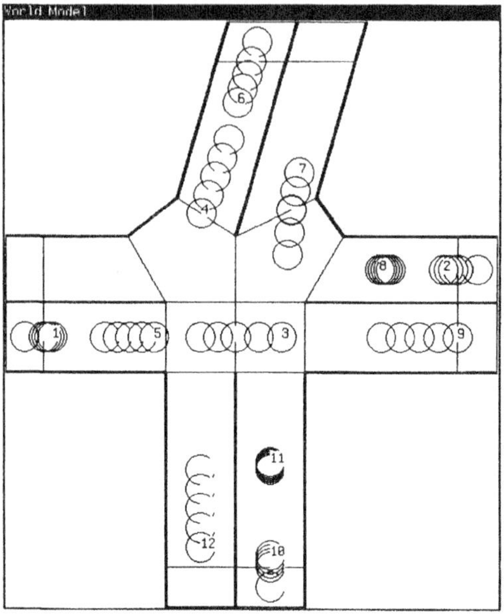

Figure 11: the simulated execution of the plan: time $t = 0$ to $t = 4$

The temporal planning process is then applied to every vehicle (coordinated and non coordinated as well) in the priority order. A temporal plan for a vehicle is a list of couples (number of the region, entrance time in the region). For a non coordinated vehicle, this temporal plan represents an estimation of the vehicle's behaviour (according to the other vehicles' behaviour). The temporal planning over the horizon $[0, 50]$ yields the following results:

```
*** temporal plans of the vehicles ***

vehicle no 12 : (17 0) (19 5)
vehicle no 11 : (18 0) (4 46) (9 50) (10 53)
vehicle no 10 : (20 0) (18 1) (4 53) (5 56)
vehicle no 9 : (5 0) (6 4)
vehicle no 8 : (8 0) (9 20) (10 25) (3 28) (4 31) (5 34) (6 42)
vehicle no 7 : (9 0) (15 2) (16 10)
vehicle no 6 : (13 0) (14 1) (10 11) (3 16) (4 18) (5 22) (6 30)
```

```
vehicle no 5 : (2 0) (3 5) (4 8) (9 11) (15 16) (16 24)
vehicle no 4 : (14 0) (10 4) (11 8) (12 13)
vehicle no 3 : (3 0) (4 1) (5 5) (6 13)
vehicle no 2 : (7 0) (8 1) (9 28) (10 33) (3 36) (4 39) (5 43) (6 51)
vehicle no 1 : (1 0) (2 1) (3 42) (17 45) (19 55)
```

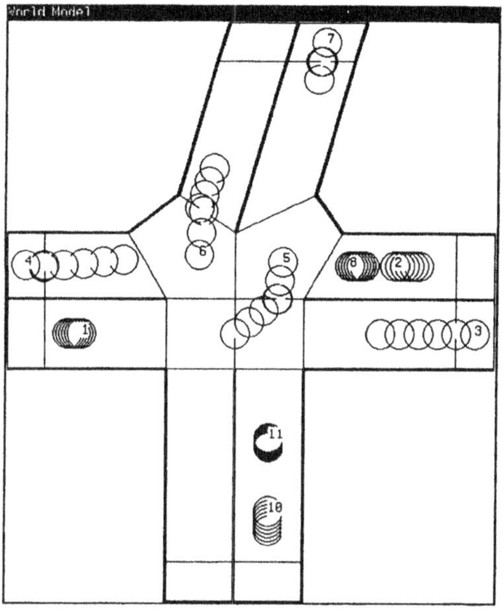

Figure 12: the simulated execution of the plan: time $t = 9$ to $t = 14$

The whole process (prioritization and temporal planning) takes less than 1 s. Figures 11 and 12 shows some steps of the (simulated) execution of the plan.

5 CONCLUSION

In this paper, we have presented a way to control a subset of car-like "coordinated" vehicles moving within an intersection and among other vehicles. A centralized "intersection manager" periodically computes a reference trajectory for every coordinated vehicle. Each vehicle is concerned with the realization of its predetermined reference trajectory. The capabilities of such a vehicle include trajectory following and local obstacle avoidance whereas the intersection manager deals with 1) reasoning about the intentions of the other vehicles and 2) motion planning in a dynamic and uncertain world.

The high-level reasoning is mostly performed by the intersection manager. It makes use of the very structure of an intersection both to estimate the behaviour of the non coordinated vehicles and to plan the motions of the coordinated vehicles. This partial centralization enables to satisfy the optimality criterion efficiently (the vehicles achieve their goals as quickly as possible). As far as the safety criterion—i.e. collision avoidance—is concerned, it is dealt with first by the intersection manager and then by each vehicle.

In order to cope with the complexity of the problem, the intersection manager applies the two principles of prioritization and path/velocity decomposition. These choices are questionable especially the second one. Indeed, the principle of path/velocity decomposition forbids one to deal with overtaking maneuvers (to overtake, one must simultaneously consider the path and the velocity).

This paper focused on the intersection manager but it is only one part of the project. Since the problem of the execution by a coordinated vehicle of its reference trajectory is also crucial, it may lead to reconsider the approach used so far. In particular, it may prove necessary to grant more capabilities to the coordinated vehicles in order to deal with the execution of a plan in a multi-agent world better.

REFERENCES

[1] J. F. Allen. Maintaining knowledge about temporal intervals. *Commun. ACM*, 26(11):832–843, Nov. 1983.

[2] J. Barraquand and J.C. Latombe. *Robot motion planning : a distributed representation approach.* Tech. Report STAN-CS-89-1257, Computer Science Department, Stanford University, May 1989.

[3] R. A. Brooks. Solving the find-path problem by good representation of free space. *IEEE Trans. on Systems, Man and Cybernetics*, 13(3):190–197, March/April 1983.

[4] W. Choi, D. Zhu, and J.C. Latombe. Contingency-tolerant robot motion planning and control. In *Proc. of the Int. Workshop on Intelligent Robots and Systems*, pages 78–86, IEEE, Sep. 1989.

[5] M. Erdmann and T. Lozano-Perez. *On multiple moving objects.* A.I. Memo 883, MIT Artificial Intelligence Laboratory, May 1986.

[6] Th. Fraichard and C. Laugier. Planning movements for several coordinated vehicles. In *Proc. of the Int. Workshop on Intelligent Robots and Systems*, pages 466–472, IEEE, Tsukuba, Japan, Sep. 1989.

[7] J.E. Hopcroft and G.T. Wilfong. *Reducing multiple object motion planning to graph searching.* Tech. Report 84-616, Cornell University, Computer Science Dept, Ithaca, N.Y., 1984.

[8] K. Kant and S. Zucker. Planning collision-free trajectories in time-varying environments: a two-level hierarchy. In *Proc. of the Int. Conf. on Robotics and Automation*, pages 1644–1649, IEEE, 1988.

[9] J.P. Laumond. Finding collision-free smooth trajectories for a non holonomic mobile robot. In *Proc. of the Int. Joint Conf. on Artificial Intelligence*, pages 1120–1123, Milan (Italy), Aug. 1987.

[10] M. Pasquier. *Planification de trajectoires pour un robot manipulateur*. PhD thesis, Institut National Polytechnique de Grenoble, Jan. 1989. in French.

[11] G. Ramanathan and V. Alagar. Coordinated motions of several disks amidst polygonal obstacles. In *Proc. of the Int. Conf. on Robotics and Automation*, pages 514–522, March 1985.

[12] J. Reif. Complexity of the movers' problem and generalizations. In *Proc. of the Symp. on Foundations of Computer Sci.*, pages 241–247, IEEE, New-York (USA), 1979.

[13] J-F. Rit. *Modélisation et propagation de contraintes temporelles pour la planification*. PhD thesis, Institut National Polytechnique de Grenoble, France, March 1988. in French.

[14] J.T. Schwartz and M. Sharir. On the piano movers' problem: III. coordinating the motion of several independent bodies: the special case of circular bodies amidst polygonal barriers. *Int. Journal of Robotics Research*, 2(3):46–75, 1983.

DECENTRALIZED A.I.
Yves DEMAZEAU & Jean-Pierre MÜLLER (Eds.)

A FRAMEWORK FOR THE RECOGNITION OF ACTIONS AND PLANS FROM VISUAL INFORMATION

Mauro DI MANZO, Alessandro CUCCHIARELLI and Salvatore VALENTI

Computer Science Department
University of Ancona
Via Brecce Bianche
60131 ANCONA (ITALY)

In a multi-agent environment, the capability of each agent to carry out tasks in a cooperative way is founded on the ability of reasoning about the actions, plans and goals of the other agents.
In the paper we present a general framework for reasoning about agents' activities based on a hierarchical modeling of facts, actions, beliefs, goals and the knowledge about them, that underlines the recognition problem as a basis for cooperative work.

1. INTRODUCTION

The cooperative interaction among agents relies on the capability of each agent to reason about the other agents' actions, plans and goals. Reasoning about plans and goals is, primarily, a matter of consciousness: they must be represented as descriptive objects causing suitable inferences [10], and each agent must maintain an explicit knowledge of his/her own goals and plans [4, 11], as well as that of the other agents.
Plans are strictly related to actions [1], which, in turn, are related to the temporal evolution of the world, rising several problems as, for instance, the frame problem, the ramification problem, the qualification problem and the temporal projection problem, approached by a number of researchers [2, 3, 6, 7, 8, 9, 12].
The stand-point of this paper is that a general framework for reasoning about agents' actions, plans and goals must take also into account a recognition problem, which is manifold. First, there are two main source of knowledge about the current state of affairs: visual information and inter-agent communications. Focusing on the former, we need conceptual structures to reason about the observability of facts, in contrast with the knowledge an agent has of them.
Second, the recognition of actions must be performed on the basis of the observed changes in the world, without waiting for their completion; this kind of inference needs facilities to support both the temporal projection in the future and the changing mind about the interpretation of past events.Third, the plan of an agent may partially or fully fit with plan of another one; this fitting must be recognized, in order to take advantage of actions performed by other agents, even if the cooperation is unintentional.
However, in most cases the recognition of an action is only provisional; a reinterpretation of

a sequence of events may cause the shifting of a plan in the future and/or a replanning activity.
In this paper we present a framework for approaching the recognition problem; this framework is based on a hierarchical modeling of facts, actions, beliefs and goals, and the knowledge about them.

2. THE CASE STUDY

The world we use to test the validity of our modeling approach contains a set of grippers that cooperate to built cubes by using simple objects.
The work plane is a table and on its surface there are elementary blocks (parallelepipoid L x L x D with oval holes along edges), connectors (angled of 90°, with a length L' < L and threaded holes), tools (screws and screwdrivers) and assembled blocks (intermediate steps towards cubes, composed by elementary blocks, connectors, screws and other assembled blocks).
Grippers are connected to the ceiling of the room by arms: they are able to move and rotate in all directions and reach any object on the table surface: each of them is an agent of the model. An assembling operation consists of putting together two blocks by using a connector and some screws. Connectors and blocks can be screwed only in fixed positions.

Geometrical relations between elements in the world are defined by using entities like point positions, reference frames, directions, numerical quantities, set of positions; such relations exist only between objects that are not part of assembled blocks: if an object A is part of a block B, spatial relations only hold between B and other objects.
To model the static aspect of the world a set of geometrical predicates and functions have been defined, whereas for the dynamic one the concept of situation, as the description of the world in a certain time instant, has been used. Time discretization is justified by the fact that part of the knowledge achieved through visual perception and image analysis takes a certain time: events too fast are imperceptible.

Moreover, the following hypotheses have been made:

(a) theories within each situation are shared by all agents and do not change when the situation does.
(b) Situations and metasituations (defined as complex situations due to the reasoning activity on a set of situations) having the same position in the sequence inside the world image of different agents correspond to a same time instant and have a same identifier.
(c) The world model is invariable with respect to situations and agents; it always contains the same objects. As some objects can be built or destroyed as a result of an activity, the world model must contain all possible objects. The set of existing objects in a given situation is explicitly reduced by an existence predicate.

3. KNOWLEDGE REPRESENTATION

The knowledge base of each agent defined in our system contains, at different cognitive levels, either the description of the observed world, or the hypotheses about the knowledge

of every other agent.
This approach allows us to make inferences under a multi-agent point of view.
In fig. 1 the knowledge base of the j-th agent is depicted.

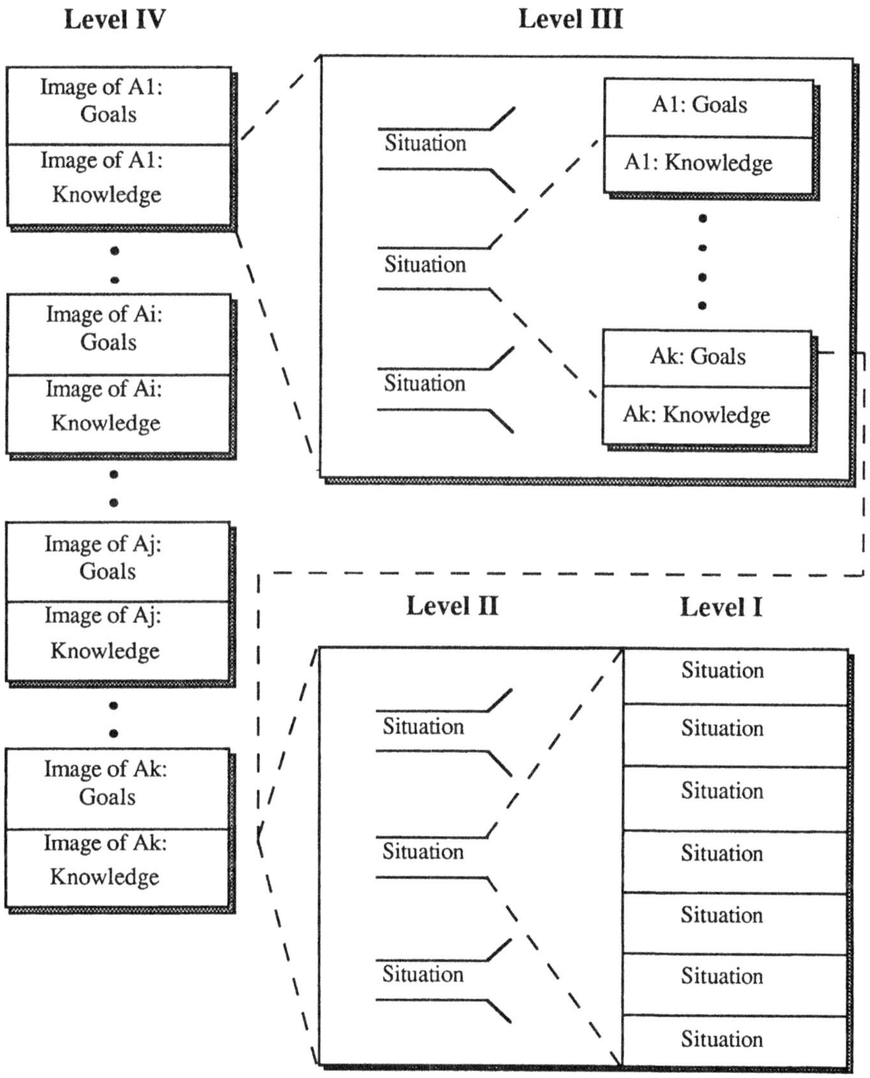

FIGURE 1
Agent knowledge base.

Note that the knowledge base of each agent can be decomposed into four cognitive levels:

level 1 - fact level
level 2 - metasituational level
level 3 - cognitive level
level 4 - metacognitive level

The level of facts (1) allows an agent to reason about the status of the world on the basis of what is observed in a given situation but with no attention to other situations. At this level, the concept of fact is defined.
The metasituational level (2) allows an agent to reason, in each situation, about facts known from past situations and foreseen for the future. At this level the concepts of events and actions are defined.
The cognitive level (3) allows an agent to reason about goals and knowledge of its own and of other agents in each situation.The concept of planning is defined at this level.
The metacognitive level (4) allows the observer to reason about what it believes an agent can desire or believe in relation to each other agent, by maintaining a metaimage for each agent. At this level it is possible to model inter-agent communication, social conventions, and so forth.
In the following part of the paper we will describe in detail each of the already cognitive level defined.

3.1. Level 1

At this level, a perceptive memory storing perceived facts, has been used to describe the knowledge of each agent about world status. The perceived facts can be described by a normal logic (considered here only at a propositional level) augmented by the observability operator O. The observability operator can be described by the following formula:

$$O\alpha \in E^i \quad \text{if} \quad \alpha \in PM^i \qquad (1)$$

where: α is a fact;
E^i is the knowledge about the world of an agent in situation i;
PM^i is the perceptive memory of the same agent in the same situation i;

stating that the fact α can be observed by an agent in the situation i if such a fact belongs to the perceptive memory PM of the same agent in the same situation. Then the operator O resembles the believe operator of the autoepistemic logic [4, 5].
At this level, each agent is allowed to reason about perceivable and not perceivable facts and between perceivable facts, about observable and not observable ones.
For instance, in the block world represented in fig. 2 the facts

ONTABLE (b), ONTABLE (c), CLEAR (c)

are perceivable by Agent A_t. On the contrary the fact

HIDDEN (b, c)

cannot be perceived by definition. Moreover, ONTABLE (c) is true and observable whilst ONTABLE(b) is true but not observable since block c is hidden from.

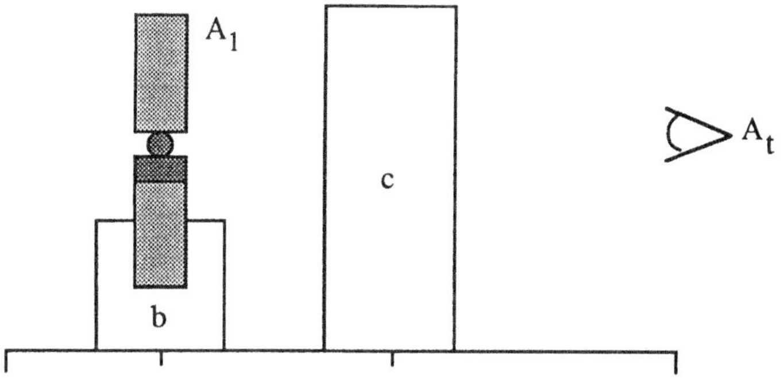

FIGURE 2
Block b is hidden by c

In our block world it is possible to draw inferences about observable and not observable facts using, for instance, the following rule stating that if object b is grasped but not observable by agent A_t, then an object should exist that stands in front of b hiding it from A_t sight:

$$(\tilde{\ } A_t \text{ GRASPED } (b, A_1) \wedge \text{GRASPED } (b, A_1)) \supset$$
$$\exists z \, (\text{BEHIND } (b, z, A_t) \wedge \text{BEHIND } (A_1, z, A_t) \wedge$$
$$\exists z' \, (\text{HIDDEN } (b, z', A_t) \vee \text{HIDDEN } (A_1, z', A_t) \supset (z = z')))$$

where:

GRASPED (x,y)	is a predicate which is true if object x is grasped by gripper y;
BEHIND (x, y, z)	is a predicate which is true if x is behind y for observer z;
HIDDEN (x, y, z)	is a predicate which is true if x is hidden by y for observer z.

In our example z can be instantiated with block c.

3.2. Level 2

At this level each situation describes the knowledge that an agent has about what has happened or is going to happen.
Temporal evolution is described by a sequence of situations with the hypothesis that each event lasts for a single transition between two observed situations.
The relation between levels 2 and 1 is represented by the predicate HOLD which allows us to state whether a given formula belongs or not to the meta-theory defined.
So

$$\text{HOLD } (\alpha, s_k) \in E^M \quad \text{iff} \quad \alpha \in E^i$$

where E^M is the meta-theory defined at this level.

For instance, if we consider the block world of fig.2 at situation s_i, we can write:

HOLD (ONTABLE (b), s_i).

If block b is put on c in situation s_j, we can write that:

HOLD (ON (b, c), s_j)

where ON (X,Y) is a level 1 predicate which is true iff object X is directly supported by Y.

3.2.1. Events

At this point we can define the concept of event as an activity that involves a product or an outcome and that occurs over two situations [1].
The occurrence of an event can be described by the predicate:

OCCURS (e, ϑ, d, q, r, s_i, s_j)

where e is the event, ϑ is the object, d is the direction, q is the quantity r is the reference and s_i, s_j are the initial and the final situation.
The relation holding between predicate OCCURS and temporal interval over which the event occurs can be described by introducing the two predicates PROS (e, ϑ, d, q, r) and PERF (e ,ϑ, d, q, r) defined at the fact level.
The former states that event e referred to object ϑ with direction d, quantity q and reference r has not yet started in the current situation. The latter states that event e, defined as before, has already terminated in the current situation.
So it is possible to state that event e referred to object ϑ with direction d, quantity q and reference r occurs between initial situation s_i and final situation s_j, by using the following formula:

$$\text{OCCURS}(e, \vartheta, d, q, r, s_i, s_j) \equiv \text{HOLD}(\text{PROS}(e, \vartheta, d, q, r), s_i) \wedge \text{HOLD}(\text{PERF}(e, \vartheta, d, q, r), s_j).$$

Note that all events considered in the model are motion events, parametrized by quantity, direction and reference .
For instance, in block world of fig. 2 it is possible to state that block B has been moved of the quantity q along a straight trajectory defined by direction d and reference r in the interval defined by situation s_i and s_j writing:

OCCURS (change_pos, b, d, q, r, s_i, s_j)

At this level, even in the hypothesis that observations are frequent enough to catch all events, some meaningful situations might pass unobserved. A typical case is that in which the beginning of an event is observed but not the end, or vice versa. In order to explain otherwise unrecognizable events, a situation can be introduced between two adjacent observed situations.

Thus, for instance, the following rule has been added stating that if an object moves on a straight trajectory between situations s_i and s_j, there exists an intermediate situation s_k over which the object still moves on the same kind of trajectory:

$$\begin{array}{l} \text{OCCURS (change\_pos}, \vartheta, d, q, r, s_i, s_j) \wedge \\ \qquad \text{AFTER} (s_i, s_k) \wedge \text{AFTER} (s_k, s_j) \supset \\ \exists q' (\text{OCCURS (change\_pos}, \vartheta, d, q', r, s_i, s_k) \wedge \\ \qquad\qquad \text{HOLD (LT} (q', q), s_k)). \end{array}$$

where :

AFTER (s_i, s_j) is a predicate stating that situation s_j follows s_i;
LT (x, y) is a first level predicate which is true if quantity x is less than quantity y.

This approach fails with longer inferential chains obtained when one or more events are completely unobserved: in such cases the recognition of situations can be carried on only through plan analysis.

3.2.2. Actions

An important class of entities defined at this level is that of actions, which can simply be interpreted as the extension of events over several situations.
The fundamental issue about action is that at this level the notion of agent appears explicitly ad the responsible for actions. In our world, an agent can only be a gripper or the gravity force.
An action can be described in our theory by defining the agent and the object involved, the initial and the final position in the reference, and the initial and the final situation along with the action occurs. Therefore, we can write:

A_OCCURS (Action, Agent, Object, p_i, p_f, r, s_i, s_f)

The relation holding between the predicates A_OCCURS() and the temporal interval over which an action occurs can be elicited by introducing the three predicates:

A_PROS (Action, Agent, Object, p_i, p_f, r)
A_PROG (Action, Agent, Object, p_i, p_f, r)
A_PERF (Action, Agent, Object, p_i, p_f, r).

The predicate A_PROS (Action, Agent, Object, p_i, p_f, r) states that the Action performed by the Agent on the Object from initial position p_i to final position p_f in the reference r, has not yet begun. The predicate A_PROG (Action, Agent, Object, p_i, p_f, r) states that the Action defined as before is on-going, while the predicate A_PERF (Action, Agent, Object, p_i, p_f, r) states that the Action is terminated.

Now it is possible to write the following formula which states that an Action should start in the situation s_i, should end in the situation s_f and should be on-going in an intermediate situation s_k :

$$\begin{aligned}&\text{A\_OCCURS (Action, Agent, Object, } p_i, p_f, r, s_i, s_f) \equiv \\ &\quad \text{HOLD (A\_PROS (Action, Agent, Object, } p_i, p_f, r), s_i) \wedge \\ &\quad \text{HOLD (A\_PERF (Action, Agent, Object, } p_i, p_f, r), s_f) \wedge \\ &\quad (\text{AFTER } (s_i, s_k) \wedge \text{AFTER } (s_k, s_f) \supset \\ &\qquad \text{HOLD (A\_PROG (Action, Agent, Object, } p_i, p_f, r), s_k)) .\end{aligned}$$

Let a_change_pos be the action of moving an object along a straight trajectory. We can introduce a rule that by using a default mechanism allows to state that to observe or to deduce a movement generates the hypothesis of an action of the kind "change position" which includes the observed movement, writing:

$$\begin{aligned}&\text{AFTER } (s_i, s_k) \wedge \text{HOLD (POS } (p_j, \text{Object}, r), s_j) \\ &\quad \wedge \text{HOLD (POS } (p_k, \text{Object}, r), s_k) \\ &\quad \wedge \text{HOLD}(\,\tilde{}\,(p_j = p_k), s_k) :\end{aligned}$$

$$\begin{aligned}&: M \; \exists\, p_i, p_f \; (\text{PRE } (p_i, p_j, \text{DIR } (p_j, p_k, r), s_k) \wedge \\ &\qquad \text{PRE } (p_k, p_f, \text{DIR } (p_j, p_k, r), s_k) \wedge \\ &\quad \text{HOLD (A\_PROG (a\_change\_pos, Agent, Object, } p_i, p_f, r), s_k))\end{aligned}$$

$$\begin{aligned}&\exists\, p_i, p_f \; (\text{PRE } (p_i, p_j, \text{DIR } (p_j, p_k, r), s_k) \wedge \\ &\qquad \text{PRE } (p_k, p_f, \text{DIR } (p_j, p_k, r), s_k) \wedge \\ &\quad \text{HOLD (A\_PROG (a\_change\_pos, Agent, Object, } p_i, p_f, r), s_k))\end{aligned}$$

where :

DIR (p_j, p_k, r)	is a first-level function returning the direction between points p_j, p_k, towards p_k, in the reference r;
POS $(p_j$, Object, r)	is a first-level predicate true when p_j is the position of Object in the reference r;
PRE (p_i, p_j, d, s_k)	is a second-level predicate which states that point p_i precedes p_j along direction d in the situation s_k.

Whilst it is possible to use knowledge about the sequence of past situations, it is reasonable to simplify the inferences about the future. For this reason we have introduced the following formula in our theory, stating that an action is completed in the next situation if is on-going in the current one:

$$\begin{aligned}&\text{HOLD (A\_PROG (Action, Agent, Object, } p_i, p_f, r), s_j) \wedge \\ &\quad \text{NEXT } (s_j, s_k) \wedge \text{CURRENT } (s_j) \\ &\qquad \supset \text{HOLD (POS } (p_f, \text{Object}, r), s_k)\end{aligned}$$

where :

NEXT (s_j, s_k):	is a level-2 predicate stating that situation s_k follows immediately situation s_j;
CURRENT (s_j):	is a level-2 predicate stating that current situation is s_j.

3.3. Level 3

At this level it is possible to reason, in each situation, about the goals of an agent, its plans and observable actions depending on such plans.
To reason about goals and knowledge of its own and of other agents in each situation each agent maintains an image of himself and of every other agent. Each image is composed by a target image, describing the desired world of the agent, and by a knowledge image which describes the world as it is known by such agent.
The relation between this level and the inner one, is obtained by two predicates Know and Want which are defined in the following part of the paper.
The predicate KNOW (A, s, a) allows us to state whether a given formula belongs or not to the meta-theory defined in the metasituation s of the knowledge image of agent A.
For instance, in our block world, we can write the following formula:

$$\text{KNOW}\ (A_t, s_i, \text{HOLD}\ (\text{CLEAR}\ (c), s_j))$$

The predicate WANT(A, s, a) allows us to state whether a given formula a belongs or not to the meta-theory defined in the metasituation s of the target image of agent A.
For instance the fact that agent A_t in the situation s_j wants block b to be posed upon block c in situation s_k, can be written by the following formula:

$$\text{WANT}\ (A_t, s_j, \text{HOLD}\ (\text{ON}\ (b, c), s_k))$$

At this level the tasks of autonomous planning and autonomous planning recognition are handled. In the following we will show some of the planning rules defined to achieve the previous result.
First planning rule: if an agent wants a future fact, which is not currently true, and does not coincide with any known future fact to be realized, and if it knows an action able to realize that fact, then it plans the execution of that action.
From the previous rule follows that if an agent has a goal for a present or future state, and it knows that the desired fact is true, then the goal is achieved; otherwise it is kept as a future goal, which will possibly generate actions in a planning process.
Second planning rule: if an agent desires an action that has a given prerequisite, then the agent desires the prerequisite. The temporal arrangement does not matter: if the prerequisite is set as a future goal, it will generate other planning actions based on the first planning rule.
Third planning rule: if an agent desires an action that is decomposable into some subactions, then the agent desires those subactions.
Fourth planning rule: if an agent desires two actions that are not feasible in parallel, then the agent must desire them sequentially.
Note that it is assumed that any agent that executes an action wants to do it (free will) and knows it is doing it (self consciousness).

3.4. Level 4

Level 4 is called metacognitive as it maintains a metaimage for each agent, allowing the observer to reason about what it believes an agent can desire or believe in relation to every other agent.
At this level it is possible to model inter-agent communication, social conventions, and so forth.

The relation between level 4 and level 3 can be described by means of the two predicates: IS_GOAL and BELIEVE.
The predicate IS_GOAL (A_i, s_k, a) allows to state whether a given formula a belongs or not to the meta-theory defined in the situation s of the target metaimage of agent A_i.

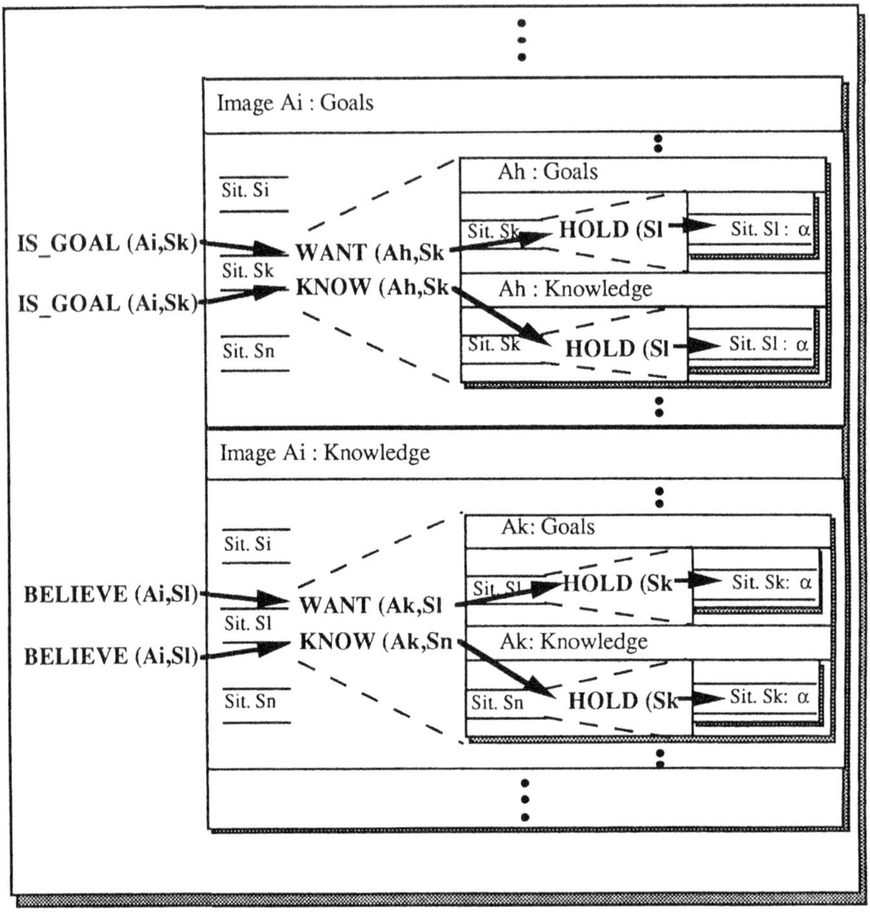

FIGURE 3
Agent inference mechanism

In our block world, the fact that agent A_i believes that agent A_t desires to put block b upon block c can be expressed by the following formulas:

IS_GOAL (A_i, s_i, WANT (A_t, s_i, HOLD (ON (b, c), s_j)))
IS_GOAL (A_i, s_i, KNOW (A_t, s_i ,HOLD (ON (b, c), s_j)))

The predicate BELIEVE (A_i , s_k , a) allows to state whether a given formula a belongs or not to the meta-theory defined in the situation s of the knowledge metaimage of agent A_i.
With respect to the previous example, we can write that:

BELIEVE (A_i, s_j, WANT (A_t, s_j, HOLD (ON (b, c), s_i)))
BELIEVE (A_i, s_j, KNOW (A_t, s_j, HOLD (ON (b, c), s_i)))

In fig. 3 the mechanism used by an agent to make inferences about goals and believes of other agents, starting from the observation of situations is depicted.

4. AN EXAMPLE

We now want to explain how the exposed theory can be used by an agent A_2 to operate within a simple world with another agent A_1 and two blocks, b and c, on the table.
The line of reasoning used by A_2 to reach its goal to have block b in a definite position will be illustrated, and the evolution of the world will be shown using the three following situations.

4.1 Situation s_1 (Fig.4)

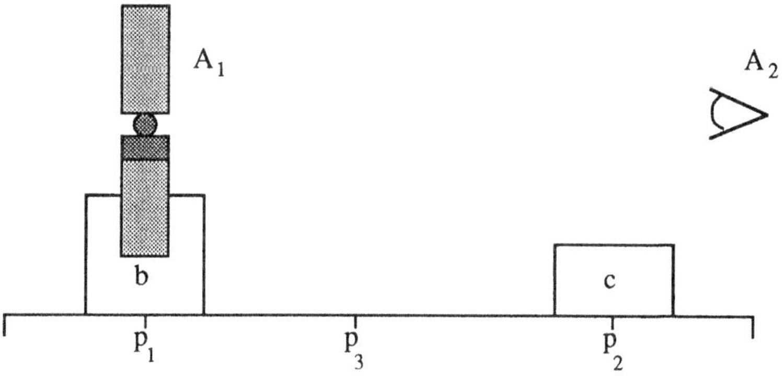

FIGURE 4

The goal of A_2 to have block b in position p_3 in a future situation s_f is expressed by the formula:

WANT (A_2, s_1, HOLD (POS (p_3, b, r), s_f))
AFTER* (s_1, s_f) (E1)

Looking at the scene, A_2 is able to assert that

KNOW (A_2, s_1, HOLD (POS (p_1, b, r), s_1))
KNOW (A_2, s_1, HOLD (GRASPED (b, A_1), s_1))
KNOW (A_2, s_1, HOLD (ON (b, table), s_1))
KNOW (A_2, s_1, HOLD (POS (p_2, c, r), s_1))

Using a default rule (d2.2), A2 can state that each known fact holds in the future unless explicit changes occur, so that:

KNOW (A_2, s_1, HOLD (POS (p_1, b, r), s_f))

and, because of a block cannot be in two different positions at the same time (1.27):

KNOW (A_2, s_1, HOLD (~POS (p_3, b, r), s_f)) (E2)

What A_2 knows about b position in s_f does not match its goal,

~(KNOW (A_2, s_1, HOLD (POS (p_x, b, r), s_f)) $\wedge$
MATCH (A_2, s_1, HOLD (POS (p_3, b, r), s_f), HOLD (POS (p_x, b, r), s_f))) (E3)

but, from the definition of a_change_pos action, it knows that b can reach position p_3 starting from a generic p'_x by the action of an agent A'_x in a defined interval s'_x, s'_f.

KNOW (A_2, s_1, A_OCCURS (a_change_pos, A'_x, b, p'_x, p_3, r, s'_x, s'_f)) $\supset$
HOLD (POS (p_3, b, r), s'_f) (E4)

Combining (E1), (E2), (E3) and (E4) and using the first planning rule (5.18), A_2 defines a new goal that is:

WANT (A_2, s_1, A_OCCURS (a_change_pos, A'_x, b, p'_x, p_3, r, s'_x, s'_f))
AFTER* (s_1, s'_f)
~AFTER* (s_f, s'_f) (E5)

so that at the end of the reasoning process in situation s_1, A_2 adds a new goal (E5) to the starting one (E1), according to what it knows about the world.

4.2. Situation s_2 (Fig.5)

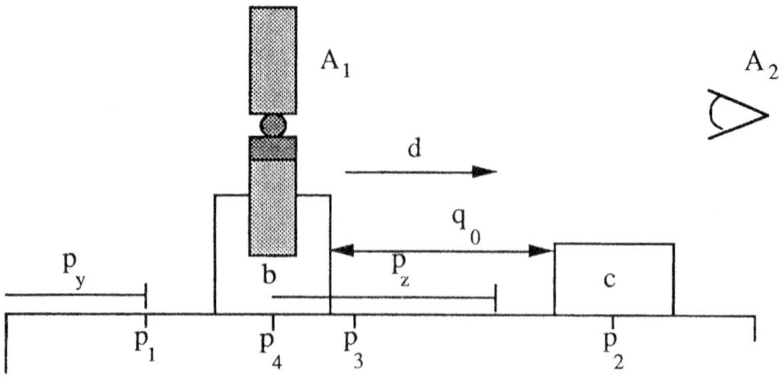

FIGURE 5

In this situation, by applying the default rule of knowledge propagation (d5.3), A2 can state that:

KNOW (A_2, s_2, HOLD (POS (p_1, b, r), s_1)) (E6)

and, looking at the scene:

KNOW (A_2, s_2, HOLD (POS (p_4, b, r), s_2)) (E7)

In the same way:

KNOW (A_2, s_2, HOLD (POS (p_2, c, r), s_1))
KNOW (A_2, s_2, HOLD (POS (p_2, c, r), s_2)) (E8)

By applying (E6) and (E7) to default rule d4.1, that states the progress of an a_change_pos action in a certain situation by the evidence of an object movement, A_2 makes in s_2 the hypothesis that A_1 is moving b along direction d from a position p_y, that precedes p_1, to p_z, that follows its current position p_4, i.e.

KNOW (A_2, s_2, A_PROG (a_change_pos, A_1, b, p_y, p_z, r), s_2))
KNOW (A_2, s_2, PRE (p_4, p_z, d, s_2))
KNOW (A_2, s_2, PRE (p_y, p_1, d, s_2)) (E9)

To have more evidence of such an hypothesis, A_2 has to verify the necessary conditions defined in its knowledge base for A_PROG (), i.e. that an event related to the action in progress is occurring.
By the rule that assumes an on-going action in the current situation completed in the next one (4.4), follows:

NEXT* (s_2, s_3)
KNOW (A_2, s_2, HOLD (POS (p_z, b, r), s_3)) (E10)

From (E7) and (E10), by using the rule that considers any object movement as being due to a motion event and the default of straight trajectory as first hypothesis on movement,

KNOW (A_2, s_2, OCCURS (change_pos, b, d, dist (p_4, p_z), r, s_2, s_3)) (E11)

About block c, by applying temporal default rule (d2.2) to (E8)

KNOW (A_2, s_2, HOLD (POS (p_2, c, r), s_3))

Because of this hypothesis, there is no movement for c between s2 and s3, and consequently no motion events on c (2.33).

KNOW (A_2, s_2, ~OCCURS (any, c, d', q', r, s_2, s_3))

So, between s_2 and s_3, we have a movement on b along direction d and no movement on c. In this situation, by the rule that defines the distance between b and c less than the quantity of movement of b if the previous conditions are satisfied (2.22):

$KNOW (A_2, s_2, HOLD (\sim LT (q_0, dist (p_4, p_z)), s_2))$

This is the proof that event (E11) is compatible with the state of objects in the world, and that (E9) is a right hypothesis.
By making the hypothesis:

$HOLD (POS (p_1, b, r), s_0) \wedge NEXT (s_0, s_1)$

and remembering (E10), is true that:

$HOLD (A\_PERF (a\_change\_pos, A_1, b, p_1, p_z, r), s_3)$
$HOLD (A\_PROS (a\_change\_pos, A_1, b, p_1, p_z, r), s_1)$ (E12)

By the rules that states that an action occurs between situation s_i an s_f iff it begins in s_i, ends in s_f and is in progress in an intermediate situation (4.2), considering (E12) and (E9) with $p_y=p_1$:

$KNOW (A_2, s_2, A\_OCCURS (a\_change\_pos, A_1, b, p_1, p_z, r, s_1, s_3))$ (E13)

Coming back to the goals of A2, by applying the default of their temporal conservation (d5.1) to (E1)

$WANT (A_2, s_2, HOLD (POS (p_3, b, r), s_f))$
$NEXT^* (s_1, s_2)$
$AFTER^* (s_1, s_f)$ (E14)

From the definition of NEXT* (...) and AFTER* (...)

$\sim AFTER^* (s_f, s_2)$

and, because of (E7),

$KNOW (A_2, s_2, HOLD (\sim POS (p_3, b, r), s_2))$
this means that s_f and s_2 are not the same situation, so that

$AFTER^* (s_2, s_f)$

and the current situation does not satisfy the goal (E14).
With the same line of reasoning used in s_1 to obtain (E5) from (E1), starting from (E14):

$WANT (A_2, s_2, A\_OCCURS (a\_change\_pos, A''_x, b, p''_x, p_3, r, s''_x, s''_f))$
$AFTER^* (s_2, s''_f)$
$\sim AFTER^* (s_f, s''_f)$ (E15)

with

$\sim AFTER^* (s''_f, s_2)$ (E16)

that unifies with (E5) moved from s_1 to s_2 (d5.1)

WANT (A_2, s_2, A_OCCURS (a_change_pos, A'_x, b, p'_x, p_3, r, s'_x, s'_f))
AFTER* (s_1, s'_f)
~AFTER* (s_f, s'_f)

The result is that in situation s_2, with respect to situation s_1, no new goal is generated by A_2, and furthermore, what A_2 knows about the movement of b (E13) is not in contrast with its goal (E15).

4.3. Situation s_3 (Fig.6)

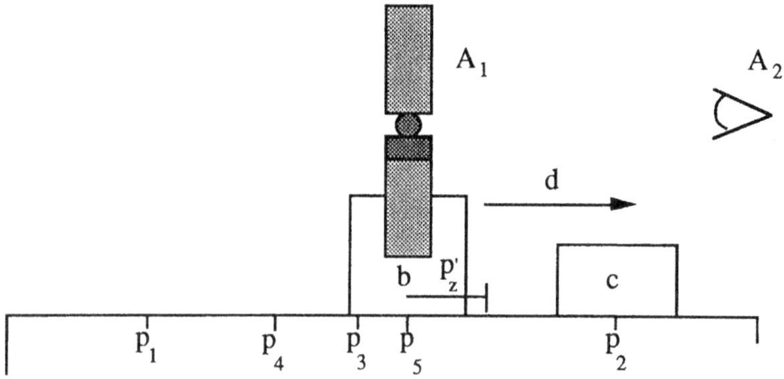

FIGURE 6

By applying the default time propagation of knowledge (d5.3) to (E13)

KNOW (A_2, s_3, A_OCCURS (a_change_pos, A_1, b, p_1, p_z, r, s_1, s_3))

and, looking at the scene

KNOW (A_2, s_3, A_OCCURS (a_change_pos, A_1, b, p_1, p_5, r, s_1, s_3))

By the same way of reasoning used to obtain (E13), it is possible to state that

KNOW (A_2, s_3, A_OCCURS (a_change_pos, A_1, b, p_1, p'_z, r, s_1, s_4)) (E17)

The goals of A_2 in situation s_3, obtained as (E14) and (E15) in s_2, are

WANT (A_2, s_3, HOLD (POS (p_3, b, r), s_f))
NEXT* (s_3, s_4)
AFTER* (s_3, s_f)

WANT (A_2, s_3, A_OCCURS (a_change_pos, A'_x, b, p'_x, p_3, r, s'_x, s'_f))
AFTER* (s_3, s'_f)
~AFTER* (s_f, s'_f) (E18)

The goal (E18) does not match with A_2 knowledge about the situation (E17): the current A_1 action on b does not match the A_2 goal that can now set up a plan to reach its purpose.

APPENDIX A. RULES OVERVIEW

1.27 $POS(p_1, J, r) \wedge POS(p_2, J, r) \supset (p_1 = p_2)$

d 2.2
$$\frac{HOLD(a, s_i) \wedge NEXT(s_i, s_j) : M\ HOLD(\alpha, s_j)}{HOLD(\alpha, s_j)}$$

2.22
$$\begin{array}{l}(OCCURS(change\_or, \vartheta, d, q, r, s_i, s_j) \wedge \\ \sim OCCURS(change\_or, x, d', q', r, s_i, s_j)) \vee \\ (OCCURS(change\_or, \vartheta, d, q, r, s_i, s_j) \wedge \\ \sim OCCURS(any, x, d', q', r, s_i, s_j)) \vee \\ (OCCURS(any, \vartheta, d, q, r, s_i, s_j) \wedge \\ \sim OCCURS(any, x, d', q', r, s_i, s_j)) \supset \\ \qquad HOLD(\sim LT(s\_dist(\vartheta, x, d, r), q), s_i)\end{array}$$

2.33
$$\begin{array}{l}HOLD(POS(p_1, \vartheta, r), s_i) \wedge HOLD(POS(p_2, \vartheta, r), s_j) \wedge SUCC(s_i, s_j) \wedge \\ HOLD((p_1 = p_2), s_j) \supset \\ \qquad \sim OCCURS(any, \vartheta, d, q, r, s_i, s_j)\end{array}$$

d 4.1
$$\begin{array}{l}AFTER(s_i, s_k) \wedge HOLD(POS(p_j, Object, r), s_j) \\ \qquad \wedge HOLD(POS(p_k, Object, r), s_k) \\ \qquad \wedge HOLD(\tilde{\ }(p_j = p_k), s_k) :\end{array}$$

$$\frac{\begin{array}{l}: M\ \exists\, p_i, p_f\ (PRE(p_i, p_j, DIR(p_j, p_k, r), s_k) \wedge \\ \qquad PRE(p_k, p_f, DIR(p_j, p_k, r), s_k) \wedge \\ \qquad HOLD(A\_PROG(a\_change\_pos, Agent, Object, p_i, p_f, r), s_k))\end{array}}{\begin{array}{l}\exists\, p_i, p_f\ (PRE(p_i, p_j, DIR(p_j, p_k, r), s_k) \wedge \\ \qquad PRE(p_k, p_f, DIR(p_j, p_k, r), s_k) \wedge \\ \qquad HOLD(A\_PROG(a\_change\_pos, Agent, Object, p_i, p_f, r), s_k))\end{array}}$$

4.2
$$\begin{array}{l}A\_OCCURS(Action, Agent, Object, p_i, p_f, r, s_i, s_f) \equiv \\ \qquad HOLD(A\_PROS(Action, Agent, Object, p_i, p_f, r), s_i) \wedge \\ \qquad HOLD(A\_PERF(Action, Agent, Object, p_i, p_f, r), s_f) \wedge \\ \qquad (AFTER(s_i, s_k) \wedge AFTER(s_k, s_f) \supset \\ \qquad\qquad HOLD(A\_PROG(Action, Agent, Object, p_i, p_f, r), s_k)).\end{array}$$

4.4
$$\begin{array}{l}HOLD(A\_PROG(Action, Agent, Object, p_i, p_f, r), s_j) \wedge \\ \qquad NEXT(s_j, s_k) \wedge CURRENT(s_j) \\ \qquad\qquad \supset HOLD(POS(p_f, Object, r), s_k)\end{array}$$

d. 5.1 $\dfrac{\text{WANT}(A, s_i, \alpha) \wedge \text{NEXT*}(s_i, s_j) : \text{M WANT}(A, s_j, \alpha)}{\text{WANT}(A, s_j, \alpha)}$

d. 5.3 $\dfrac{\text{KNOW}(A, s_i, \alpha) \wedge \text{NEXT*}(s_i, s_j) : \text{M KNOW}(A, s_j, \alpha)}{\text{KNOW}(A, s_j, \alpha)}$

5.18 AFTER* (s_k, s_f) $\wedge$ WANT (A_1, s_k, HOLD (α (x_1, ..., x_n), s_f)) $\wedge$
KNOW (A_1, s_k, HOLD ($\sim\alpha$ (x_1, ..., x_n), s_f)) $\wedge$
$\sim$(KNOW (A_1, s_k, HOLD (α (x'_1, ..., x'_n), s_f)) $\wedge$
MATCH (A_1, s_k, HOLD (α (x_1, ..., x_n), s_f), HOLD (α (x'_1, ..., x'_n), s_f))) $\wedge$
KNOW (A_1, s_k, A_OCCURS (α, A_t, ϑ, p_i, p_f, r, s'_i, s'_f) $\supset$
HOLD (α (x_1, ..., x_n), s'_f)) $\supset$
AFTER* (s_k, s'_f) $\wedge$ $\sim$AFTER* (s_f, s'_f)) $\wedge$
WANT (A_1 s_k, A_OCCURS (α, A_t, ϑ, p_i, p_f, r, s'_i, s'_f))

5.21 WANT (A_1 s_k, A_OCCURS (α, A_t, ϑ, p_i, p_f, r, s_i, s_f)) $\wedge$
$\sim$AFTER* (s_f, s_k) $\supset$
(KNOW (A_1, s_k, A_OCCURS (α', A'_t, ϑ', p'_i, p'_f, r, s'_i, s'_f)) $\wedge$
MATCH (A_1, s_k, A_OCCURS (α, A_t, ϑ, p_i, p_f, r, s_i, s_f),
A_OCCURS (α', A'_t, ϑ', p'_i, p'_f, r, s'_i, s'_f)) $\supset$
($s_i = s'_i$) $\wedge$ ($s_f = s'_f$)) $\vee$
($\sim$KNOW (A_1, s_k, A_OCCURS (α', A'_t, ϑ', p'_i, p'_f, r, s'_i, s'_f)) $\wedge$
$\sim$MATCH (A_1, s_k, A_OCCURS (α, A_t, ϑ, p_i, p_f, r, s_i, s_f),
A_OCCURS (α', A'_t, ϑ', p'_i, p'_f, r, s'_i, s'_f)) $\supset$
$\sim$AFTER* (s_i, s_k))

REFERENCES

[1] Allen, J.F., Toward a general theory of Action and time, Artificial Intelligence, 23 (1984) 123-154.

[2] Ginsberg, H.L., Smith , D.E., Reasoning about action I. A possible world approach, Artificial Intelligence, 35 (1988) 155-195.

[3] Ginsberg, H.L., Smith , D.E., Reasoning about action II. The qualification problem, Artificial Intelligence, 35 (1988) 311-342.

[4] Konolidge, K., Belief and incompleteness, in: Hobbs J.R., Moore R.C., (eds.), Formal Theories of the Commonsense World, (Ablex Publishing Company, 1985) pp. 359-403.

[5] Konolidge, K., On the relation between default and authoepistemic logic, Artificial Intelligence, 35 (1988) 343-382.

[6] Lifschutz, V., Formal theories of actions, Proceedings IJCAI-87, Milan (1987), 966-972.

[7] Lifschutz, V.,Miracles in formal theories of actions, Artificial Intelligence, 38 (1989) 225-237.

[8] McCarthy, J., Hayes, P., Some philosophical problems from the stand-point of artificial intelligence, in: Meltzer B., Mitchie D. (eds.), Machine Intelligence 4, (Edinburgh University Press, 1969) pp. 463-502.
[9] McCarthy, J., Applications of circumscription to formalizing common-sense knowledge, Artificial Intelligence, 28 (1986) 89-116.
[10] McDermott D.V.,Reasoning about plans, in: Hobbs J.R., Moore R.C., (eds.), Formal Theories of the Commonsense World, (Ablex Publishing Company, 1985) pp. 269-317.
[11] Moore, R. C., A formal theory of knowledge and actions, in: Hobbs J.R., Moore R.C., (eds.), Formal Theories of the Commonsense World, (Ablex Publishing Company, 1985) pp. 319-358.
[12] Shoham Y., Chronological ignorance: experiments in nonmonotonic temporal reasoning, Artificial Intelligence, 36 (1988) 279-331.

Interaction between Perceiving Capabilities

DECENTRALIZED A.I.
Yves DEMAZEAU & Jean-Pierre MÜLLER (Eds.)

COOPERATION BETWEEN DISTRIBUTED AGENTS THROUGH SELF-ORGANISATION

Luc Steels

VUB AI Lab
Pleinlaan 2.
1050 Brussels Belgium

The paper uses a behavior-based approach to tackle the problem of cooperation between distributed agents. It focuses on the use of self-organisation and dissipative structures to establish emergent functionality. Other principles such as randomness, the subsumption architecture, and the gradient field are also used. Results of computational experiments are presented.

1. INTRODUCTION

The paper discusses some central issues in the cooperation between distributed agents using the following case study:

> The objective is to explore a distant planet, more concretely to collect samples of a particular type of precious rock. The location of the rock samples is unknown in advance but they are typically clustered in certain spots. There is a vehicle that can drive around on the planet and later reenter the spacecraft to go back to earth. There is no detailed map of the terrain although it is known that the terrain is full of obstacles, hills, valleys, etc.

The case study is designed to require autonomy. It is not feasible to plan and steer the whole thing out of earth because communication from and to the planet has a considerable time delay and may be cut off during certain periods. Although one solution could be that the vehicle itself wanders around and collects the rocks, it is obvious that a larger terrain could be covered much more quickly if there is a group of mobile robots that perform the task of searching and carrying the rocks to the vehicle. This would make the solution also less fault tolerant because loss of one robot is not fatal. Because the desired samples are clustered in certain spots, the robots better cooperate to accomplish the task. This gives us the problem addressed in this paper: how can these distributed robots cooperate to find samples and to carry them to the collecting vehicle. If the present case study seems somewhat far fetched, the cleanup of toxic waste or household garbage collection can be viewed as comparable tasks.

Evaluation criteria

The following criteria will be used to evaluate different solutions. These are criteria relevant for AI systems in general but they are particularly appropriate for mobile robots operating on a distant planet.

1. Robustness: The system should be able to recover when a certain action is not correctly executed. For example, when a sample is not picked up although the instruction was given, this should not lead to further malfunction.

2. Graceful performance degradation: Loss of one robot should not be fatal although it could give decreased performance.

3. Flexibility: When conditions in the environment change, this should not require major changes or incapability to function. For example, the vehicle could move while the robots are searching around, the rock samples could be exhausted in one location requiring a rerouting of resources to explore another location, there could suddenly be new obstacles on a path between the samples and the vehicle.

4. Hardware economy: This refers to the complexity of the proposed hardware and the resources (e.g. in energy) that is needed to keep the hardware operational.

5. Cognitive economy: This refers to the amount of internal representations needed. The more complex this representation the less economical the system will be.

6. Communicative economy: This refers to the amount of information that needs to be exchanged between the subsystems involved to get the task done (e.g. between the robots or between the robots and the vehicle). Less communication is more desirable if only because all communication requires substantial amounts of equipment and processing.

7. Predictability. This refers to the amount of regularity that has to be present in the environment for the total system to keep functioning. Ideally the system should be able to cope with unpredictable situations.

8. Prior knowledge. This refers to what has to be known in advance to have a successful system. For example, does a map of the terrain have to be available? Less prior knowledge is more desirable.

There are also some quantitative criteria concerning the optimality of the solution. For each sample i there will be the time needed by a robot to find the sample $t_{e(i)}$, and the time needed by the same robot to carry the sample back to the vehicle $t_{c(i)}$. The total time t(n) needed to carry a set of n samples is therefore equal to:

$$t(n) = \sum_{i=1,n} t_e(i) + \sum_{i=1,n} t_c(i) \qquad (1)$$

Let us assume that d is equal to the distance between the location of the sample and the location of the vehicle. We also assume that the time needed by a robot to cover one unit of distance is equal to one unit of time. Then the optimal performance with only one robot is given by

$$t(n) = 2nd \tag{2}$$

When m robots are available, the optimality is given by

$$t(N) = 2\frac{n}{m}d \tag{3}$$

Therefore if we have as many robots as samples, we can optimally carry all samples in as much time as it takes a single robot to carry one sample. This proves that parallelism helps (if we can keep the other design objectives such as fault tolerance, communicative economy, etc. optimal).

2. TWO PARADIGMS

Work on distributed cooperating agents started in the late seventies (Lenat (1975), Steels (1979), Lesser (1979), Smith (1980), Kornfeld and Hewitt (1981)). The basic assumption was that the agents were complex entities of the sort then proposed for a single artificial intelligence, i.e. each agent had substantial internal reasoning powers so that they could build up models of the world, relate and update these models with sensors that interpret the world, and communicate through complex messages for example to negotiate a solution or to exchange partial views of a plan. All of this was firmly within the symbolic AI tradition. More recently, there has been a revival of research on distributed agents, particularly in logic-based AI (see e.g. Konolidge (1982), Rosenschein and Genesereth, 1987). The reasoning powers of the agents are assumed to be even more pronounced than proposed in earlier work. Each agent is now a strictly rational agent using a logical description of the world and performing logical inference to plan its action and cooperate with other agents.

The logical approach

Applying the logic-based approach to our case study we would end up with the following proposal:

1. Each robot is equiped with a logical inference machine of the sort described by Genesereth and Nilson (1987). It has a representation of the world in the form of expressions in an extended form of predicate calculus (e.g. this representation records the position with respect to other agents and the vehicle). The robot builds up this representation progressively by sensing and reasoning. It can plan its actions by reasoning logically about the world and about possible actions it could take. It performs temporal and spatial reasoning and has axiomatic representations of the preconditions and effects of an action. Thus the robot can form plans to decide in which direction it should move next, whether it should pick up some object, whether it should go back to the site on which it earlier

found a rock, and so on. The robot is capable to translate these plans into concrete action by activating its effectors and adapt the plan when changes in the world have made it obsolete or when an action did not get executed as planned.

2. To handle the cooperative part, each robot has additional functionalities: It is able to engage in a dialog with other agents or the vehicle. This dialog involves exchanging something close to logical formula. It could for example ask another agent where it is located or whether it found something and where. Each agent develops not only a model of itself and its own actions but also of what other agents know and belief. It performs meta-level reasoning to think about how it should relate its own actions to other agents and when it should engage in communication or in cooperation.

The position taken in this paper is that the above scheme is entirely unrealistic for the following reasons:

1. The technological complexity required in each agent is too high. If the agent has to be equipped with a logical inference machine, it would need at least several megabytes of memory and a processor fast enough to execute the tens of thousands of logical inferences required per second. This implies that the agent has to carry a computer around of the size of a powerful workstation. This computer has to remain operational in difficult circumstances (assuming it survives the trip to the planet). To establish communication between agents, we would need moreover radio equipment, components that formulate requests to other agents, and components that decode requests and formulate answers. The more complex the nature of the messages between agents, the more complicated these components will be.

2. So far we have no working programs that demonstrate how an agent can extract a logical description of the world from currently available sensors, and worse no such programs seem to be forthcoming. Existing vision systems require vast amounts of computation which would have to be added to the logical inference machinery. Known algoritms do not get much further than (unreliably) extracting elementary information from the image, making some leading vision researchers question the idea whether a general purpose vision system that can extract a complete symbolic description from the image in real time is at all feasible (Ullman, 1987). Even such seemingly simple problems such as knowing where each agent is located are much more difficult than is commonly assumed.

3. Logic-based AI faces a set of fundamental problems which have not found adequate solutions and which would be needed in this application. These problems include the frame problem, effective reasoning about time and space (particularly the combination of the two), coping with the dynamics (and therefore non-monotonicity) of the world, and so on. These are the research problems that logic-based AI has been studying for the past few decades, but the fact that no solution seems within reach for non-toy problems indicates serious fundamental difficulties.

The behavior-based approach

An alternative to knowledge is behavior. Behavior is unconscious and without much deliberation or volition. It is typical for tasks involving perception, locomotion, speech and other skills. Nobody can explain for example how he is able to parse a speech signal, or which muscles he is moving to pick up a suitcase. Professional typists when asked cannot immediately give declarative descriptions of the keyboard although they exhibit behavior that implies 'knowing' something about the arrangement of the keys.[1] Skilled typing is therefore a clear case where behavior rather than knowledge seems to be at the heart of the task. AI research and engineering so far has stressed knowledge-based approaches. This is entirely appropriate for tasks such as computer configuration, theorem proving, or legal reasoning, where the problem solver is capable to explain how he is solving the problem and what knowledge he brings to bear. But it is not necessarily the case that all tasks related to intelligence should be solved using knowledge-based techniques. In any case this paper explores the use of behavior instead of knowledge to handle the task proposed in the case study.

3. CHARACTERISTICS OF BEHAVIORS

There is no consensus yet on what the distinctive features are of a behavior based approach to AI. In our own research we have been exploring the following characteristics (Steels, 1988)

1. ANALOGICAL REPRESENTATIONS

Logical descriptions of the world are avoided almost entirely. There is no such thing as a central fact base that contains a description of the relevant state of the world in terms of a set of facts (or possibly another equally symbolic representation, such as a semantic network or frames). Instead representations are exploited that are a lot closer to the world itself. These representations will be called analogical because they keep some part of what they represent *implicit* in the representation. For example, suppose we have to handle relations in space. Two representations could be used (see Fig 1):

- The symbolic representation uses facts based on predicates like *left-of*, or *position (x,y)*.
- The analogical representation uses a grid where the objects occupy positions mirroring the positions they take in the world.

The main reason for using analogical representations is that they are closer to the sensors and require no (or a much simpler) categorisation of the world before they can be used. For example a sonar sensor or a camera, can give us a bitmap in which objects occur as blobs occupying a position analogous to the position they occupy in reality. A heat sen-

[1] You can try this yourself (if you can type 'blindly'): What letter is under your right hand index finger on the middle bar?

left-of (object-1, object-2)
square (object-1)
round (object-2)

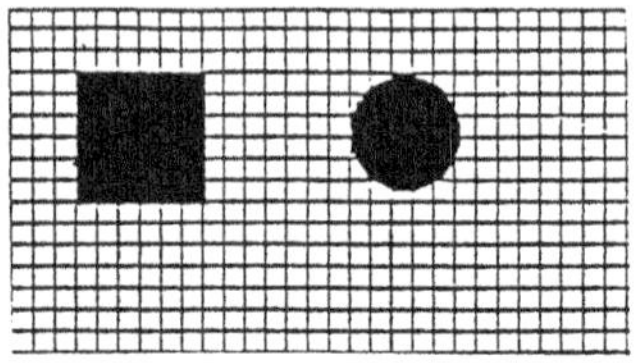

Fig 1. a. Symbolic representation. b. Analogical representation.

sor gives us immediately an analogical and continuous representation of how warm it is.

2. ANALOGOUS DYNAMICS

Using mainly analogical representations makes it no longer possible to use logical inference as primary mechanism for decision making. The first thing we will do is directly link analogical representations with perception and action. A very simple example of this is a system with a thermometer that is linked to a valve. The higher the temperature the more the valve is closed. The thermometer is an analogical representation of temperature: the higher the temperature the higher the position of the thermometer. There is a direct connection between the world and this representation. There is also a direct connection between the representation and the action of the valve.

The second thing we could do is execute various operations over analogical representations to transform it and give us more information. One example of this is a gradient field which is established on an analogical representation of a terrain. The process of creating the gradient can be seen as a diffusion operation starting from the target and going around obstacles until it reaches the vehicle. The route followed by the vehicle is given by following the highest gradient towards the target. (see Payton (1989) for a similar example).

3. EMERGENT FUNCTIONALITY

It is typical for behaviors that the required functionality does not get established by explicit design but that it emerges as a side effect of (i) the internal dynamics and/or (ii) the (dynamical) interaction with the environment. A typical example of the first phenomenon is a tensile structure, such as the geodesic domes built by Buckminster Fuller, in which different stresses interact to reach equilibrium and thus a stable structure capable to carry weight. It is only when the last component is put in that the whole structure suddenly obtains its functionality (fig 2 from Kenner, 1976). This contrasts with a building constructed with bricks or concrete in which the capacity to carry load comes from the rigidity of the component materials.

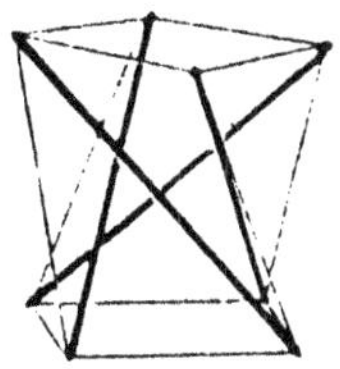

Fig 2. Tensile structure illustrating emergent functionality through internal dynamics.

An example of the second phenomenon is the forward movement of certain kinds of worms which are not capable to generate movement on their own, but when they are put in water with a certain density, the skin spontaneously starts to contract and stretch locally leading to forward movement (Oster, et.al, 1983). The movement is therefore a consequence of the interaction between the behavior of the medium in which the worm is located and the behavior of the skin.

In this paper, we will explore specifically how functionality can emerge based on self-organisation. Self-organisation is a technical term from the theory of complex systems (Prigogine (1976), Nicolis and Prigogine (1978)). It refers to a phenomenon in which a so-called dissipative structure spontaneously emerges out of the interaction of the behavior of many elements. A typical example is the formation of vortices in fluid flow. Self-organisation is now understood to be a fundamental process in biology (particularly in evolution, pattern formation, or the immune system), and in physics and chemistry (Babloyantz, 1987). There is no reason why it should not be of equal relevance to AI.

To get dissipative structures which are the product of self-organisation the following properties must be fulfilled:

1. There must be a basic underlying dynamical system which shows an equilibrium behavior, i.e. the system keeps evolving until it reaches a state of rest. The state of rest is still dynamic from the viewpoint of the underlying objects but there are no major macroscopic properties of the system changing. For example, when two closed containers with different gas pressures are connected, the joint system will evolve until there is equal pressure in both containers, although the movement of the molecules responsible for the pressure is still going on.

2. The dynamical system must be exposed to an outside disturbance, i.e. it must be open. In the case of the water flow, the disturbance is the force causing the fluid to flow. In the case of a selectionist system, the disturbance is environmental pressure.

3. The dissipative structure forms itself in response to this external force. It feeds on itself, which implies that the dynamics is going to be non-linear, and it is

present as long as as the force is present. This implies that there is not only a mechanism that establishes structure but also one that breaks it down again. Thus the vortices in the water will be present as long as the water keeps flowing at a rapid rate. When the flow is no longer there, the water will move back to an equilibrium state.

All of this is mapped onto the case study as follows. We will design a system of interacting robots whose equilibrium behavior consists in exploring the terrain around the vehicle. The presence of rock samples constitutes a disturbance. The desired dissipative structure consists of a spatial structure (i.e. a path) formed by the robots between the samples and the vehicle. This structure should spontaneously emerge when rock samples are present, it should enforce itself to maximise performance and should disappear when all samples have been collected.

4. STEP 1: THE IMPORTANCE OF RANDOMNESS

Before we can build this system we have to get the basic behaviors of the agents implemented. Some solutions, which may seem obvious at first, have to be rejected if we want to maximise the design criteria stated in the beginning. For example, a complete map of the terrain and knowledge where a robot or the vehicle are located on this map, or a complete vision system that is telling us what kind of object a robot has in front of it and what the exact boundaries are of this object, are luxuries that will not be assumed to be present.

Instead we start from the following simple behaviors:

Movement behavior

1. *Choose randomly a direction to move.*
2. *Move in that direction*

Handling behavior

1. *If I sense a sample and am not carrying one, I pick it up.*
2. *If I sense the vehicle-platform and am carrying a sample, I drop it.*

The handling behavior establishes a direct connection between sensors and effectors and runs parallel with the movement behavior. There is no sophisticated control strategy or internal reasoning of any sort. To handle obstacles, an additional behavior is added:

Obstacle avoidance

If I sense an obstacle in front, I make a random turn.

The moving behavior and the obstacle avoidance behavior are coupled using a subsumption architecture (Brooks, 1987), i.e. when there is an obstacle, obstacle avoidance behavior overrides random movement (fig 3).

---

random behavior

---

obstacle avoidance

Fig 3. Subsumption architecture. Bottom-level layers take precedence over top-layers.

Will this solution solve the problem? Yes and no. The robots clearly perform a random walk or Brownian movement. Hence they will accidentally stumble into the samples and later on find back the vehicle. The following is a classical theorem from probability theory:

> **The random walk theorem**: *Starting from any point in a random walk restricted to a finite space, we can reach any other point any number of times.* (Chung, 1974).

It follows from this theorem that the robots will find the rock and they will find back the vehicle. The only problem is that it may take a very large amount of time. Nevertheless this solution has some of the features that we want:

1. There is robustness. If a sample sensor malfunctions temporarily no harm is done. If the pick up action did not get executed properly, the sample sensor will still be on and the robot will pick it up again. If the vehicle-platform sensor malfunctions, the robot will wander around until it stumbles again on the platform. If the sample is accidentally dropped it will be picked up again or possibly found by another robot which will then carry it to the vehicle.

2. There is flexibility because changes in the vehicle, the rock samples or sudden obstacles can all be handled.

3. There is extreme cognitive and communicative economy, and no prior world knowledge is required.

4. Most importantly, parallelism can be exploited without additional overhead.

To understand how parallelism helps, it is useful to go back to equation (1):

$$t(n) = \sum_{i=1,n} t_e(i) + \sum_{i=1,n} t_c(i) \qquad (4)$$

Clearly when the number of robots increases, the probability that one of them will reach a particular point in the space increases as well. So, if the number of robots increases to a (possibly very large) number M, we may evolve towards the theoretical optimum for the needed exploration time:

$$\lim_{1 \to M} \sum_{i=1,n} t_e(i) = nd \tag{5}$$

However no improvement with parallelism can be expected for the corresponding carrying time t_c because each robot carrying a sample must find its own way back. This puts an important limit on this solution. It shows that to optimise the total time we necessarily need more mechanism. It is not enough to just multiply the number of robots.

To test these theoretical insights, a number of experiments were conducted to study the relation between the number of robots and the overall time needed to solve the task. These experiments were implemented in an actor-based complex dynamics language RDL (Steels, 1989)[2]. The interface to the system is shown in fig 4. There are different windows each displaying one aspect of the simulation. One window called ROBOT shows the positions of the different robots. The size of the square indicates how many robots there are in that location. A second window called CARRYING-SAMPLE shows the positions of the robots carrying samples. Other windows show the remaining rock samples, and the collected samples already at the vehicle.

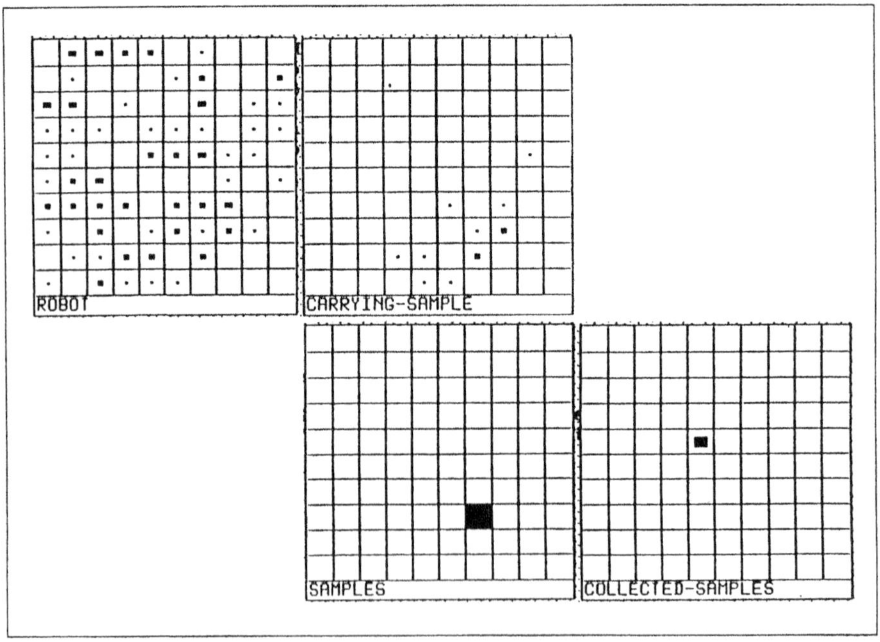

Fig 4. Snapshot of simulation environment.

The number of samples n is equal to 100. Starting with 8 agents, parallelism was raised by a factor of 2 up to 256 agents. The results of the experiments are displayed in fig 5.

[2] Development of this language is partly sponsored by ESPRIT project P440.

The x-axis represents 4×2^x. The y-axis gives the average time for 50 experiments. 8 agents require close to 30.000 time steps which decreases to about 8000 time steps for 256 agents. As expected we see a steady but limiting increase in the overall efficiency as parallelism increases.

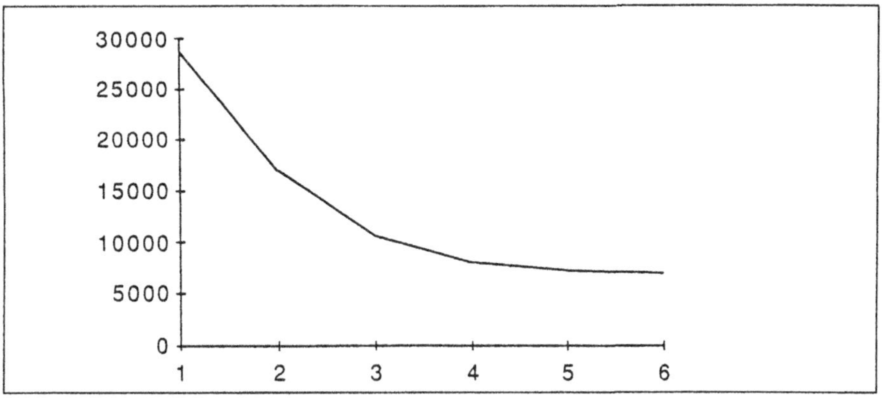

Fig 5. Relation between parallelism and efficiency.

The results are better understood when the average total time needed t(n) is decomposed into t_e and t_c, as in fig 6. As predicted, t_e decreases but t_c remains constant at about 7800 which is the average time for a robot to find back the way to the vehicle.

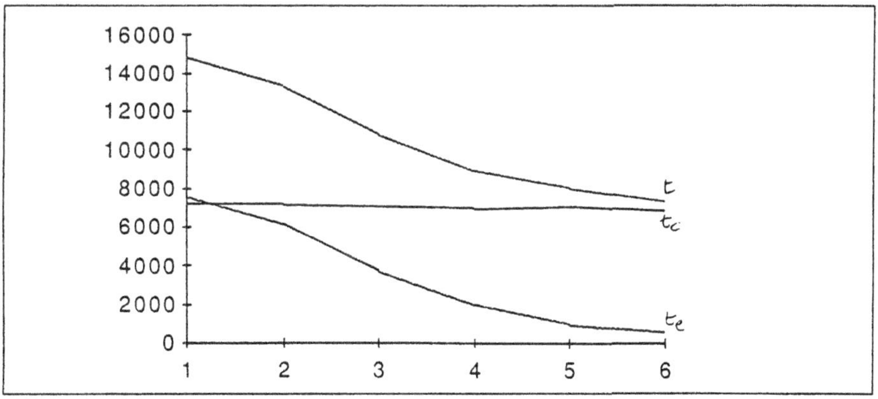

Fig 6. Decomposed parallelism relation.

5. STEP 2: THE GRADIENT FIELD

A gradient field is a field emanating from a certain point and diminishing in strength as the distance to the point increases. Gradient fields are extremely common in nature. They play a key role for example in the formation of structures such as shells, plants, and neural networks (Meinhardt and Gierer, 1982). Physical phenomena such as magnetism, radiation, or diffusion are all instances of mechanisms that establish a gradient field.

A gradient field will be used here to solve the following problems:

1. We have seen that t_c is not optimised through parallelism. The gradient field must solve this problem. It must be a guide to the robots how to get back to the vehicle.

2. We also want the robots to keep moving within a bounded area around the vehicle. This will increase the probability that they will find the samples in that area. When the vehicle moves forward, the robots should move along with it.

A gradient field is established through a diffusion process. Let p =<i,j> be a position in a discretised spatial representation, and n(p) the von Neumann neighbourhood of p = <i,j>:

$$n(p)=\{p' \mid p' = <i+k,j+q>, -1 \leq k \leq 1, -1 \leq q \leq 1, p' \neq p\} \quad (6)$$

Let g (t,p), a non-negative integer, represent the gradient at a time t in a position p. The diffusion processes used in the experiments is defined using the following difference equation:

$$g(t_k+1,<i,j>) = \sum_{m \in n(i)} \frac{g(t_k,m)}{8} \quad (7)$$

Boundaries are assumed to be dissipative. An additional rule helps further in the decay process:

$$g(t_i+1,p) = 0 \text{ if } g(t_i,p) \leq 8 \quad (8)$$

Note some important consequences of this diffusion process:

1. There is a decay, consequently continuous supply of g is needed.

2. The extent of the field depends on the amount of g originally available. This implies that we can engineer the system to specify how far robots may wander away from the vehicle by increasing g.

A physical way to implement g is by the emission of a sound wave from the vehicle. Increasing g then means increasing the sound level.[3] Each robot must have a sensor that can detect the sound and determine the direction where it came from. If the vehicle, which is responsible for emitting g, moves, the field will move along.

Let us now turn to the behaviors that use the principle of the gradient field.

The robot can be in two modes:

- Exploration: In this mode the robot moves away from the sound source, i.e. it follows the lower gradient.

[3] An alternative, which was also verified in computational experiments, is that the robots put themselves markers on the ground as they are exploring the area around the vehicle. There also then needs to be a process of collecting the markers similar to the mechanism that we will discuss in section 6.

- Return: The robot moves back to the sound source, i.e. it follows the higher gradient.

These modes determine two additional moving behaviors:

Return movement

If I am in return mode I chose the direction of highest gradient.

Explore movement

If I am in exploration mode I chose the direction with the lowest gradient.

The following behavior regulates which mode the robot will be in:

Mode determination

1. If I am in exploration mode and I sense no lower concentration than the concentration in the cell on which I am located, I put myself in return mode.

2. If I am in return mode and I am at the vehicle-platform I put myself in exploration mode.

3. If I am holding a sample, I am in return mode.

These behaviors are coupled using a subsumption architecture to the other moving behaviors as in fig 7:

random movement

return movement

exploration movement

obstacle avoidance

Fig 7. Subsumption relation between moving behaviors.

Fig 7 illustrates what happens when there are no rock samples. On the left we show an additional window called SOUND that implements g. Next to it there are a series of successive snapshots showing the distribution of the robots.

There is clearly a pulsating wave of robots coming out of the vehicle until they reach the boundaries of the SOUND diffused from the vehicle located in the middle of the space and returning back to the vehicle. The robots clearly explore systematically the area around the vehicle. When the vehicle moves the SOUND area will also move and the

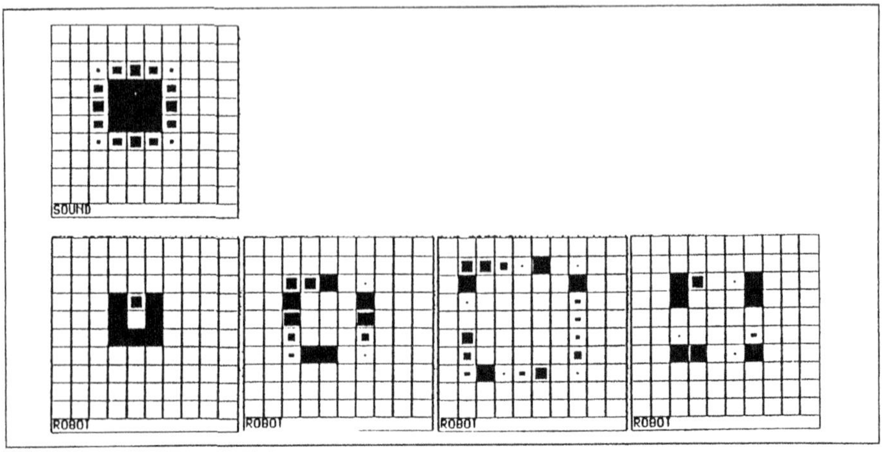

Fig 8. Exploration around the vehicle in waves.

robots will be attracted to the new location of the vehicle. Given that the movement is not too fast none of them will be lost. If one of them is lost it will fall back on random behavior.

When a rock sample is discovered, it will efficiently be brought back to the vehicle guided by the gradient field.

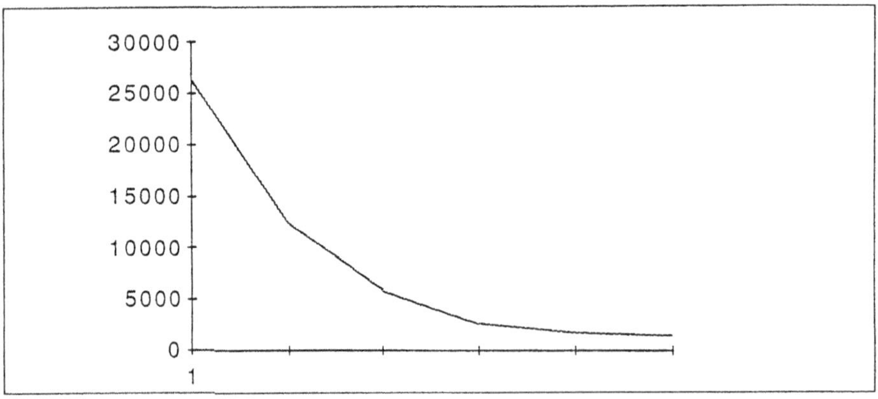

Fig 9. Absolute times with gradient fields.

The following experiments confirm this. Fig 9 represents again the evolution in (average) absolute time with parallelism increasing from 8 to 256 by a factor of 2. The time needed t(n) drops from about 25000 to about 500. Fig 10 gives the decomposition in t_e and t_c. We see that the second term in the computation t_c has dropped dramatically to be constant and equal to the distance between the sample location and the vehicle.

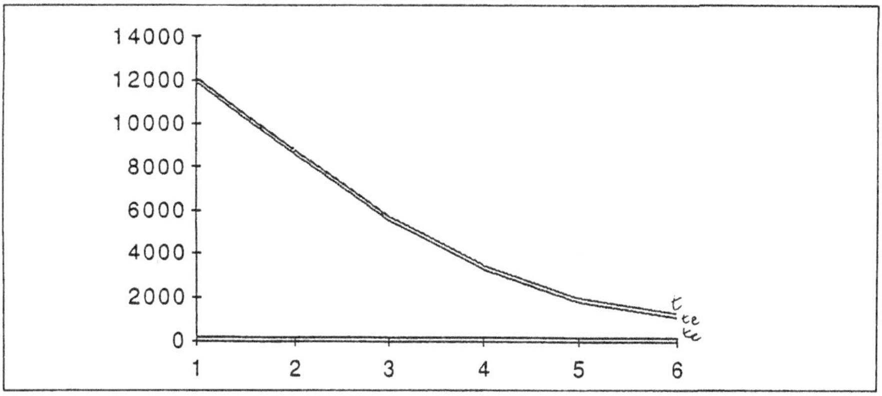

Fig 10. Decomposition of average time with gradient fields.

6. STEP 3: SELF-ORGANISATION

We are now ready to focus on how the principle of self-organisation could be applied. Specifically we want to optimise the first term t_e by establishing cooperative behavior between the distributed agents. When one robot has discovered the samples, it should communicate its finding to others and efficiently establish a path between the sample location and the vehicle. The means of communication between the robots will be a trail composed of 'crumbs'. The crumbs should be easily detectable by a robotsensor. Each robot has a certain supply of these crumbs and is capable to put them down and pick them up.

The following behaviors are added to the repertoire of the mobile robots to make this all happen:

Crumb handling

1. If I carry a sample, I drop 2 crumbs.

2. If I carry no sample and crumbs are detected, I pick up one crumb.

(1) will establish the path. (2) will break it down again. Note that the speed of break-down is less than the speed of buildup, although it does not really matter how much. We also need a new movement behavior:

Path attraction

If I am not carrying a sample and I sense crumbs, I move towards the highest concentration of crumbs.

This behavior is integrated with the other movement behaviors using the subsumption architecture (fig 11).

random movement

return movement

exploration movement

path attraction

obstacle avoidance

Fig 11. Subsumption relation between moving behaviors.

Fig 12 contains a few snapshots of a simulation in progress. Fig 12 a. is taken when one robot has discovered the samples which are located in the bottom right. Consequently there is a small square in the CARRYING-SAMPLE window at that position. The robots are scattered around randomly in the area to be explored around the vehicle.

Fig 12 b. illustrates the formation of a path. A second robot has now discovered the sample and the first one has arrived back at the vehicle (given a first small square in the COLLECTED-SAMPLES window). Note that crumbs have been put down by the first robot and that there is already a grouping of the robots because of attraction to the crumbs path.

In fig 12 c. we see several of these robots coming back with samples to the vehicle and the set of collected samples has already increased. Notice however that the crumbs path has been broken down considerably because more robots without samples are walking

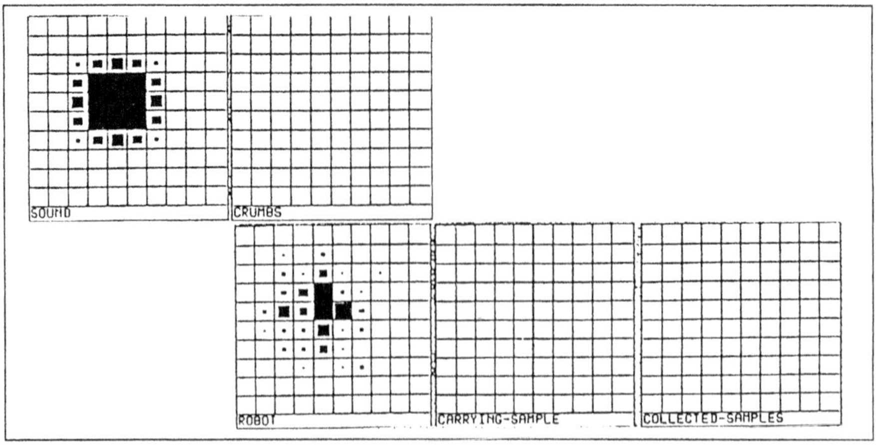

Fig 12a. Different snapshots of simulation in progress.

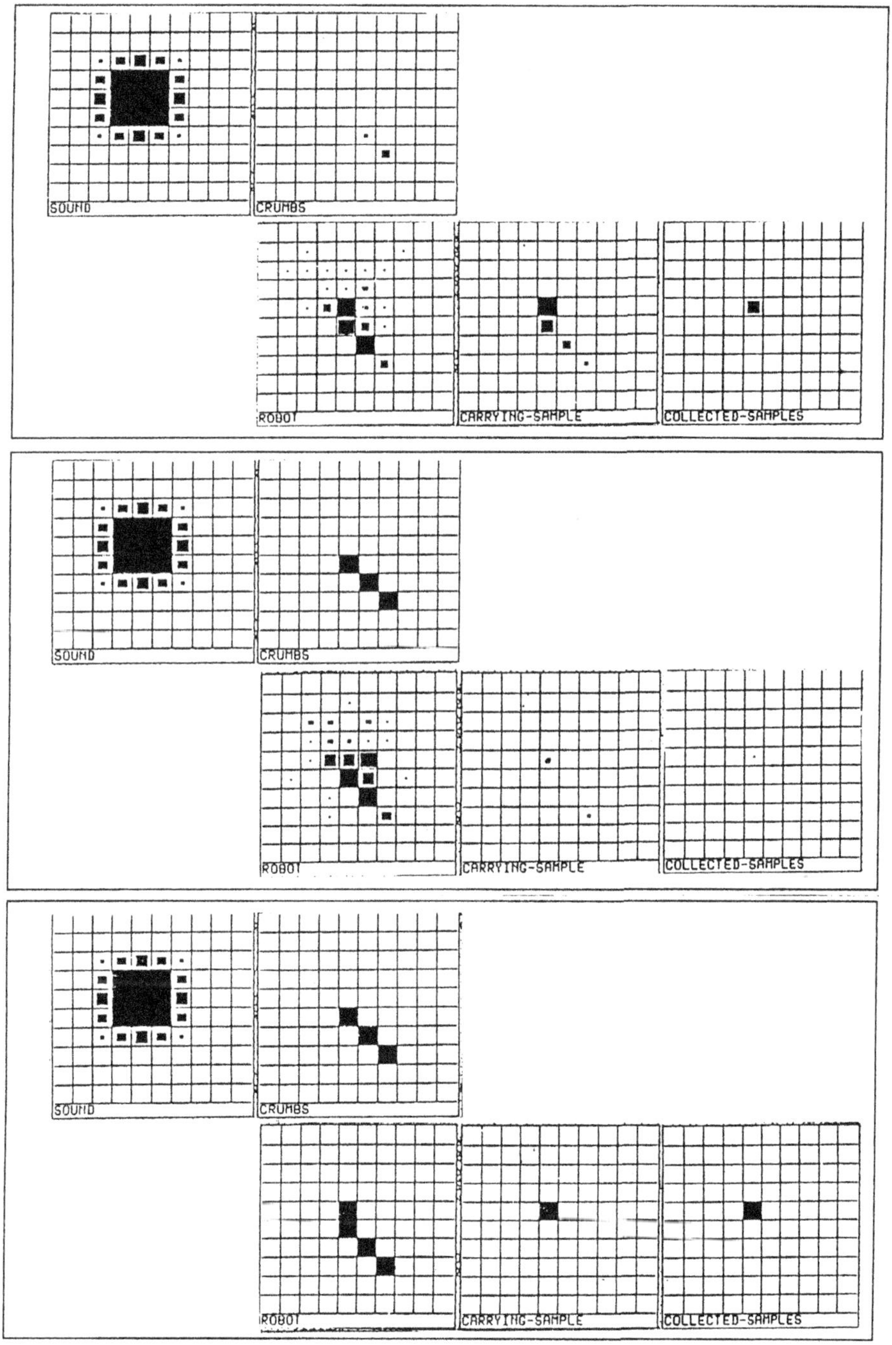

Fig 12bcd. Different snapshots of simulation in progress.

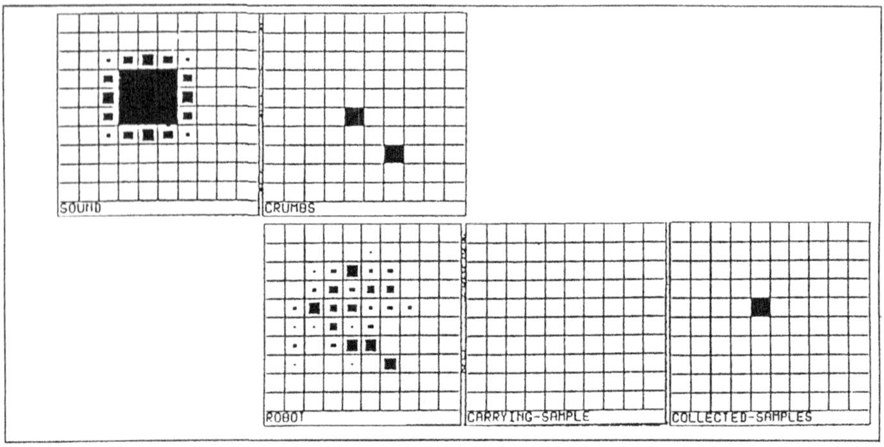

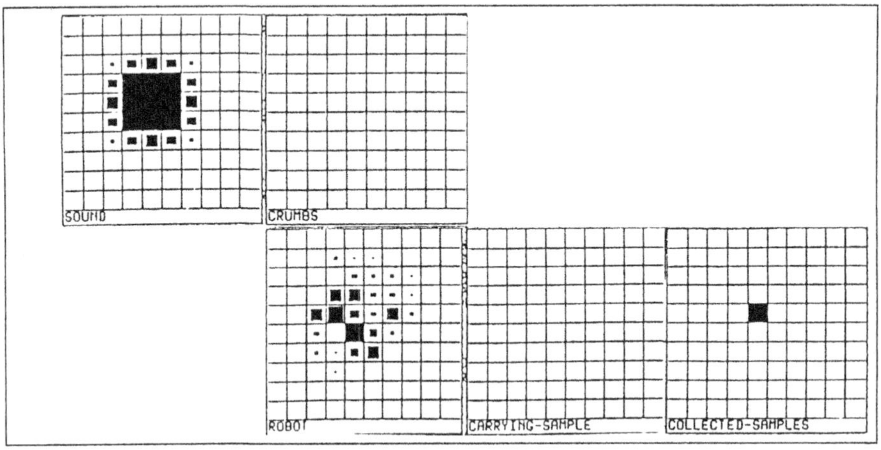

Fig 12ef. Different snapshots of simulation in progress.

along the path to the samples (and thus breaking down the samples) than there are robots returning with samples and thus reestablishing the path.

Fig 12 d. shows that the crumbs path has been reestablished again by returning robots. We also see that robots now maximally cooperate in the task. There is only one robot that is not on the path.

In fig 12 e. the samples are exhausted and the path is being broken down again. Robots are already scattered around in search of new samples. In fig 12 f. the system has returned to the original equilibrium behavior.

The experimental data confirm that almost optimal performance is reached after a few time steps. Fig 13 contains again the average times t(n) needed by an increasing number of robots (going from 8 to 256). We go from about 2500 timesteps which is a drastic reduction from 30000 timesteps to slightly under 1000 time steps with 256 robots.

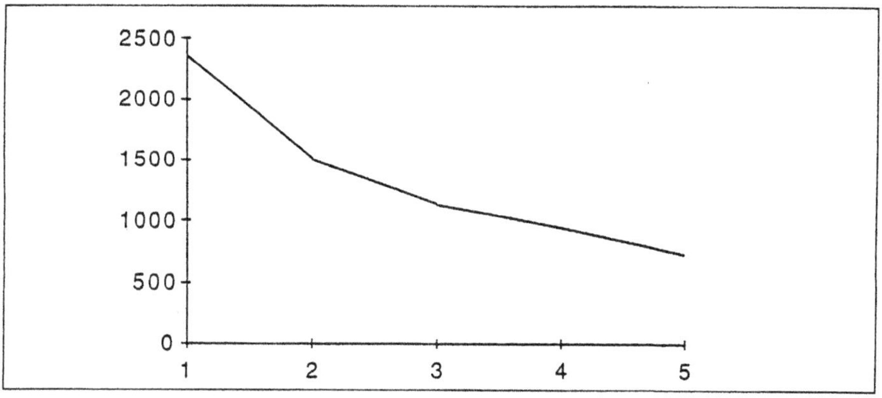

Fig 13. Total time with dissipative structure in place.

Further inspection reveals that most of the remaining non-productive time is spent in the initial phase when the first sample needs to be found. Once the sample is found, an efficient path is established fairly quickly even with a small group of robots. To illustrate this better fig 14 shows the exploration time t_e needed for each sample in one experiment with 16 robots. The x-axis represents the discovery order of a sample. The y-axis represents the time needed to discover a particular sample. Starting from roughly the 17th sample, the time is equal to the distance between the vehicle and the sample (except for sample 26 and 27 which were discovered by robots with a longer discovery path). The initial search phase can only be made smaller when more robots are available to scan the area around the vehicle.

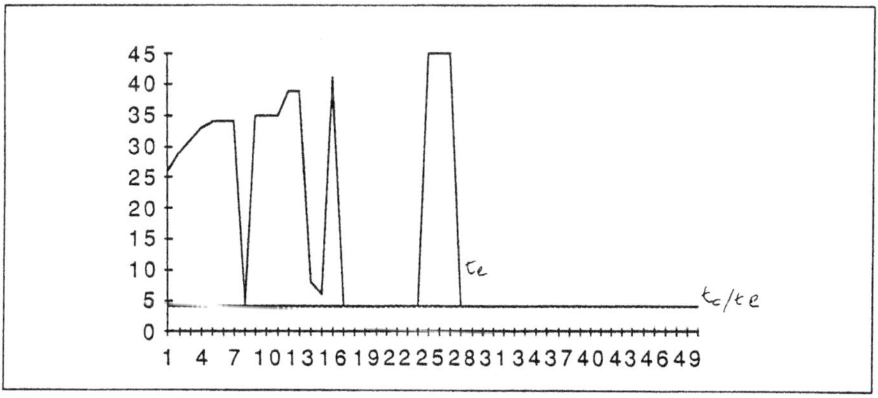

Fig 14. Time needed to discover each sample.

This experiment illustrates particularly how functionality can be made to emerge:

1. The strengthening of a path is not programmed in but is due to the non-linear interaction of the behaviors: Robots not carrying samples are attracted by the path which increases the chances that they will arrive at a sample and on return contribute to the establishment of the path.

2. The breakdown of the path also follows from the interaction between the environment and the robots. When there are no more samples, this will lead to less crumbs being put down, and because there is a depletion process the path will eventually disappear.

3. Also the fact that robots follow the path towards the vehicle and not away from it is, surprisingly, not programmed in but follows from the fact that on average more crumbs will be located nearer to the rock samples. Most robots by the way start on the path from the vehicle to which they return due to the pulsating in/out movement.

7. CONCLUSIONS

The solution we arrived at scores high on the various evaluation criteria proposed in the beginning of this paper:

1. The solution is robust because the improper execution of an action is not fatal to the whole system.

2. The solution is fault tolerant, because loss of a robot is not fatal either, although loss of the vehicle would of course be fatal. If there are fewer robots this will lead to a graceful performance degradation, but even with two robots (or one) the total system still remains operational.

3. The solution is flexible. Environmental changes have little impact. Any kind of object can be on the way between the robot and the vehicle.

4. There is extreme cognitive economy. The internal representation consists only of the state of the robot (exploration mode or return mode). There are no complex representations of time or space, no explicit representations of action, no representation of where the other robots are or where the vehicle is.

5. There is extreme communicative economy. The robots use the world to communicate among themselves: They leave markers behind in the world. Never is there any point to point communication. There are no complex messages to formulate or decode.

6. The environment does not have to be very predictable. For example, things would work equally well when there are two or more sources of rock samples.

7. Finally no prior knowledge in the form of terrain maps or other information is needed.

The robots themselves are definitely constructable using current technology. They do not require very sophisticated sensors or effectors. The assumed subsumption architecture has been well tested now in a number of applications. The solution satisfies also the quantitative criteria. We have moved from a very inefficient solution involving random search to an efficient cooperation between the robots as soon as a sample has been found.

The real importance of this paper is however not in the adequacy of the found solution but in the underlying principles. These principles can be summed up as follows: We have a number of dynamical mechanisms at our disposal: (partially) random movement, a gradient field, a dissipative structure. Each of these mechanisms is dynamical in the sense that it depends on the non-linear interactions with the environment. Structures grow dynamically and decay again. Although gradient fields have been used in other work, this is the first paper experimentally illustrating the use of dissipative structures. The idea was already proposed in Steels (1987) which contains suggestions on other applications.

The relation to ant societies is obvious but not as straightforward as one may think. Many ant societies use individual recruiting (one ant fetches another one), and if they do mass recruiting they are typically much less effective (30 % or even 5 %) than the robot ecology proposed in this paper (Deneubourg, et.al. 1985).

8. ACKNOWLEDGEMENT

I am indebted to several members of the VUB AI lab dynamics group (particularly Bernard Manderick and Jo Decuyper) for help in understanding complex dynamics in its many manifestations, and to Pattie Maes and Walter Van de Velde for their invitation to the Lagos Workshop on Autonomous Agents which prompted the writing of this paper.

9. REFERENCES

Babloyantz, A. (1986) Molecules, dynamics, and life. An Introduction to Self-organization of matter. Wiley, New York.

Brooks, R. (1986) A robust layered control system for a mobile robot. IEEE Journal of Robotics and Automation, 2:14-23, 1986.

Chung, K. L. (1974) Elementary Probability Theory with Stochastic Processes. Springer-Verlag. New York.

Deneubourg, J., J. Pasteels and J. Verhaeghe (1983) Probabilistic Behaviour in Ants: A Strategy of Errors? In J. Theor. Biol. (1983) 105, 259-271.

Genesereth, M. and N. Nilsson (1987) Logical foundations of artificial intelligence. Kaufmann, Los Altos.

Kenner, H. (1976) Geodesic math and how to use it. University of California Press. Berkeley.

Konolidge, K. (1982) A first-order formalization of knowledge and action for a multi-agent planning system. Machine intelligence 10. Ellis Horwood, Chichester.

Kornfeld, W. and C. Hewitt. (1981) The Scientific Community Metaphor. IEEE Transactions on Systems, Man, and Cybernetics. SMCS-11(1):24-33, January 1981.

Lenat, D. (1975) Beings: Knowledge as interacting experts. Proceeding IJCAI-4, pp. 126-133. Kauffman, Los Angeles.

Lesser, V. et.al. (1979) Working papers in distributed computation: Cooperative distributed problem solving. Dept Comp. Science Amherst.

Nicolis, G. and I. Prigogine (1977) Self-Organization in Nonequilibrium Systems. Wiley-Interscience, New York.

Oster, G.F., J.D. Murray, and A.K.Harris (1983) Mechanical Aspects of Mesenchymal morphogenesis. Journal Empryol. exp. Morph. 78, 83-125.

Payton, D. (1989) Internalized Plans: a representation for action resources. Hughes AI Center, Calabasas, Ca.

Prigogine, I. (1980) From Being to Becoming. Freeman, San Francisco.

Rosenschein, S. and M. Genesereth (1987) Communication and Cooperation Among Logic-Based Agents. In Proceedings of the 6th Conference on Computers and Communications, p. 594-600. Phoenix.

Smith, R. (1980) The contract net protocol: High-level commjnication and control in a distributed problem solver. IEEE Trans. Comput. vol. C-29, pp. 1104-1113.

Steels, L. (1979) Reasoning modeled as a society of communicating experts. MIT AI Lab. Technical report. Cambridge, Ma.

Steels, L. (1987) AI and complex dynamics. Proceedings of the IFIP workshop on concepts and techniques for knowledge-based systems. Mount Fuji, Japan.

Steels, L. (1988) Steps towards common sense. In ECAI-88, Munchen. Pitman Pub. London.

Steels, L. (1989) CDL: A complex dynamics language based on localised actors. VUB AI Lab Memo 89-5.

DECENTRALIZED A.I.
Yves DEMAZEAU & Jean-Pierre MÜLLER (Eds.)

AN EXPERIMENT IN COOPERATION

David Connah and Peter Wavish

Artificial Intelligence Group,
Philips Research Laboratories, Redhill,
UK, RH1 5HA.

This paper describes an experiment in cooperation between two simulated, autonomous agents. The cooperation is achieved not by explicit planning but by the operation of situated action on the part of the two agents. Their behaviour during the scenario, which is displayed graphically, may nevertheless be interpreted by an observer as being based on beliefs and plans. A short section is also included on the way in which the system has been implemented.

1. INTRODUCTION

The term agent is becoming increasingly fashionable both in the field of Artificial Intelligence and, more generally, in other computing contexts. It has almost as many meanings as there are instances of its use and this has been the source of considerable confusion. It might be as well therefore if we were to explain our use of the term at the outset. In this paper we will regard agents as complex and autonomous 'beings'. For the most part they will be artificial in the sense that they are programmed in software or constructed from electronic hardware but our use of the term also allows us to regard people as agents. The word agent in other contexts (for example in Distributed Artificial Intelligence) often refers to simpler and more specific entities which are controlled in a hierarchical manner in such a way that a group of them can be organised to carry out some fairly complex task. In general, agents of the type described here would be expected to have a continuing existence in a complex and changing environment and would have to be able to cope with such changes.

The natural consequence of defining agents in this way is that they will normally form part of heterarchical rather than hierarchical systems. Furthermore there will be a variety of agents in the world and communication between them will have to be flexible and natural; that is to say growing out of the perceptions and actions that are part of their general behaviour patterns.

We are interested in agents of this kind because it seems to us that a system consisting of a number of such agents interacting freely with each other can be mapped onto a large number of application scenarios. This makes it possible to do research at a more abstract and therefore more general level without any sacrifice of applicability. The sort of abstractions that we are considering include negotiation and cooperation between agents as well as communication, the role of beliefs, plans and reasoning. This paper is concerned with one small experiment on the nature of cooperation between very simple agents. The main motivation for this experiment is to demonstrate a way of achieving cooperation which differs considerably from that normally suggested (see next section). Although a simple type of cooperation forms the focus of the experiment, questions are also raised about the nature and role of communications, plans and beliefs. We intend to take up these issues at greater length in future reports.

The rest of the paper is organised as follows. In the next section previous work is briefly mentioned and some of the work that forms the foundation of our approach is introduced. Section 3 is a general discussion of how we see cooperation acting between agents and sections 4 and 5 deal with the experiment proper. In section 6 we examine what we have learned from the experiment and after a note about the way in which the experiment was implemented we conclude by mentioning the direction in which we expect our future work to go.

2. PREVIOUS WORK

There is an extensive literature on such topics as beliefs, plans, commitment, conflict and negotiation , for example (Cohen & Levesque 1987, Galliers 1988, Konolige 1986, Rosenschein & Genesereth 1985). Much of this literature is characterised by the fact that it treats what one might call reasoning agents. It is worth making a distinction between rational agents and reasoning agents. According to our use of these terms an agent is rational if it adopts actions, goals and strategies which are, in some sense, conducive to the success of the agent. Normally a perfectly rational agent would adopt optimally successful strategies of this kind. Needless to say according to this definition, people are not perfectly rational although one would expect all agents which have survived in the world to be rational to some degree. Just as people are not perfectly rational one would not expect agents to be perfectly rational. It is in any case very difficult to construct a perfectly rational agent and such a project is almost certainly misguided. A reasoning agent, on the other hand, is one which explicitly reasons about its own actions and the actions of other agents. This is not a pre-requisite for rationality as expressed above.

With reference to reasoning agents, whilst there is a place for the investigation of such high-level and essentially problem solving activities it has to some extent led to a neglect of the role of much humbler processes, first of all in the everyday actions of agents and secondly as a basis on which to develop the higher level activities. Our principal concern is in the investigation of these lower level activities.

There are two other ways in which we see our work as differing from most of the previous work: we intend to implement our theories (that is to say ours is to some extent an engineering enterprise) and we do not wish to build folk psychological theories into the agents at the lowest level.

In (Connah, Shiels & Wavish 1988) we described a testbed for investigating the behaviour of interacting agents and many of the ideas inherent in that testbed have been used in the present work albeit with some implementational changes. We described there the way in which we see cooperation (and other aspects of agent interaction) as emerging from two concepts: situated action and the idea of agents being embedded in their environment.

Suchman gives an extensive account of the idea of situated action in (Suchman 1987) and some other work based on similar ideas was undertaken by (Chapman & Agre 1986, Agre & Chapman 1987). The nub of situated action is that agents can react directly to a situation; that the various aspects of any situation index directly a reasonably small set of actions on the part of the agent. This set is of course unique to the agent and is presumably acquired by a combination of evolutionary, cultural and individual learning. How this is done does not concern us at present; we simply assume the result. The idea is deceptively simple. What is not immediately apparent is the set of consequences for such things as plans, beliefs and communication that flow from the acceptance of the idea. The experiment described here is a simple exploration of some of those consequences.

The question of embedding in the world is also of great importance (Clark 1987). Without a world in which to embed the agent the concept of situated action doesn't make much sense. The consequence of embedding to which we attach most importance is that it is possible in an embedded agent to ensure that there is a direct loop embodying perception of the world and action upon it which is threaded through the agent and the world. Furthermore it is a tenet of our approach that as far as possible the world should act as its own model; that is to say that instead of the agent building internal representations of the world it should use its perceptions of the world directly. Thus what might in other circumstances be thought of as manipulations of an internal model are on this understanding seen as interactions with the real world.

This approach sometimes leads to a misunderstanding. We do not think that situated action can be used directly in all situations. Rather we believe strongly that it has a direct application in some cases, particularly where there is no time for deliberation, and that it also underlies, in some sense, more sophisticated modes of behaviour.

3. COOPERATION

In this section we first mention some of the motivations for cooperation between agents and then we discuss a strategy for achieving cooperation in this scenario.

Why should any agent ever do anything to help another agent achieve a goal which it does not itself share? There seem to be at least three classes of motivation which can be exploited when help is required:

1) benevolence; a motivation which, provided that no great cost is incurred, allows help to be offered without thought of direct benefit to one's self

2) altruism; a motivation which, even at great cost to one's self, allows help to be offered often to a particular class e.g close relatives, the young and vulnerable etc.

3) self–interest; a motivation which allows help to be offered in the expectation that some future benefit (money, help, the assuagement of guilt, avoidance of punishment etc.) will be obtained.

There is conceivably a fourth class, self preservation, where help is offered because it is the only way that survival can be ensured but it might be argued that this is just another example of self interest. In any event self interest in one form or another is arguably the commonest reason for help being offered. Of course in sophisticated agents (such as people) all of these motivations are likely to be present and very often entangled with each other but for the rest of this paper it will be assumed that self interest is what motivates both agents in their attempts at cooperation.

Another important issue concerns the strategy for cooperation. At one extreme an agent might have a conscious and deliberate plan for obtaining help when it finds itself in difficulties. At the other extreme, its in–built behaviour might be such that it achieves cooperation by a series of reactive moves and signals; in other words the agent, in the right circumstances, acts in such a way that it achieves cooperation with another agent without any intervening planning process and possibly without the need for explicit negotiation. Of course there are a number of concealed assumptions here but it is precisely this concealment in which we are interested. The actions of the agents in these circumstances lead to the achievement of their goals because their response to the situation has been learned (in people at least) from similar situations in the past.

4. THE EXPERIMENTAL SCENARIO

What we have done is an experiment in that it should be possible for us and others to repeat it and obtain the same (or a substantially similar) result. We have however suppressed most of the implementational details in order to avoid obscuring our main point which is to do with the ways in which cooperation between agents can be achieved. A short note on the implementation is presented later.

The scenario that has been used for this experiment is that of furniture removal. There are a number of reasons for choosing this example: it is a situation that is easily understood without any special expertise, it is in a concrete rather than an abstract domain and it lends itself easily to a simple (two dimensional) form of graphical representation.

In more detail, the scenario involves a room in a house which has a doorway in one wall and which contains a sofa and a table. Two agents are in the room. At the beginning of the scenario each agent has a task (given to it by the designer or experimenter): one has to carry the sofa to the doorway and the other has to carry the table. When both of these tasks have been completed the scenario is at an end. The catch is that the weights of the sofa and table are such that an individual agent is unable to pick up either piece of furniture unaided; the only practical solution to the problem is to enlist the help of the other agent.

A point worth noting here is that although the two goals mentioned above are initially 'given' to the agents, the agents are allowed to generate and modify goals including, in principle, the ones they were originally given. Clearly, this could in certain circumstances lead to paradoxical results. We will return to this point in section 6.

5. DETAILS OF THE EXPERIMENT

The course of the experiment as it unfolds can be described with the aid of some diagrams taken from the graphics produced by the system. All the objects and agents are represented on the screen by icons. Objects are point objects and so at various times the (transparent) icons will appear superimposed on one another.

At the beginning of the experiment the two agents are in a room which is empty but for the presence of a table and a sofa (fig. 1).

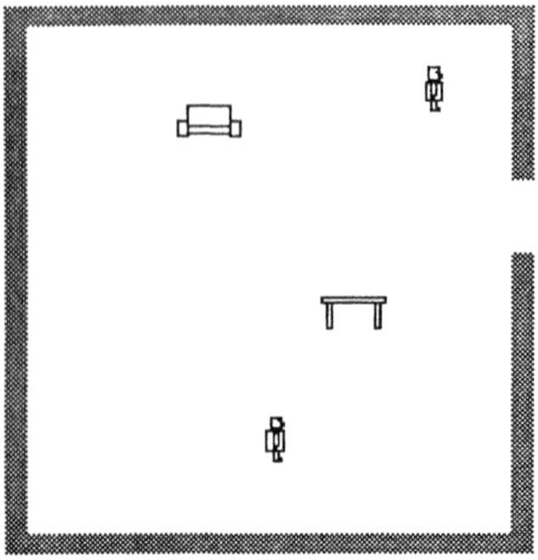

FIGURE 1

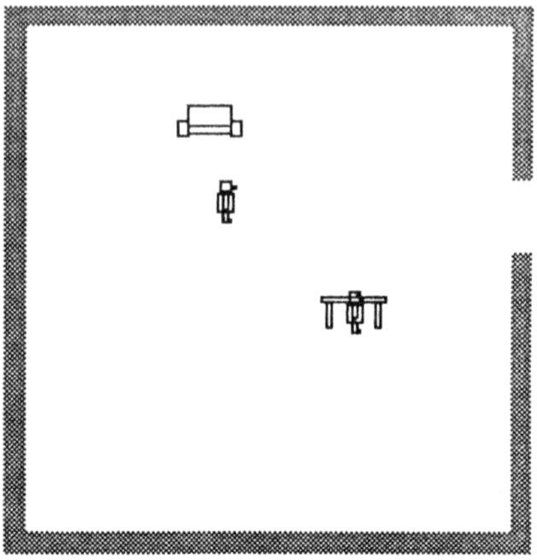

FIGURE 2

The goal of agent1 (at the top of the diagram) is to carry the table to the doorway and the goal of agent2 (at the bottom) is to carry the sofa to the doorway. The agents are not at first near the furniture that they have to remove from the room and so the first effect of their goals is to make them move to the appropriate item of furniture (fig. 2).

Agent1 reaches the table first and immediately tries to lift it. Attempting to lift something takes a finite time and agent1 discovers during this process that the table is too heavy. It puts the table down and the failure triggers a sequence of behaviour in which the help of another agent is ultimately invoked. This behaviour sequence is entered upon not as the result of reasoning about the situation but as a simple reaction to a failure to lift which, in turn, resulted from the object's being too heavy. The actions of the agent can however be described as if they did result from a reasoning process and, indeed, an outside observer might be tempted to ascribe such reasoning to an intelligent agent in these circumstances. The presumed internal monologue might go as follows:

"This table is too heavy for me to lift by myself" (fig. 2)

"Nobody is offering to help me but if I offer to help anyone else who needs help perhaps they will help me in return so I will make a general offer of help". (fig. 3).

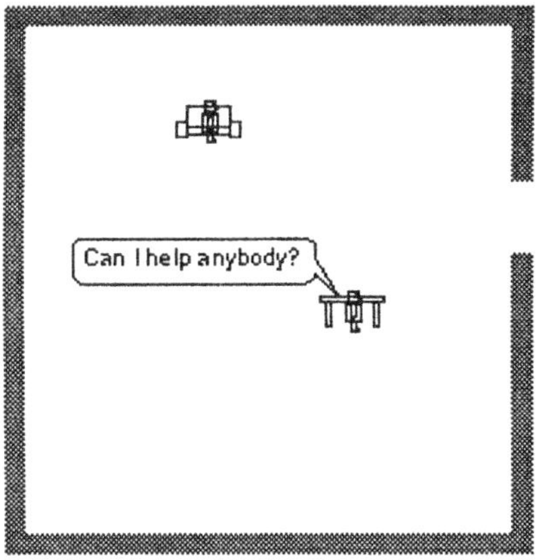

FIGURE 3

FIGURE 4

The agent is now in a 'helping mode' and changes its goal of carrying the table to the door into an analogous joint goal to be effected with the help of another agent at the appropriate time.

In the meantime agent2 has reached the sofa having heard agent1's offer of help along the way and it, in turn, discovers that the sofa is too heavy for it to lift. The internal dialogue of agent2 might be something like this (note that although the agents are identical their behaviour is different because of the difference in their circumstances):

"This sofa is too heavy for me to lift by myself" (fig. 3)

"Agent2 is looking for somebody to help, perhaps I can help it in return. I'll say 'I need help' ". (fig. 4).

FIGURE 5

On hearing this, agent1 says 'O.K.' and is now specifically in the position of helping agent2; its part of the contract is complete and it now waits for agent2 to say what has to be done (fig. 5).

FIGURE 6

When agent2 hears agent1 say 'O.K.' it replies by enunciating its goal and is then in a state of 'being helped' and is also in a state of obligation to agent1 (fig. 6).

Agent1 adopts agent2's goal. The situation now is that both agent1 and agent2 have the goal of getting the sofa to the doorway and in addition agent1 has converted its original goal of getting the table to the doorway into a deferred goal of doing it with agent2's help. Agent1 is helping agent2. Agent2 is being helped and is also obliged to agent1. Agent2 is by the sofa and agent1 is by the table. Agent1's goal triggers its movement (as before) and it sets off for the sofa (fig. 7).

When agent1 reaches the sofa both agents attempt to lift it and this time they succeed because their combined strength is sufficient. Their (shared) goal now triggers movement towards the door and since they are holding the sofa it goes with them (fig. 8).

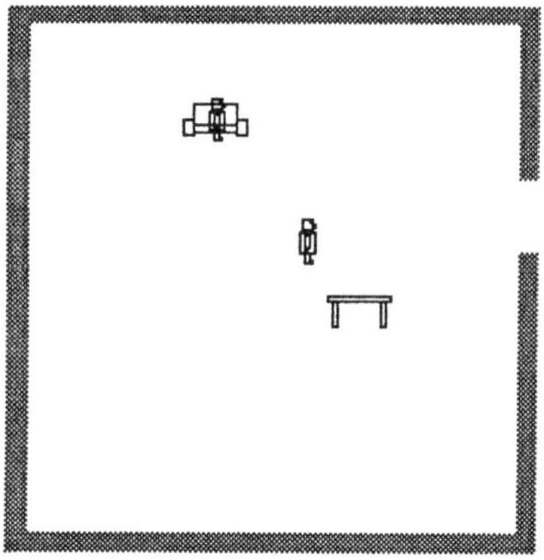

FIGURE 7

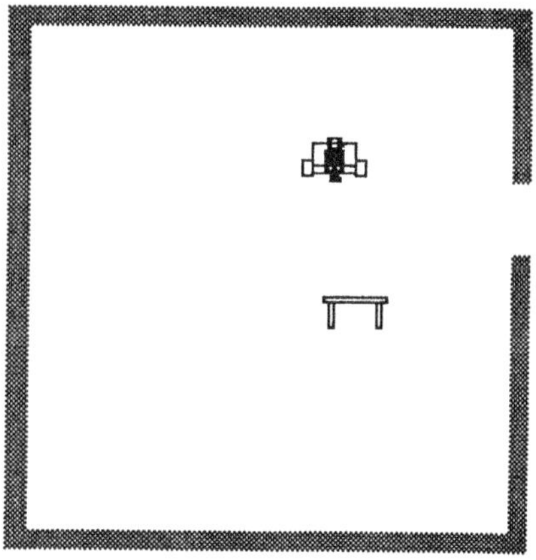

FIGURE 8

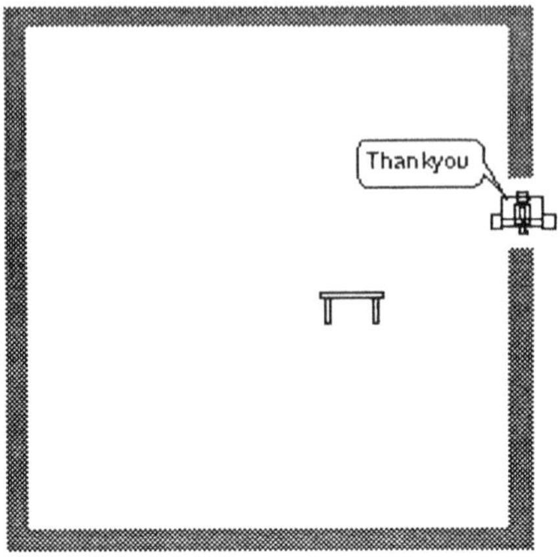

FIGURE 9

When they reach the doorway with the sofa they both realise that they have achieved this particular goal (fig 9). They both put the sofa down and agent2 says 'Thankyou'. Both agents get rid of this satisfied goal and agent1 converts its joint goal back into an ordinary goal. The roles are switched and because agent1 'knows' that agent2 is under an obligation to help, it immediately communicates its goal to agent2 (fig. 10) i.e. to take the table to the doorway.

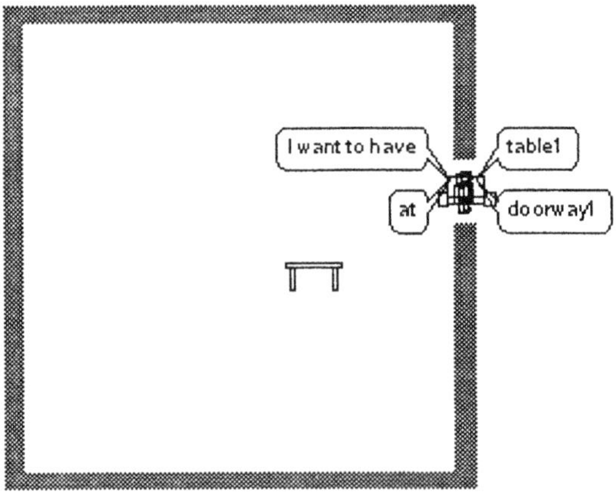

FIGURE 10

Agent2 adopts this goal and they both set off for the table (fig. 11).

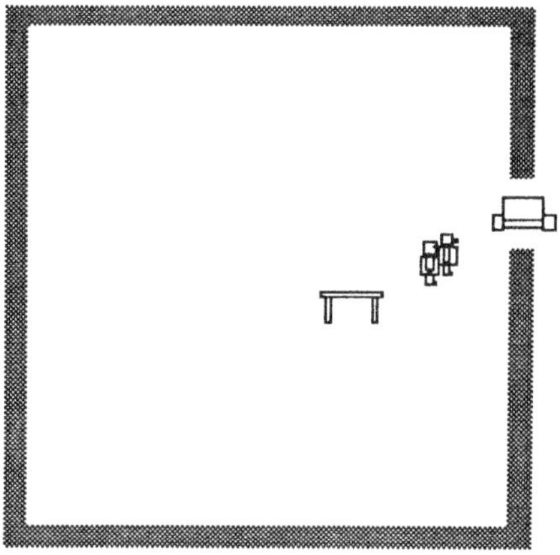

FIGURE 11

They then pick up the table and move off towards the doorway (fig. 12). When they reach the doorway both agents have achieved their goals and all obligations and the roles of helper and being helped are removed from their current behaviour patterns.

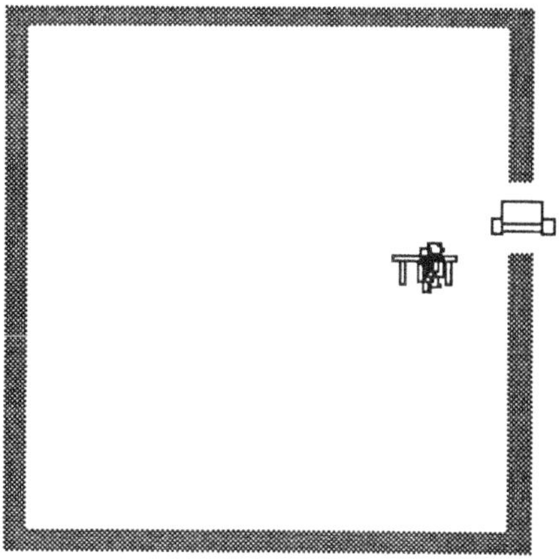

FIGURE 12

A final point about this experiment is this. The agents are identical in their reactions to situations although initially they have been given different goals. If no changes to the system are made except that the initial positions of the agents are altered in such a way that agent2 is nearer to the sofa than agent1 is to the table (the reverse of the situation described above) then their roles throughout will be reversed: agent2 will be the first to offer help and agent1 will accept; the table will be moved to the doorway before the sofa and so on. This illustrates quite nicely that the actual behaviour of an agent is a function not only of its architecture and history but of the specific situation in which it finds itself. This is not in itself surprising but it is encouraging that the implementation should demonstrate it so simply.

6. DISCUSSION OF RESULTS

In this section we will use the experiment we have just described to illustrate three areas which are of particular interest to us: the question of models and representation, the role of plans and beliefs and the nature of communication between agents. Let us take these issues in turn.

It should be clear from what has been said so far that the agents do not construct any internal model of the world. Any actions that they take are taken on the basis of their immediate perception of their surroundings. If they need to move a table and they do not currently see the table then they look around for it and move off towards it when they have found it. It is worth pointing out here that the agent's situation can be thought of as being in two parts: the external situation and the internal state of the agent.

Turning to beliefs and plans, the presumed internal monologue of section 5 illustrates clearly how actions which are situated, in the sense that they are a direct response to the situation, can appear to an outside observer to be the result of beliefs held or plans constructed by the agent. What we mean by implicit beliefs, for example, is that the behaviour of an agent in certain circumstances is the behaviour that would be expected of that agent if it did in fact hold the corresponding explicit beliefs. It is important to recognise in this regard that in any agent having implicit beliefs there may also be (as it were) an internal observer which makes the same kind of belief ascriptions as would an external observer. Thus on being asked "Do you believe X?" an agent may have to make such an internal observation before it is able to answer the question. During this process its implicit belief becomes explicit and may then be subject to the kind of treatment that other workers have described.

The point is not that there are no such things as explicit beliefs or knowledge or plans; clearly there are. However it is our contention that most of the simple, everyday actions that an agent is called upon to perform do not make use of them and, more importantly, even the explicit variety are based on a very large vocabulary of implicit actions. The emphasis in AI in the past has been on the explicit and because there has been no substructure on which to base these explicit beliefs and plans far too much effort has been devoted to representing, reasoning about and manipulating the explicit variety directly often with rather implausible results. The experiment described here has shown that a simple kind of cooperation is possible using only situated action.

Although the experiment only touches upon the question of communication it nevertheless does illustrate the way in which communication between agents has to be seen in the context of a number of situated actions. The utterances shown here are almost completely atomic in the sense that they are not parsed in the usual way but can be seen as whole chunks of text ('speech') which trigger particular actions. This is not quite the whole story since when an agent states its goal ('I want to have table1 at doorway1') the other agent does an extremely crude parse of this in order to acquire for itself a suitable form of this goal. What is at issue here however is not the nature of this parsing but the fact that much of the significance of the utterance is contained in the situation and not in the utterance at all. At this point in the unfolding of the scenario a goal statement is *expected* of the other agent and any parsing that takes place (whether crude or sophisticated) ought to take account of this fact.

The experiment described here is, for several reasons, rather unreal. In particular there are two aspects of agents that we need to improve if they are to achieve real autonomy. In an earlier section it was pointed out that it was perfectly possible for the agents to modify or abandon their goals (this is clearly essential in anything but a very simple agent) and that this included the possibility of abandoning their original given goal. There is no reason why they should do this in the present example but in general one would want to understand the circumstances in which this might be necessary. What is lacking in the present set-up is any sort of motivation at a higher level which might control the behaviour of the agents. Why do agents do anything at all? Why do they pursue the goals given to them by their designer? Implicit in this example is the idea that they pursue their original goals because that is literally their *raison d'etre*. This could be made explicit and goals given by the designer could have a different status from those generated by the agents themselves. This is not a very satisfactory solution. Dretske (Dretske 1988), amongst others, has pointed out the close relationship between behaviour and desires and what is required in our agents is a set of desires which have an overall driving influence on their behaviour.

The second way in which the example is unsatisfactory is that the behaviour of the agents is extremely one-dimensional. Originally they have only one goal each and their programming is limited to the accomplishment of this goal. Real autonomous agents would have to be able to accommodate many goals simultaneously. Furthermore in a simple example it is possible in principle to anticipate all the specific situations that are likely to arise whereas in more realistic examples this is not the case. The answer to this is to develop more abstract strategies for dealing with unexpected problems and for the opportunistic satisfaction of goals. For example agents might inadvertently get involved in tight loops and a strategy for recognising and dealing with this will be necessary. A simple example of the kind of situation envisaged is that of trying to put a (bad) coin into a vending machine. The machine rejects the coin and the client tries again perhaps two or three times but eventually recognises that he is in a loop and tries another coin. Although it is impossible to predict the details of every situation an agent will encounter, it should be possible at a sufficiently high level of abstraction to adopt strategies for coping with whole classes of unexpected occurrence.

7. A NOTE ON IMPLEMENTATION

It is not the main purpose of the paper to describe in detail how this experiment has been implemented. However a brief sketch of the method might help in understanding the fundamental ideas on which the demonstration is based.

The experiment was conducted with the aid of a language called ABLE (Agent Behaviour LanguagE) and a software tool called LYDIA (Let's You Develop Interacting Agents). LYDIA incorporates an interpreter for ABLE as well as some tools to aid in simulation and debugging. As its name implies, ABLE is a language which allows behavioural descriptions to be written down. These descriptions apply not only to agents but to any objects in the universe of discourse. There are constructs in the language which allow dependencies between behaviours to be described and time is incorporated into the language at a fundamental level. The language is essentially rule-based and situated actions can be written as rules in the language. The process of encoding an experiment such as this consists of encoding behavioural descriptions of agents and objects such as chairs, tables and so on and then of encoding the laws of 'physics' that determine the interactions between these.

The interpreter works by going through a cycle in which the next event in the world is predicted from an inspection of the behaviours and causal relationships that exist at that time. The language is not a logic (not even a temporal logic) since there are no concepts of truth or falsity and no necessity to undertake the proof of theorems in the language.

Much of the language's power comes from the fact that all the terms that can be written down are behaviours (including the rules themselves) and thus it is possible to nest simple behaviours and rules describing behaviour in an arbitrarily complex way. Furthermore, because everything is described in terms of aspects of behaviour, it is easy to integrate perception and other cognitive activities with actions and the behaviour of physical systems.

In some ways it is tempting to see agents and objects in terms of an object oriented programming paradigm. This is misleading however. Agents do not, at the lowest level, pass messages to each other; their interaction is accomplished by means of rules describing the physics of the world. Their actions have effects on the world and these effects in turn affect other agents. Thus the mechanism is more like a broadcast than direct message passing. A simple form of communication can be achieved at this level although of course the mechanism is not specifically connected with communication. More directed communications can be built on top of this.

From a practical point of view it is not difficult to generate quite large numbers of rules during the construction of an experimental scenario and this, naturally, can lead to a rather slow simulation of the behaviour of the entire system. However it turns out that it is very easy to distribute the execution of the rules over a number of processors without changing the basic code at all. In other words the problem of partitioning that often arises when concurrent execution is attempted is trivial (indeed might be said to be non–existent) using this approach. We have successfully taken the existing code running on one processor and distributed it over four Sun 3s without any rewriting of the application and achieved some speeding–up as a result. There are of course overheads associated with the partitioning and the amount of speed up depends on how well the load is balanced over the machines. With more rules the overheads and the imbalance will have a smaller effect and a closer approach to a linear speed up should be achievable.

Although our chief interest is in the ways in which agents interact, the software which we have developed seems to have applications outside that sphere which we are also trying to explore and which we will report on at another time.

8. FUTURE WORK

There is still a lot of mileage in the furniture moving scenario; the present example is only a tiny fragment of what is involved in (say) clearing an entire room full of furniture with fairly realistic constraints about collisions, resolving conflicts between agents and carrying out the task in an acceptable order. We intend to explore this further in the belief that what we learn about cooperation, negotiation and conflict resolution will have much more general applicability in the long run.

All the agents that we have so far constructed have been both simple and 'flat' in the sense that they have had no internal architecture to speak of. The central part of our work is the investigation of appropriate agent architectures. We believe that we have most of the tools available now and we intend to extend our work in that direction towards the end of this year.

Finally this example has not involved us in considering the role of situated action in the communication between agents to any great extent. We think there is much to be gained from approaching communication from the low–level pragmatic end and building on top rather than the other way round and this is an area we intend to explore in the near future.

ACKNOWLEDGEMENTS

We would like to acknowledge our debt to Martin Shiels for many interesting and constructive discussions on this and related topics when he was working in this project group.

REFERENCES

Agre, P.E., 1985, 'Routines', MIT AI Memo 828.

Clark, A., 1987, 'Being there: why implementation matters to cognitive science', Artificial Intelligence Review, Vol 1, 231–244.

Cohen, P.R. and Levesque, H.J., 1987, 'Persistence, Intention and Commitment', Proceedings of 1986 workshop on Reasoning about Actions & Plans, Timberline, Oregon, ed. Georgeff and Lansky, Morgan Kaufman.

Connah, D.M., Shiels, M.A. and Wavish, P.R., 1988, 'A Testbed for Research on Cooperating Agents' Proc. ECAI Munich 1988, 445–447.

Dretske, F., 'Explaining Behaviour. Reasons in a World of Causes', Bradford Books, MIT Press 1988.

Konolige, K., 1986, "A Deduction Model of Belief", Pitman, London and Morgan Kaufmann Inc. Los Altos, California.

Rosenschein, G. and Genesereth, M., 1985, "Deals among Rational Agents", Proceedings of 9th. IJCAI, Los Angeles.

Suchman, L., 1987, 'Plans and Situated Actions: the problem of human machine communication', Cambridge University Press.

Practical Issues for Information Exchange

DECENTRALIZED A.I.
Yves DEMAZEAU & Jean-Pierre MÜLLER (Eds.)

MODELING AUTONOMOUS AGENTS AND THEIR GROUPS

Takeo Maruichi, Masaki Ichikawa and Mario Tokoro

Department of Computer Science
Keio University
3-14-1 Hiyoshi, Yokohama 223
JAPAN

This paper describes a model for representing an *autonomous agent* and a *group* of agents. Object-oriented concurrent computing [Hewitt 1977] [Yonezawa 1987] provides the basis for modeling autonomous agents and their communication by passing messages, but there are two important issues in realizing an organization of autonomous agents :

- an object does not have a function to realize *autonomy*.
- cooperating objects are considered to form a group, but such a notion of a group is not provided.

We first define an autonomous agent as a concurrent object, but one which has its own *message-interpreter* to realize autonomy. A message-interpreter searches for important messages from the local message queue while maintaining internal consistency and protocols for cooperation with other agents, fetches the message, and executes it. Second, we define the notion of an *environment* where agents exist and are considered to form a group. An agent can multicast a message to all the agents in an environment.
The fundamental model, which adds these two new functions to object-oriented concurrent computing, is called an *organizational model of computation.* These two new functions help in modeling democratic and dynamic organizations found in many natural and social systems where multiple autonomous agents cooperate with one another. To evaluate this organizational model of computation, an example called the *distributed schedule-boards* is presented.

1 Introduction

Various natural and social systems, such as honeybee colonies, companies, sports games, or traffic facilities in a town, can be represented as a collection of groups of cooperating intelligent individuals (also called *autonomous agents*) [Decker 1987] [Hewitt 1983] [Huhns 1987] [Koestler 1978]. In such systems, each autonomous agent, which is a coarse-grained intelligent computational unit controlling its own execution, solves its local or partial problems and cooperates with others to solve an entire problem given to their group or organization. One of the important issues in achieving such a dynamic and democratic organization is establishing a fundamental computational model.

Object-oriented concurrent computation [Hewitt 1977] [Yonezawa 1987] is one of the effective models for describing cooperating agents. Specifically, message passing is important in realizing communication. However, in object-oriented concurrent computing, a receiver usually obeys the incoming messages without considering whether the message should be executed or not. Additionally, an object does not communicate with multiple objects or a group of objects simultaneously. Thus, since the functions provided in object-oriented concurrent computing are simple and restricted, it is difficult to realize a multi-agent world or, alternatively, a democratic organization. In order to design a higher, abstracted model to represent such a multi-agent world, the following two issues in object-oriented concurrent computing have to be considered:

- **autonomy of an agent**

  An agent is naturally modeled as a concurrent object. However, when an object receives a message, it usually executes a method associated with the message without evaluating its meaning or the status of the agent, because it does not have a control mechanism for message execution. Therefore, an object is not considered to be *autonomous*. In order to realize *autonomy*, an object needs to have a function to control message execution while considering its internal state or environmental conditions.

- **a group of agents**

  In complex cooperation in the real world, an agent is considered to influence other agents by multicasting a message to a number of other agents at the same time. In addition, an agent sometimes sends a message to unknown agents as well. Such cooperating agents are considered to form a group in communication. Therefore, a mechanism for multicasting a message to a group of agents is required to realize *group communication*. The notion of a group of agents is important and is referred to as an *environment* in this paper.

In this paper, we will discuss principles for realizing these two functions and establish an *organizational model of computation* by adding these functions to object-oriented concurrent computing. First, we describe an autonomous agent model based on the concept of a concurrent object. Next, we describe a group model of autonomous agents using the notion of an environment. Thirdly, an example of the *distributed schedule-boards* is presented using the organizational model of computation. Additionally, an implementation of the model is also described. Finally, comparisons to related work, and directions for future research are discussed.

2 The Autonomous Agent Model

An agent can be easily represent as a concurrent object. However, an object is not an autonomous entity, and the following requirements are necessary for realizing an autonomous agent:

- In asynchronous systems, the order of message arrivals from different agents is not guaranteed. Thus, an autonomous agent has to deal with arrival messages in any order.
- Though an object usually obeys an incoming message, an autonomous agent needs to evaluate the message before its execution because the agent has to keep its internal consistency to process its task.

These requirements can be summarized by saying that an agent has to control its behavior while considering incoming messages and the agent's internal state. In order to fulfill the requirements, a *message-interpreter* is combined with a concurrent object to make an autonomous agent.

2.1 An Agent Machine

The structure of an agent resembles that of a concurrent object. The internal structure of an agent machine is shown in Fig.1. An agent has one message queue and several methods. The biggest difference between an agent and a concurrent object is that an agent has its own message-interpreter, which manages *messages* in the message queue, *tasks*, and *protocols* while keeping internal consistency. The main role of a message-interpreter is to maintain the message queue.

We will use the example of a cyclic-buffer-agent to discuss the autonomy of an agent. The cyclic-buffer-agent class is defined as shown in Fig.2, which is almost identical to that of object-oriented programming languages [Goldberg 1983]. An instance is created from

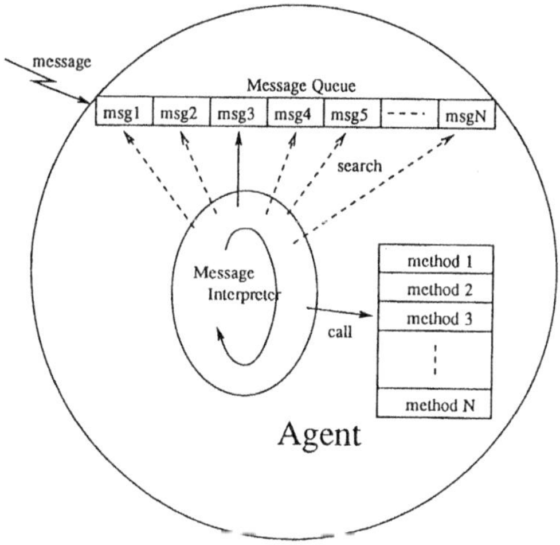

Fig.1. The definition of an agent machine

```
(defagent  cyclic-buffer-agent
           (super-agents        agent)
           (instance-variables
                (state          'empty)
                (top            0)
                (bottom         0)
                (buffer-size    10)
                (buffer         (make-array 10))))

(defmethod  put  ((self cyclic-buffer-agent) value)
   (setf (aref (@ buffer) (@ top)) value)
   (incf (@ top))
   (if (>= (@ top) (@ buffer-size))
       (setf (@ top) 0))
   (if (buffer-full? self)
       (setf (@ state) 'full)
       (setf (@ state) 'enough)))

(defmethod  get  ((self cyclic-buffer-agent))
   (prog (retval)
         (setq retval (aref (@ buffer) (@ bottom)))
         (incf (@ bottom))
         (if (>= (@ bottom) (@ buffer-size))
             (setf (@ bottom) 0))
         (if (buffer-empty? self)
             (setf (@ state) 'empty)
             (setf (@ state) 'enough))
         (return retval)))
```

Fig.2. The definition of cyclic-buffer-agent class

the class by specifying its message-interpreter as follows:

```
(setq  instance
       (new  ($$ cyclic-buffer-agent) #'buffer-interpreter 'name1))
```

The created agent has its own interpreter, `buffer-interpreter`, and a unique name, such as `name1`. One agent can send a message to another by specifying the target's name as follows:

```
(send  name-of-target-agent  a-message)
```

2.2 Message Interpreter

When an agent is created, its message-interpreter starts to execute. When a message arrives at an agent, the message causes an interrupt to be added into the message queue. The message-interpreter searches for an important message in the queue, retrieves it, and invokes suitable methods. This message selection mechanism realizes the autonomy of an agent.

We will discuss the autonomy of an agent using an instance of cyclic-buffer-agent class. A task assigned to a cyclic-buffer-agent is to keep values in the internal buffer. A cyclic-buffer-agent processes its task by accepting `:put` or `:get` messages. Because the agent has a finite-sized buffer, `:put` or `:get` messages cause errors when the buffer is `full` or `empty`, respectively. The reason can be seen in the state transition diagram of the agent illustrated in Fig.3. In order to avoid errors, the agent should not process `:put` or `:get` messages when it is `full` or `empty`. This behavior is considered part of the agent's autonomy and is written in the message-interpreter as shown in Fig.4. In the figure, `<-` is a macro for calling an internal method, and `@` is a macro for referencing an instance variable. This example of a cyclic-buffer-agent shown that message selection and method invocation are important for realizing the autonomy of an agent. As a result, the message-interpreter can control the behavior of an agent and realize an autonomous agent.

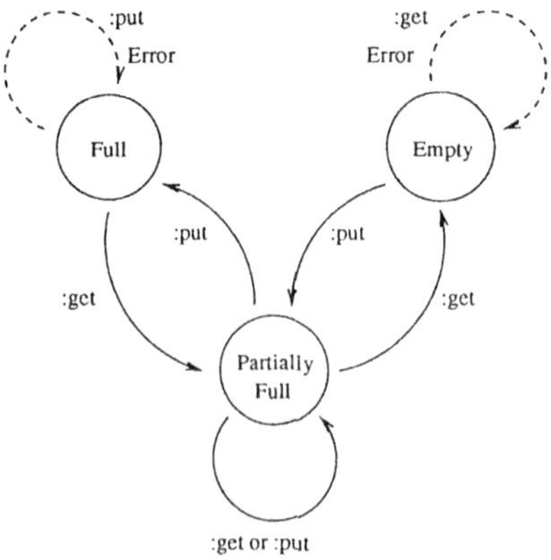

Fig.3. A state transition diagram of a cyclic-buffer-agent's task

```
(def-interpreter  buffer-interpreter
                  ((self cyclic-buffer-agent))
  (prog ((flag t))

     (while flag

        (RECEIVE-IF
            (AND (eval (not (eq (@ state) 'full)))
                 (put))
            (THEN
                 (<- self :put (@ (msg-ref 0) value))))

        (RECEIVE-IF
            (AND (eval (not (eq (@ state) 'empty)))
                 (get))
            (THEN
                 (SEND (@ (msg-ref 0) target)
                       (msg-def reply
                           (value (<- self :get)))))))))
```

Fig.4. A message-interpreter of a cyclic-buffer-agent

2.3 Functions used in Message-Interpreter

The basic and important role of a message-interpreter is to manage a message queue. As shown in the example of the cyclic-buffer-agent, the message-interpreter searches for the messages by considering the state transition diagram of the assigned task. In order to search for a message in the message queue, the following primitive operations are provided:

- `(receive)`

  This primitive retrieves the first message in the message queue and returns it. If there are no messages in the message queue, this operation does not wait for a incoming message and returns `nil`.

- `(receive-block)`

  This primitive is a blocked version of `receive`. When this primitive is called from a message-interpreter, and there are not any messages in the message-queue, this primitive waits until the arrival of the next incoming message.

- `(receive-peek)`

  This primitive just peeks at the first message in the message queue. Thus, even if this primitive returns a message, the message is still in the message queue.

- `(receive-put-back` *message*`)`

  This primitive puts the *message* back to the end of the message-queue.

- `(message-queue-length)`

  This primitive returns the current number of messages in the message-queue.

- `(receive-if` *conditions actions*`)`

  This primitive searches the message-queue, and fetches the first message that satisfies *conditions*, and then executes *actions*.

- `(receive-if-all` *conditions actions*`)`

  This primitive is an extended version of `receive-if`. While the `receive-if` finds only the first message found in the message-queue, `receive-if-all` searches and collects all the messages satisfying the given *conditions* and makes a list of collected messages, and then executes *actions*.

In object-oriented concurrent computing, because a message is associated with a method, it is difficult to represent the processing of more than one message at the same time. For instance, consider the situation where a customer wants to buy a product from a company by sending money through a bank. A customer sends an `order-message` to a company and a `remittance-message` to a bank, the latter specifying the amount of money to send and the company that should receive it. For the company, the arrival order of these two messages can not be evaluated and is not guaranteed, so two possible scenarios must be handled: the `order-message` is faster than the `remittance-message`, and the opposite case. It is not easy to represent this kind of autonomy of a company agent in traditional object-oriented concurrent programming languages.

When using a message-interpreter, multiple messages can be processed using the operations `receive-if` or `receive-if-all`. Thus, the order of arrival messages is not important because two messages are not processed until the *conditions* in the expression is satisfied as follows:

```
(receive-if                            ;; searching in the message queue.
      (AND (eval (@ product-list))                 ;; there is a product.
           (order-message              ;; a message for an order.
                 (category      'an-order)
                 (task-id       ?taskid))
           (remittance-message         ;; a message for sending money.
                 (task-id       ?taskid)
                 (from          'a-bank)))
      (THEN
           (<- self :send-a-product-to-customer
                     (msg-ref 0) (msg-ref 1))))
```

The expressions `(msg-ref 0)` and `(msg-ref 1)` refer to the messages: `order-message` and `remittance-message`, which satisfied the given conditions.

A message-interpreter may be thought of as a scheduler that manages the execution of messages and provides autonomy to an agent. In this model, since there is only one activity in an agent, the methods in the same agent do not execute in parallel.

2.4 Inheritance

An agent class can inherit the internal structure and methods from super agent classes. In this model, an agent class may have multiple super agent classes as in many other object-oriented programming languages [Stefik 1986]. The inheritance chain is created in a depth-first left-to-right order. However, an agent does not inherit its message-interpreter from its super agents. Instead, an agent can have any message-interpreter that may be different from that of another agent, even if both agents are created from the same class. In a similar way, people may be said to possess some of the same functions (*instance variables* and *methods*) while their characters (*message-interpreters*) are different.

3 The Group Model of Autonomous Agents

In the real world, there are many cases where an agent can send a message not only to a single agent, but also to multiple agents at the same time. We have already demonstrated the effectiveness of broadcasting a message to multiple agents in the simulation of a school of fish [Maruichi 1987]. Broadcasting a message is considered to be similar to multicasting a message to the all the agents existing in the same environment, which is the place where agents exist. Using the notion of an environment, a group is represented and a message is multicasted to all the agents in the group.

A large organization such as a company can be represented as a collection of groups of agents. Fig.5 shows an example of groups of autonomous agents that represent the computer science department at our university. A dashed-line represents a group or an environment where agents exist, while a small circle represents an autonomous agent representing a professor or student. Agents existing in the same environment can be considered to form a group. As shown in the figure, an agent may belong to more than one group (or environment) at the same time. In the complex cooperation arising at a meeting or in group communication, a message, such as a voice or gesture, is transferred to multiple agents through the environment, and each agent processes the message and takes an action. Thus, the notion of a group of agents is needed in order to represent a multi-agent world such as a company or a democratic organization. The advantages of using the notion of an environment are:

- Since an agent does not need to specify all the names of targets to send a message, an agent becomes independent from other agents. As an agent just specifies the name of an environment (or a group of agents) to send a message, a school of fish or a flock of birds for example is easily represented.
- If an agent can enter/exit a group (or environment), dynamic and complex organizational schemes that include many groups can be easily modeled.

By using the notion of an environment, the message passing primitive **send** will be extended as discussed in the following section. Additionally, the other primitives for accessing an environment are presented.

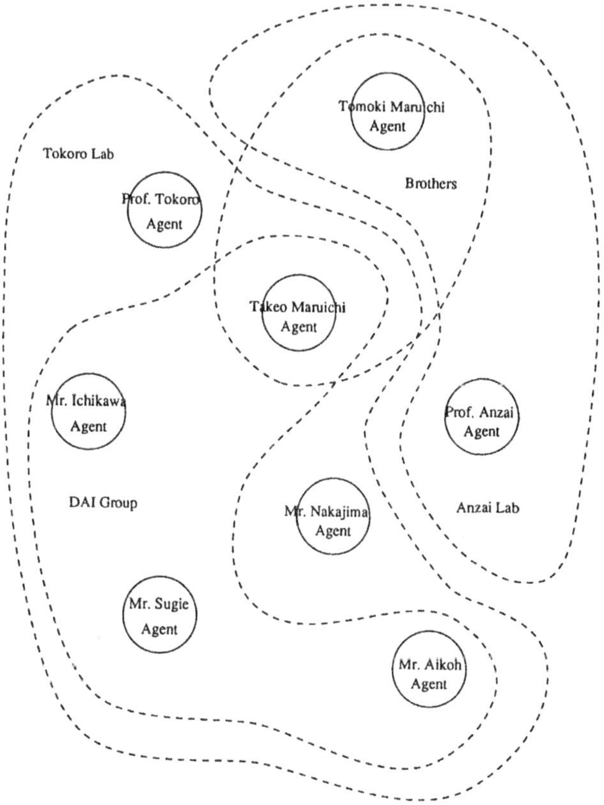

Fig.5. An example of groups of agents

3.1 Extended Send Operations

A **send** operation is used when an agent needs to send a message to a target by specifying the target's name. Though a **send** operation supports only point-to-point communication, the operation is extended to realize multicasting using the notion of an environment as follows:

- **(send-all** *environment-name message* **&key :except-me)**

  By specifying *environment-name*, an agent can send a message to all of the agents in the environment without specifying the names of particular targets. This is done by sending a message to an environment, where all the members of the specified environment receive the same message copied from the original message. This operation is illustrated in Fig.6. In the figure, agent **A** may be either in the environment or not. If agent **A** is in the environment without specifying the **:except-me** keyword, the message is sent to agent **A** as well. This function is performed as an atomic action and returns a list of names of agents which will receive the *message*.

- **(send-to** *environment-name agent-name message*)

  In addition to multicasting a message, an agent can send a message to one specified target. This is almost identical to point-to-point communication. This operation is realized by specifying the name of an environment, *environment-name*, and the name of the target agent, *agent-name*. If the *agent-name* does not exist in the *environment-name*, this function returns nil and does not send a message. This operation is also performed as an atomic operation and is illustrated in Fig.7. In the figure, again, agent **A** may be either in the environment or not.

Using an environment, group communication is realized by indirect message passing through an environment.

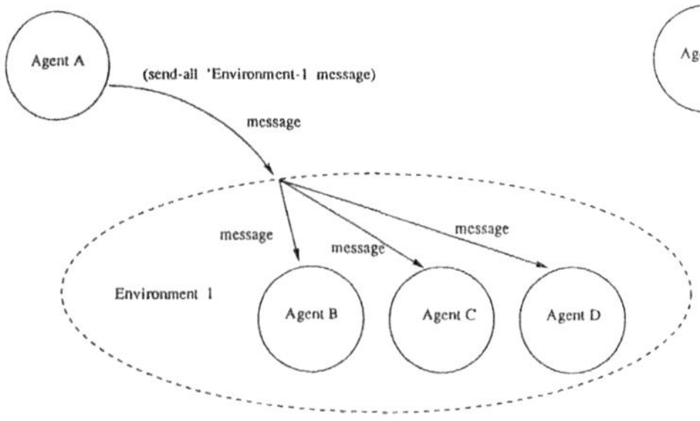

Fig.6. The send-all primitive

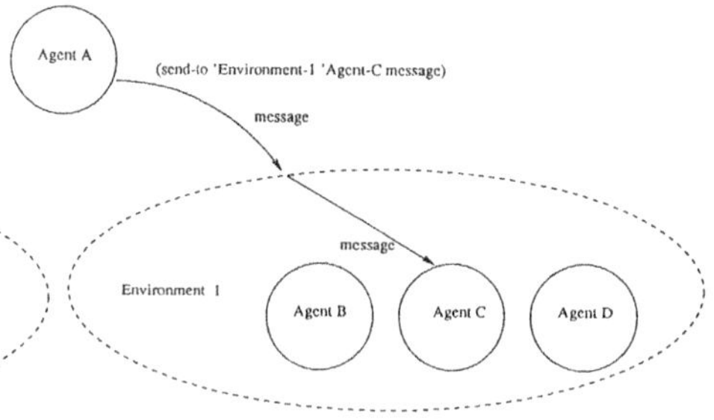

Fig.7. The send-to primitive

3.2 Creating/Deleting and Entering/Exiting an Environment

An environment can be created or deleted like an agent by using the following operations:

- `(new` *environment-class environment-name*`)`

  The environment named *environment-name* is created.

- `(destroy` *environment-name*`)`

  If the environment named by *environment-name* is empty, this function destroys the environment and returns `t`. If not, this function does nothing and returns `nil`.

One of the most important features of using the notion of an environment is that an agent can enter/exit an environment by itself. An agent can enter/exit an environment by specifying the name. In addition, some primitives are provided for getting information from an environment.

- `(enter` *agent environment-name*`)`

  An agent enters the environment named *environment-name*. After entering to the environment, *agent* receives any messages sent to the environment. If there is no *environment-name* in the system, this function returns `nil`.

- `(exit` *agent environment-name*`)`

  An agent exits the environment named *environment-name*. After exiting the environment, *agent* does not receive the messages sent to the environment, but may still receive messages sent directly to it.

- `(number-of-agents` *environment-name* `&key :except-me)`

  This function returns the number of agents in the environment. If the caller agent is in the environment and the `:except-me` key is specified, the agent is not counted.

- `(name-list-of-agents` *environment-name* `&key :except-me)`

  This function returns the list of names of agents in the environment. If the caller agent is in the environment and the `:except-me` key is specified, again, the agent is not contained in the list.

An agent can belong to more than one environment simultaneously. As a result, an organization which includes many environments and many autonomous agents can be represented, as in Fig.8. We call this model the *organizational model of computation* [Maruichi 1989], and it consists of three components: *(1) agents*, *(2) messages*, and *(3) environments*. Each autonomous agent influences others by sending a message to an environment, and is, in turn, influenced by receiving the messages sent to the environments to which it belongs.

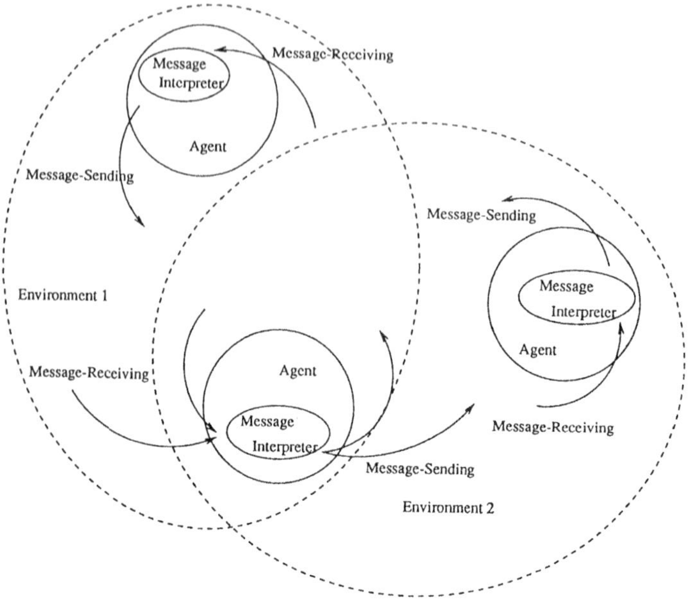

Fig.8. The organizational model of computation

4 Examples: Distributed Schedule-Board Agents

This section describes the methodology for representing organizational problem-solving using autonomous agents and their groups. In this section, we discuss a simple example of *distributed schedule-board agents*, where each autonomous agent cooperates with other agents to decide a meeting plan in a democratic style.

In the example of distributed schedule-boards, a user using a workstation has his own `schedule-board-agent` as shown in Fig.9. Each user can give a command to the agent in order to make a meeting plan by mutual agreement with other agents. Additionally, a meeting room is reserved. This kind of problem-solving is an instance of basic organizational problem-solving commonly found in many companies or committees [de Jong 1988]. The nature of this kind of problem-solving is that autonomous agents cooperate with others in a democratic style.

In order to achieve successful cooperation among agents, each agent must keep *protocols* to guide group communication (i.e., agents discussing the shared problem). Fig.10 shows the form of an organization that includes three schedule-boards and two meeting rooms. Each of the five agents belong either to a group named `office-environment` or to a group named `meeting-room-environment`.

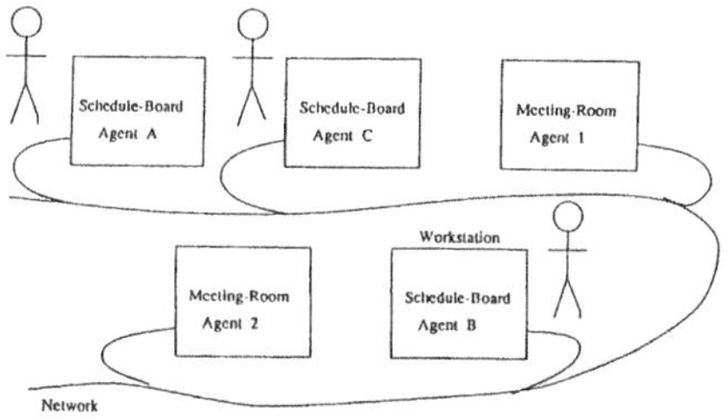

Fig.9. The distributed schedule-boards problem

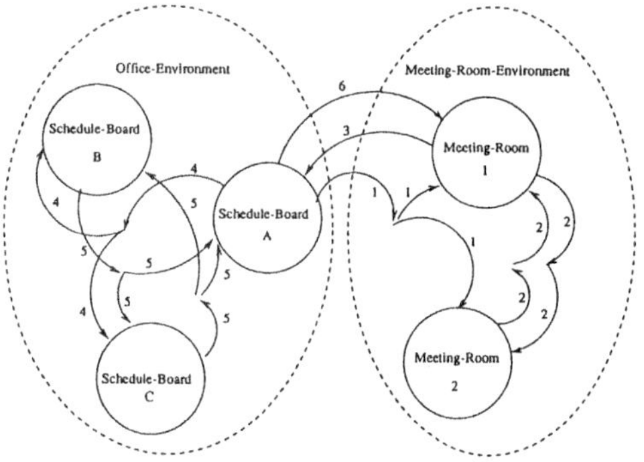

Fig.10. A representation of the distributed schedule-board-agents

4.1 Group Communication among Schedule-Board Agents

Consider the situation in which "Schedule-board-agent `A` wants to make a meeting plan with both B and C for four hours this week". As shown in Fig.10, schedule-board-agent `A` first looks for four hours in the local schedule-board and asks for `meeting-room-environment` to book the four hours (1). If any meeting-room-agent replies to `A` (3), `A` proposes the meeting plan to both `B` and `C` by multicasting a message into the **`office-environment`**(4). If `A` receives an **`OK-message`** from both `B` and `C`(5), `A` reconfirms the meeting room (6).

If `B` or `C` replies to `A` with a **`Not-OK-message`**, `A` will cancel the meeting-room and a new-leader is selected from the group, excluding `A`. Changing the leader in a group of autonomous agents is important for making a fair decision in a democratic organization. This mechanism is described in the agent's message-interpreter as shown in Fig.11. In this case, an agent who was not the leader is selected. In order to do this, all the agents in a group have to have the same evaluation functions.

In order to achieve successful cooperation, the behavior of an agent has to be guided by *protocols*. Specifically, in asynchronous systems, received messages have to be managed by the message-interpreter which keeps *protocols*. For instance, a protocol for cooperation among schedule-board agents is illustrated in Fig.12. In this figure, each arrow represents a message passing event.

4.2 Best Selection between Meeting-Room Agents

Meeting-room-agents are asked by the leader of schedule-board agents to check their local schedules and then to multicast the state message to others in the `meeting-room-environment` ((2) in Fig.10). Each agent can understand the others' state and decide whether it is the best available room or not (Fig.13). This algorithm is similar to that used in a group of schedule-board agents. In a group of meeting-rooms, there is not a group leader. However, each agent can make a decision as to whether or not it is the best available room because each agent has the same evaluation function for calculating a value which represents availability.

```
(def-interpreter  board-interpreter
                  ((self schedule-board))
  (prog ((alive t)
         stack leader answer agent-num leader-msg)

      (<- self :initialize)

      (while alive

         ;; My user let me make a new plan.
         (RECEIVE-IF
             (AND (eval (eq (@ state) 'Idle))
                  (meeting-request-msg
                        (category     'Make-A-Meeting-Plan)))
             (THEN
                  (<- self :look-for-a-meeting-room (msg-ref 0))
                  (setf (@ state) 'Wait-For-A-Room)))

         ;; I receive the reply from the selected free room.
         (RECEIVE-IF
             (AND (eval (eq (@ state) 'Wait-For-A-Room))
                  (room-plan-msg
                        (category     'Booking-And-Reply)))
             (THEN
                  (setq leader t)
                  (setq answer t)
                  (setq agent-num
                        (<- self :multicast-my-plan (msg-ref 0)))
                  (setf (@ state) 'Group-Discussion)))

         ;; I'll check each local schedule, if I am not a leader.
         (RECEIVE-IF
             (AND (eval (eq (@ state) 'Idle))
                  (meeting-request-msg
                     (category          'Propose-A-Meeting-Plan)))
             (THEN
                  (setq answer (<- self :check-my-plan (msg-ref 0)))
                  (setq agent-num (1- (length (@ (msg-ref 0) to))))
                  (setq leader-msg (msg-ref 0))
                  (setf (@ state) 'Group-Discussion)))

         ;; I'm collecting the replies from other members.
         (RECEIVE-IF
             (AND (eval (eq (@ state) 'Group-Discussion))
                  (meeting-request-msg
                        (category     'Accept-Or-Refuse-The-Plan)))
             (THEN
              (push (msg-ref 0) stack)
              (if (eq (length  stack) agent-num)
                  (then
                    (if (null leader) (push leader-msg stack))
                    (setf (@ state) 'Idle)
                    (if (and (everybody-say-yes? stack) answer)
                        (then
                          (if leader
                              (<- self :reconfirm (msg-ref 0)))
                          (<- self :accept (msg-ref 0)))
                        (else
                          (if leader
                              (<- self :cancel (msg-ref 0)))

                          (if (<- self :should-I-make-new-plan?
                                    leader-msg stack)
                              (then
                                 (<- (@ window) :print-line
                                             "I BECOME A LEADER....!")
                                 (<- self :look-for-a-meeting-room
                                          (msg-ref 0))
                                 (setf (@ state) 'Wait-For-A-Room)))))
                    (setq leader nil)
                    (setq leader-msg nil)
                    (setq stack nil))))))

      (<- self :finish)))
```

Fig.11. The message-interpreter of a schedule-board-agent

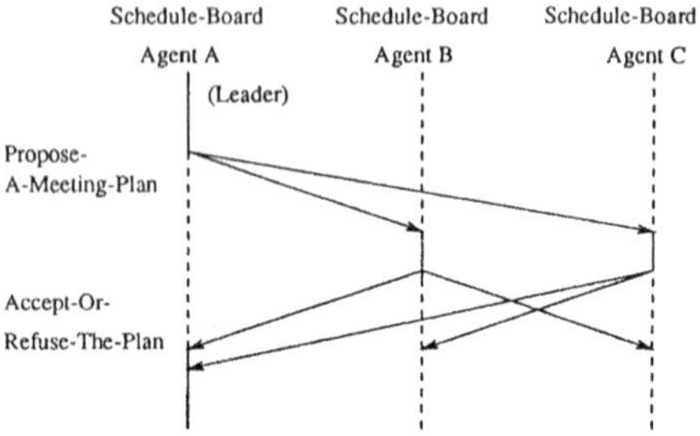

Fig.12. A protocol used in a group of schedule-board-agents

```
(def-interpreter  room-interpreter
                  ((self meeting-room))
  (prog ((alive t) stack reply-target)

      (<- self :initialize)

      (while alive

         ;; When I am asked to be free or not, ...
         (RECEIVE-IF
             (AND (eval (eq (@ state) 'Idle))
                  (room-plan-msg
                        (category 'Room-Request)))

             (THEN      ; I will check my schedule and reply.

                  (setq reply-target (@ (msg-ref 0) from))
                  (<- self :check-and-inform-the-plan
                           (msg-ref 0))
                  (setf (@ state) 'Group-Discussion)))

         ;; I compare my schedule with other's schedule.
         (RECEIVE-IF
             (AND (eval (eq (@ state) 'Group-Discussion))
                  (room-plan-msg
                        (category 'Room-Information)))
             (THEN
                  (push (msg-ref 0) stack)
                  (if (all-messages-received? stack)
                      (then
                         (if (<- self :should-I-reply? stack)
                             (then
                                (setf (@ state) 'Booking)
                                (<- self :reply-to-target
                                         (msg-ref 0) reply-target))
                             (else
                                (setf (@ state) 'Idle)))
                         (setq stack nil)))))

         ;; I'm waiting for the reservation, because of booking.
         (RECEIVE-IF
             (AND (eval (eq (@ state) 'Booking))
                  (room-plan-msg
                     (category 'room-reservation)))
             (THEN
                  (<- self :reserve-this-room (msg-ref 0))
                  (setf (@ state) 'Idle))))

      (<- self :finish)))
```

Fig.13. The message-interpreter of a meeting-room-agent

4.3 Experimental Result

Fig.14 shows an interaction among five autonomous agents in the example described in the preceding section. Each arrow represents an asynchronous message passing event, and the vertical line represents the passage of five agents. In the figure, A, as a leader, first manages a group discussion with B and C. However, the first plan is not accepted by either B or C. Next, B becomes the new leader and suggests a meeting plan, which is accepted by the others.

Fig.15 shows the screen snapshot displaying the agent's schedule. The upper three windows are displayed by the three schedule-board agents in the group `office-environment`. In addition, the lower two windows are displayed by the two meeting-room agents in the group `meeting-room-environment`. In each schedule's time-table, a white rectangle represents a private schedule, while a black rectangle represents a group's meeting schedule.

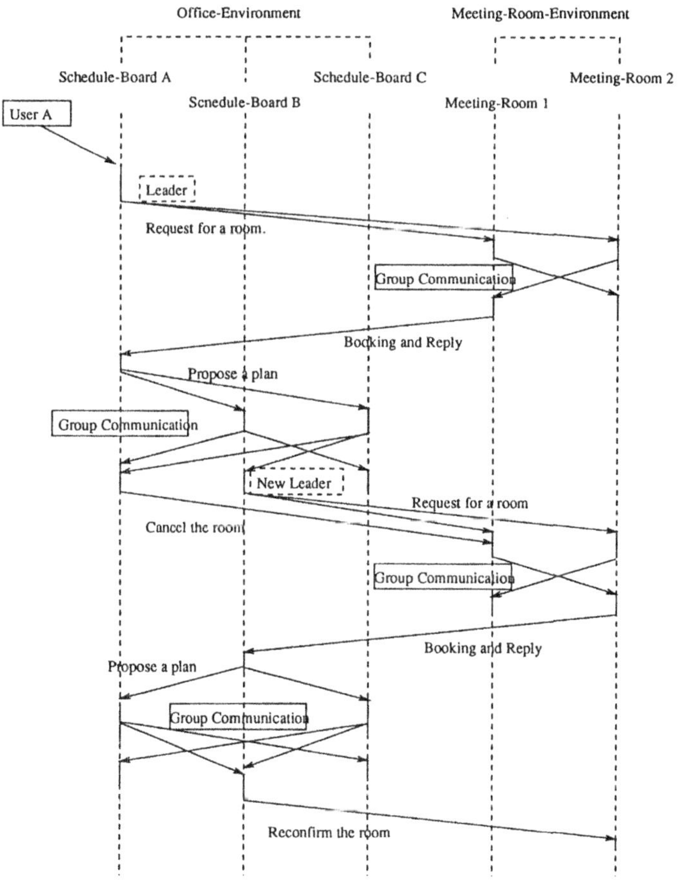

Fig.14. Interactions among agents along the time axis

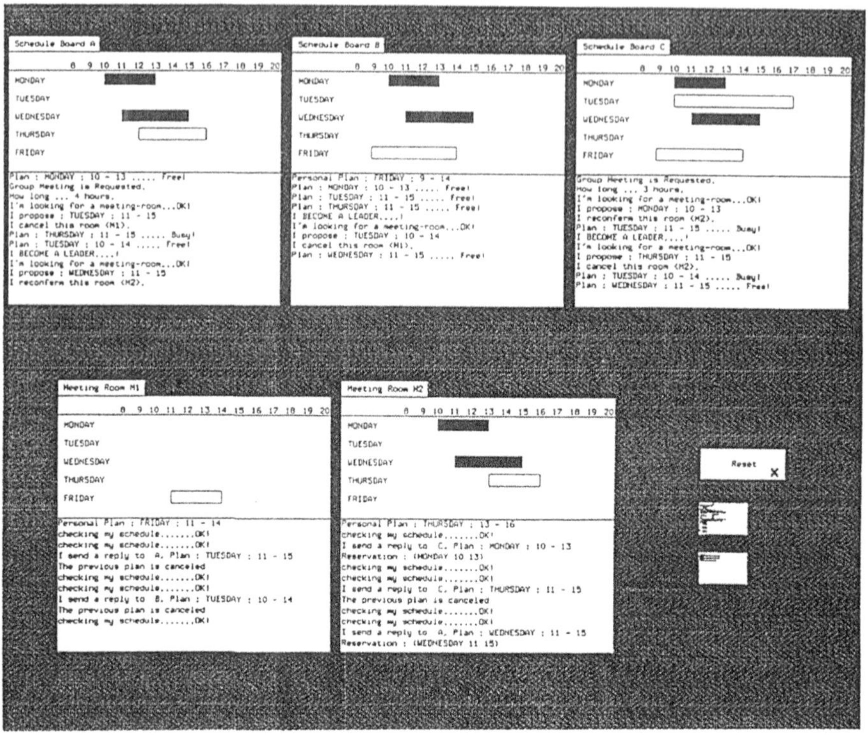

Fig.15. A screen snapshot

5 Implementation

This section describes an implementation of autonomous agents and environments in an object-oriented concurrent computing system. In order to realize the organizational model of computation, three components (agents, messages, and environments) are required, and these are represented as three kinds of objects:

- **agent** - an active object which is assigned to a processor and whose message-interpreter is always running.
- **message** - a passive object that is transferred from a sender to one or more receivers.
- **environment** - a passive object that is referred by an agent and contains a name-list that keeps the names of agents.

The organizational model of computation is implemented on the object-oriented programming system called PANDORA-II, which is implemented on KCL [Yuasa 1985]. PANDORA-II runs on a single workstation, but connects to other PANDORA-IIs running on different hosts. Thus, an environment can be extended over the network.

5.1 Distributed Implementation

In order to implement the organizational model of computation, the names of environments and agents are assumed to be unique in the network. An environment may exist over several PANDORA-IIs connected by the network. When an environment is created on any host, the environment becomes a server and the name of that environment is sent to other hosts. If an agent on the different host enters the remote environment, the name of the agent is sent to the remote environment and kept in its name-list. Using this mechanism, an environment can be extended over many hosts.

For instance, Fig.16 shows the environments shared by agents running on three different hosts: **host-1**, **host-2**, **host-3**. In this case, agents called a, b, c exist in the **host-1**, but **environment-1** contains a, c, h. Each agent knows that actually there are three agents in **environment-1**.

Not only operations **enter** and **exit**, but also other operations such as **send-all** or **send-to** are extended for the distributed environment. To send a message through the remote environment, it is sent to the environment, copied, and sent to all the agents in the environment.

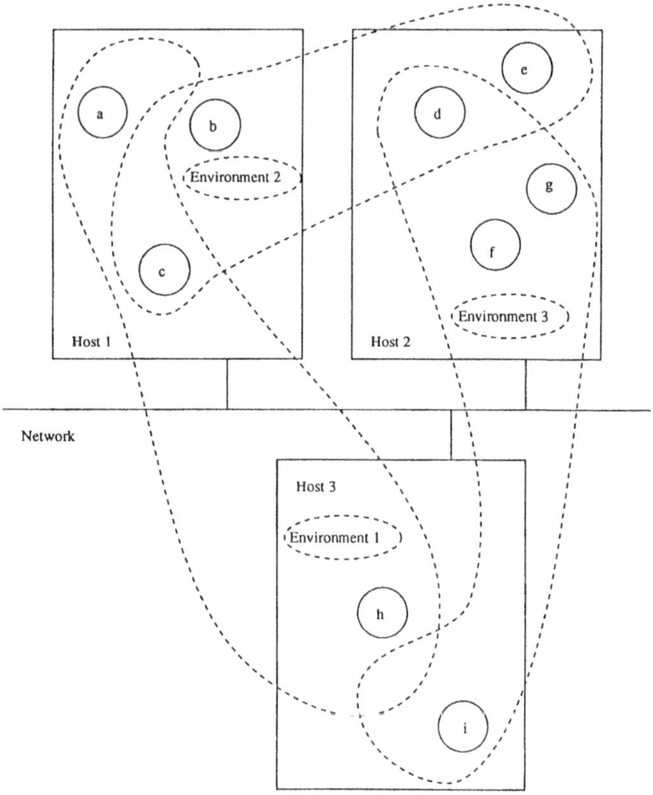

Fig.16. Distributed implementation

6 Discussion

As an organization, committee, or team which is actually made up of groups of autonomous agents, an autonomous agent model and a group model presented in this paper are effective for representing such a multi-agent world. In this section, we compare these two features in the organizational model of computation to related work.

6.1 Autonomous Agents vs. Concurrent Objects

In the actor model [Hewitt 1977], the order of message arrivals is not guaranteed even if those messages are sent from the same actor. If the order of messages needs to be rearranged, a *serializer* is used.

A *meta object* [Maes 1987] [Watanabe 1988] is an object that is in the meta-level of an object, and controls the object from the meta-level. The purpose of a meta object is to modify the behavior of an object.

Both a *serializer* and a *meta object* can be used as a message-interpreter in order to realize the autonomy of an object. However, these are conceptually different objects from the controlled object. The difference between these models and our agent model is that in our model a message-interpreter is an internal mechanism of an agent. In spite of this difference, a meta object or a serializer can have a meta-meta object or a serialized serializer in a recursive style, while a message-interpreter does not have another interpreter. As a result, the nature of a message-interpreter should be easy for programmers to understand and implement.

6.2 Environments vs. Other Communication Mechanisms

In order to achieve complex cooperation, agents need to communicate with each other. Communication between autonomous agents is done in several ways, *environments* presented in this paper being one of these ways. This section classifies communication styles used in previous models or systems for comparison with an environment.

The actor model is one of the important concurrent object models that provides a message passing mechanism which is a communication method to construct asynchronous systems. A message-passing mechanism provides point-to-point communication and does not require a shared medium.

Cammarata's *Distributed Air Traffic Control* [Cammarata 1983] is a distributed planning problem consisting of a simulated airspace with planes arriving at various airports located within the air space. In order to avoid collisions in the airspace, each airplane communicates with the others in turn by specifying its name because only point-to-point communication is supported.

Lesser's *Distributed Vehicle Monitoring Testbed* [Lesser 1983] sets up a simulated environment with moving vehicles that make sounds which can be picked up by acoustic sensors. Processing is done in a generic blackboard architecture partitioned into levels such as "signal," "group," "vehicle," and "pattern." Since each knowledge source communicates with others via the blackboard, synchronization is required between knowledge sources.

Table 1: A comparison of communication and control between multi agents

name	*agent*		*communication*		
	type	*creation*	*control*	*mechanism*	*synchronization*
Distributed Air Traffic Control	process	static	passive	one way, point to point	asynchronous
Distributed Vehicle Monitoring Testbed	knowledge source	static	active	bidirectional, shared medium (blackboard)	synchronous
Contract Nets	process	static	active	one way, broadcast	asynchronous
Scientific Community Metaphor	daemon	dynamic	passive	one way, broadcast	asynchronous
Business Applications by Ubik	actor	dynamic	passive	one way, point to point	asynchronous
Distributed Behavior Simulation	actor	dynamic	passive	one way, broadcast	asynchronous
Tuple Space Computational Model	process	static	active	bidirectional, shared memory	synchronous
The Organizational Model of Computation	agent	dynamic	semi-active	one way, multicast	asynchronous

Contract Nets [Davis 1983] is the most common functionally accurate negotiation-style protocol. The basic architecture is comprised of nodes with *manager* and *contractor* roles; any node can be at any one time both a manager and a contractor for different tasks. This protocol consists of three steps: *announce*, *bid*, and *contract*. Though broadcasting is used to announce a task, each node has to respond actively to the manager to get the task.

Scientific Community Metaphor [Kornfeld 1981] is one of the organizational problem solving models for highly parallel systems. An individual called *a sprite* behaves as a daemon that communicates with others by broadcasting in the scientific community. *Sprites* are organized around general problem-solving goals. Since the role of a sprite is already defined, a sprite does not have any chance to change the course of problem solving. The most important feature of a scientific community metaphor is that only broadcast communication is used.

Ubik [de Jong 1988] is based on an actor model of computation and is a programming system to design business organizations or applications. Ubik consists of a basic computational object called a *Ubik configurator* that sends messages by *output* operations in parallel, and each receives message by *input* operations. Communication between Ubik configurators is done in point-to-point style.

[Maes 1987] Maes, P., *Concepts and Experiments in Computational Reflection,* in Proceedings of OOPSLA-87, 1987.

[Maruichi 1987] Maruichi, T., Uchiki, T., and Tokoro, M., *Behavioral Simulation Based On Knowledge Objects,* in Proceedings of ECOOP-87, 1987.

[Maruichi 1989] Maruichi, T., *Organizational Computation,* Ph.D thesis, Keio University, 1989.

[Reynolds 1987] Reynolds, C., *Flocks, Herds, and Schools : A Distributed Behavioral Model,* in Proceedings of SIGGRAPH-87, 1987.

[Stefik 1986] M. Stefik, and D. Bobrow, *Object-Oriented Programming : themes and variations,* The AI Magazine, Vol.6 No.4, pages 40-62, Winter 1986.

[Watanabe 1988] Watanabe, T., and Yonezawa, A., *Reflection in an Object-Oriented Concurrent Language,* in Proceedings of OOPSLA-88, 1988.

[Yonezawa 1987] Yonezawa, A., Shibayama, E., Takada, T., and Honda, Y., *Modeling and Programming in an Object-Oriented Concurrent Language ABCL/1,* in Object Oriented Concurrent Programming, A.Yonezawa and M.Tokoro, eds, MIT Press, 1987.

[Yuasa 1985] Yuasa, T. and Hagiya, M., *Kyoto Common Lisp Report,* Kyoto University, 1985.

DECENTRALIZED A.I.
Yves DEMAZEAU & Jean-Pierre MÜLLER (Eds.)

EXPERIENCES ON SEMI-AUTONOMOUS USER AGENTS

Heikki HÄMMÄINEN, Jari ALASUVANTO, Risto MÄNTYLÄ

Department of Computer Science
Helsinki University of Technology
Espoo, Finland

The objective of user agents is to support users in the execution of cooperative multilateral tasks. The interest in extending agent systems with various automated features is increasing along the fast developing communication networks.

This paper first identifies the basic characteristics of user agents agents and presents a coarse classification for some existing implementations. The same framework is then employed in describing experiences on building and using semi-autonomous user agents to manage semi-automated office tasks. The experiments are based on agents constructed with an agent shell called PAGES which is used as a reference system throughout the text. The work described is part of the DIMUN* project which investigates the potential benefits of integrated communication networks in industrial applications.

1. INTRODUCTION

The term *agent* is often used of separate entities, e.g. computer processes, able to cooperate with other similar entities in some rational way. Correspondingly, agents representing human users and supporting them in their cooperation with other users are referred to as *user agents*. When such agents operate asynchronously and concurrently on several tasks, with several other agents, with incomplete knowledge about the environment, and without the continuous attendance of users, they fall into the category of *semi-autonomous user agents*.

Considering the current state-of-the-art in offices, any office tasks that are well-structured, i.e. programmable, and cost-effective to automate, are likely to be already computerized. Consequently, the research is being focused on the integration of a variety of semi-structured tasks which have not been technically possible or cost-effective to automate until recently. Semi-automated user agents are widely seen as a promising new approach in this field.

From the user's point of view, an ideal user agent is able to handle tasks resembling those of a human secretary. The agent should complete routine tasks on its own and pass others appropriately to the user. Typical routine tasks include, for instance, fixing dates for meetings, filtering mail, responding to well-defined requests, and keeping track of pending activities. These tasks tend to be partially different for each user implying that agents should be adaptable to specific tasks according to the user requirements.

When considering the modeling of a system which associates users with computational agents, the collaborative patterns of human societies are a natural basis [4, 8]. For instance,

---

* Distributed Manufacturing Using Existing and Developing Public Networks [5]. DIMUN is a pilot project (R1039) in the RACE programme [25] sponsored by the Commission of the European Communities.

the organization amongst the agents is dynamic, adapting itself to the requirements of the changing human organization. Further, instead of being homogeneous, agents possess some specific skills representing the expertise of their users. The degree of benevolence, which specifies the nature of cooperation between agents, can be derived from the user side as well; if the user or his role within the organization requires accommodative behaviour, his agent is also expected to support that pattern. Even the personal and organizational goals of the user are to some extent reflected in the tasks of his agent. However, the involvement of agents is likely to remain modest regarding the achievement of the goals, since (1) several goals, e.g. the optimal allocation of working hours, cannot be easily defined in formal terms and (2) several negotiation acts, e.g. face-to-face meetings, tend to by-pass agents.

Notably, the partial automation of user agents raises some intriguing questions concerning the imitation of human intellect. The attempt to distinguish whether an invisible dialogue partner is a man or a machine has traditionally been considered as the touchstone for artificial intelligence. In some sense, user agents turn this problem into a very practical one, because messages are assumed to be more or less understandable to users and their agents at the same time. For instance, the user may not know whether a structured request or response arriving from another agent was created manually or automatically. The relevance of this knowledge, of course, depends on the application. Let us consider e.g. the existing automatic voice-based calling and answering machines attached to telephones - the half done imitation of human interaction may create confusion.

We explore the opportunities and constraints of user agents by reviewing different existing approaches and by discussing some experiments implemented with PAGES agents [12]. Although the primary objective of user agents is to support users interactively, our discussion concentrates on the autonomous aspects of semi-automated agents.

2. DIFFERENT APPROACHES

The table below (fig. 1) classifies agent implementations according to selected criteria for the underlying model, agent concept, and message paradigm. Instead of aiming at a complete analysis, the chosen systems and criteria are biased to expose interesting contrasts. In particular, our simplified evaluation may appear unjust to some systems, because certain features would deserve a more sophisticated assessment than the plain existence.

The table identifies some obvious categories of agents. The X.400/MHS user agent [32] and the ODA editor [16], as specified in the current standards, belong to the simple *manual agents* which help users to interchange human readable messages. The administrative applications based on EDIFACT converters [17] operate as simple *integrated agents* in the inter-system messaging. The KMMS [2] and ISCREEN [24] agents are *mail filters* specialized on the automatic interpretation of human readable text messages. The AMIGO [18], FMN [29] and Coordinator [31] systems apply *coordination agents* to manage explicitly modeled communication tasks and office procedures. The Information Lens [21], Object Lens [19] and PAGES [12] systems employ *semi-automated agents* in managing combinations of human and agent readable messages. The Imail (Intelligent Mail) [11], Envoy [9] and PAGES systems extend the agent model by exploiting programmable messages as *mobile agents* between user agents. The BOSS [13] and Contract Net [4] models consist of closed sets of *problem solving agents* which cooperate to fulfil their global mission.

Considering the aspects of collective problem solving, user agents typically deal with routine tasks and self-interested negotiations rather than well-structured distributed problems. Thus, they represent *decentralized* rather than *distributed* artificial intelligence [22], since (1) their goals are often conflicting and must be dynamically adapted to an existing organization, (2) their existence is not directly justified by the existence of other agents, (3) the granularity of the inter-agent interaction is relatively coarse, and (4) the agents operate with imperfect and changing knowledge about each other. Consequently, the interaction between user agents is likely to follow the principle of *direct messaging* rather than *shared memory.*

System / Model	X.400	ODA	EDIFACT	FMN	Mediator	Inf. Lense	Obj. Lense	KMMS	ISCREEN	Coordinator	PAGES	Imail	Envoy	Contract net	BOSS
Model															
• bilateral	x	x	x	x		x	x	x	x	x	x	x	x		
• multilateral				x	x		x				x	x	x	x	x
• negotiation					x					x	x			x	x
Agents															
• programmable			x	x	x	x	x	x	x		x		x	x	x
• specialized			x		x					x				x	x
Messages															
• natural language	x	x		x				x	x	x	x		x		
• structured (typed)		x	x	x	x	x	x				x		x	x	x
• programmable											x	x	x		
• types migrate											x				

FIGURE 1. A simplified classification of selected agent implementations.

Each system in our list captures some desired functional aspects of an ideal user agent. The system must cope with bilateral and multilateral cooperation in benevolent and non-benevolent mode. Agents must be user programmable to allow the flexible maintenance and specialization. These properties set notable requirements to the nature of the inter-agent messages. In the first place, messages must be readable to human users and to their agents, which forces a compromise between the use of natural language and structured message types [19]. The continuous evolution of user agents and their tasks makes the inter-agent migration of new message types and related knowledge necessary [12]. In some applications it seems useful to allow *programmed messages*, i.e. self-contained active objects, to travel between agents in accomplishing specific independent tasks [30].

The ability of an agent to execute proper actions as a response to a message depends on its ability to interpret the message within its local context. The problem of automated message handling can be classified into [26]: (1) linguistic analysis of natural language messages (2) knowledge-based analysis of natural language messages by using keywords, patterns, and context databases, and (3) standardized message types, e.g. ODA and EDIFACT. Linguistic analysis of natural language messages is a challenging approach, but because of the inherent complexity of the area the developments so far have been rather modest, see e.g. [24]. When aiming at advanced automated features in multi-agent operations, natural language seems to be comparatively fruitless. For this reason, our presentation concentrates on the assumption of strictly typed messages.

3. OVERVIEW OF PAGES SYSTEM

PAGES agents [12] are asynchronous, active, interactive, and user programmable. They cooperate by interchanging *form objects* through direct (inter-process) and indirect (electronic mail) communication links over local and public networks. The basic agent model is rather general and captures a variety of applications. Its objective is to provide a single abstraction for different categories of agents, i.e. personal agents, role agents, and organizational group agents. For instance, Ms. Smith operates her own user agent, but at the same time she may

Considering the typical personal and organizational contexts, however, the situation is often more favorable, because the receivers are able to classify most senders and their potential objectives in advance. On the other hand, the value of information depends greatly on its expectability, the most unexpected being the most valuable. This observation suggests that sophisticated guesses may become very costly. Thus, due to the semantic and pragmatic obscurity of messages, the automated operations remain as *information filters* rather than being initiators of some critical irreversible inter-agent procedures.

The objective of filters is to optimize the user's reading effort by deciding about forwarding, deletion, or preservation of messages. This requires a rough assessment of the significance of a message to the receiver. The knowledge employed in filtering can be considered consisting of the *social, economic* and *cognitive* aspects of information sharing as discovered in the organizational studies by, for instance, [21].

User agents clearly need to handle natural language, both as separate messages and as part of structured ones. To cope with natural language messages and ordinary mail senders in an open electronic mail network, PAGES agents hold a standard form class which turns incoming messages into standard forms, and vice versa. Consequently, rules can be applied on these messages like on any forms, except that the actual contents of a message resides in a single field as a bulk of text.

4.1.1. Social filtering

The social aspect of message filtering is based on the organizational relationship between the sender and the receiver instead of on the actual contents of messages. The practical exploitation of social factors requires that the user can identify the roles of important persons and groups and that this information is made available to his agent.

In PAGES, the problem is solved with forms containing information about classified senders and groups. These forms are accessible from the rules of other form classes.

Ex.
```
// Mail/Entrance: agent of a sales manager receiving messages from, e.g., customers
IF this.SenderGroup ("Customers") THEN
    this.MailOut ("SalesSecretary@myCompany")  // Forward to a secretary for closer inspection
    this.Delete                                // Local duplicate is not necessary
```

The example shows an entrance rule in the standard *Mail* class of a sales manager. The rule uses group information to identify the messages coming from customers and to forward them to a sales secretary. The usability of this approach clearly depends on the regularity of the mapping between the user groups and the objectives of their messages.

4.1.2. Economic filtering

Persons tend to apply some implicit cost-benefit comparisons as the basis of their message filtering. In addition to organizational aspects, these comparisons involve technical information such as the size of a message and the number of other recipients.

Ex.
```
// Mail/Entrance: the immediate prompting of brief, i.e. cheap, messages
IF this.Size < 200  THEN
    this.Open        // Open the message in a separate prompt window on the screen
```

However, the usability of the cost-benefit analysis based on the number of recipients is reduced by the trade-off between quality and personalization. A large group of recipients makes the message less personal and less valuable to an individual, but at the same time the large circulation motivates the sender to improve the quality of information, which increases its value to the receiver. Thus, it can be argued that rules ignoring the contents of messages are of weak nature.

4.1.3. Cognitive filtering

As opposed to the social and economic filtering aspects, the cognitive one is based on the identification of the message contents. When dealing with natural language, the rudimentary mechanisms employ simple keyword matching.

```
Ex.  // Mail/Entrance: sales manager's agent forwards customer complaints by looking for keywords
     IF this.SenderGroup ("Customers") and TextBody.HasPattern ("guarantee") THEN
          this.MailOut ("TechSupport")                    // Send to the technical staff
```

Filtering becomes more robust if the receiver can assume that the senders behave well and preserve some additional attributes, i.e. tag lines, in their response messages. Tags enable an agent to accurately match the messages belonging to a given conversation. The benefit from this is that rules can be better focused on expected responses. For instance, interrelated messages can be semantically linked to provide hypertext-like browsing mechanisms. The simple example below shows how the arriving message is automatically double-linked with the original request.

```
Ex.  Mail/Entrance: PAGES user communicating with an ordinary mail user
     IF TextBody.HasPattern ("TagLine:") THEN
          TagVariable = Text.AfterPattern ("TagLine:")  // Retrieve tag value, i.e., form id
          that = "Mail".TagVariable                     // Set 'that' to refer to the original question
     IF that.Exists THEN
          that.Write ("NextMail", this.Name)            // Set link from the question to this answer
          PreviousMessage = TagVariable                 // Set a field to refer to the question
```

If we further assume that it is possible to apply commonly agreed keywords and patterns in messages, stronger rules and automated responses can be incorporated. This approach can be illustrated with a mail server agent returning some information to authorized requestors.

```
Ex.  Mail/Entrance: an agent running as an information server for a certain research project
     IF TextBody.HasPattern ("Help") or TextBody.HasPattern ("help") THEN // Match a request
          that = "Mail"."HelpText"                  // 'that' refers to a help message
          that.MailOut (this.Sender)                // Return a copy of the help message
     IF Text.HasPattern ("Calendar") and this.SenderGroup ("Partners") THEN // Check the authorization
          that = "Mail"."DIMUNCalendar"             // 'that' refers to a project calendar
          that.MailOut (this.Sender)                // Return a copy of the calendar
```

The simplicity of this concept has gained some popularity. For instance, together with the anonymous file transfer, the public mail servers have become a widely used method in the Internet community for delivering heterogeneous information such as software, technical descriptions, and price lists.

The analysis of complex text messages and the automatic composition of tailored responses requires a multi-layered agent architecture and a library of response text fragments as described by, e.g. [26]. The main problem of the message analysis is that each agent must be carefully tuned for the expected user-specific spectrum of messages, which seems to be an inordinate effort regarding the level of the existing expert system tools in general. Moreover, the efficient processing of the rule bases and large glossaries requires significant computing resources.

4.2. Structured Messages

When dealing with free-text messages, the rule designer spends his effort in trying to characterize the message contents and the objectives of the sender. By adopting an agent readable structure, for instance a simple set of attribute-value pairs, the problem of message ambiguity becomes obsolete. The continuous spectrum of natural language messages is, in fact, restricted by making it discrete. Consequently, messages can be handled accurately in the rules attached to the corresponding types.

Ex. ProductOrder/Entrance: a salesman's agent filtering customer orders

```
IF ProductId == 132 and OrderedQuantity > 100 THEN      // Match an expensive order
    that.MailOut ("salesManager")                       // Forward it to manager
```

The notion of *message type*, or form class in the case of PAGES, simplifies the lexical, syntactic, semantic and pragmatic interpretation of messages. Typical message types for user agents can be derived from the general classification of human communication acts [27]: *directive* (request to act), *assertive* (request to confirm an act), *commissive* (promise to act), *declaration* (confirm an act), and *expressive* (express a state of affairs). If these categories are refined into sufficiently detailed application-specific message types, the rule programmer may concentrate on organizing the effective domain knowledge and operations instead of trying to recognize messages. The experiments of Malone et al. indicate that a comparatively small set of common message types may significantly improve the efficiency of organizational message handling [21]. The wide exploitation of shared message types requires, of course, notable efforts on the sound standardization of the hierarchical message taxonomy. As a practical drawback, the structured types must be known to both the sending and receiving users, wherefore a high degree of uniformity is required from the software of the interacting agents.

Manually oriented systems such as the Coordinator model [31] generally employ a minimal fixed set of types, whereas active systems such as the Information Lens [21] and Strudel systems [28] provide inheritance-based hierarchies of message types. The PAGES type mechanism differs from the Lens system by assuming an open network where the agents cannot share a centralized type storage. Types are shared through explicit inter-agent interchange.

The interchange of knowledge encapsulated into form classes introduces the problem of a common knowledge representation scheme and a knowledge interchange protocol [15]. As a generalized problem this would be very difficult to solve. Instead, in PAGES knowledge conversion is not a major issue, since agents are based on the same software and know the same specialized rule language.

4.3. Programmed Messages

Traditionally, active agents interchange passive messages. Another field of applications, however, is captured by viewing messages as active programmable objects or "mobile agents" which migrate between immobile user agents. Such objects can carry and gather information, and make decisions about their routing and appearance. This approach involves some analogy with the conventional office forms which tend to migrate from one person to another while being filled out. Although migrating objects involve significant security problems, it can be argued that some aspects such as synchronization, consistency, recovery, and exceptions in general are best handled by the individual message objects [6].

The nature of migration systems is largely characterized by the granularity of message objects. Migrating objects can be for instance Unix shell processes [11], Smalltalk objects [9], Zetalisp objects [30], or standard form objects as in PAGES. Regardless of the implementation techniques, objects consist of some *private variables*, *internal rules*, and *interface functions*.

The basic components of migration models are (1) the local object-agent interaction and (2) the global coordination between a user agent and its objects migrating elsewhere. Notably, migration extends the notion of object identity with object ownership, i.e. each active object belongs to somebody. Moreover, the safety of user agents requires that objects can prove their origin through authentication and that proper authorization mechanisms and run-time monitoring reduce the risk of misuse.

4.3.1. Local Interaction

The local interaction, or dynamic coupling, between arbitrary foreign objects and user agents occurs within the limits of the imperfect knowledge they have about each other. In a simple case, the agent provides an abstract machine which enables the migrating object to run and interact with the user. In more sophisticated applications, both parties may access each other through some standard interface functions, either in read-only or read-write mode. The initiative tends to be biased in favor of the migrating object, because its designer may employ some knowledge about the services of other agents whereas the users of agents are inherently ignorant about the objectives of foreign objects.

In PAGES, migrating objects consist of a form class and its instance which migrate together. This is normally the way to transfer knowledge, i.e. class definitions, between agents, but the same mechanism supports programmable messages provided that the users have enabled the automatic introduction of new form classes in their agents. The form-agent interaction is based on the standard rule language and the interface functions common to all forms and agents.

Ex.
```
// CircularLetter/Automatic:  currently in the agent of one of the users in the circulation list
IF agent.Today > MyArrivalDate + 1 THEN   // Stay for at most one day within each user agent
        VisitNext = VisitNext + 1         // Set counter to point to the next user of the address list
        this.MailOut (AddressList(VisitNext))  // Go to the next user
IF agent.Today > Deadline THEN            // Return after deadline, regardless of the current location
        this.MailOut (this.Creator)       // Return to the originator
```

The rules above characterize the time constraints of an interactive circular letter, e.g. a collector of opinions, performing its autonomous mission. The standard interface of agents allows the retrieval of information such as the current date and location which the form needs in its spatio-temporal decisions. On the other hand, agents may use standard functions to access forms. Technically, the interaction between the migrating and local forms is possible, but to reduce the problems of security and complexity that coupling is normally disabled.

4.3.2. Global Coordination

The user who initiates migration needs to preserve some global control over the location and state of his mobile objects. This inherently centralized coordination is often implemented with special immobile monitor objects, e.g. *overseers* [6] or *heads* [30], which control the migrating objects by maintaining loose contact with them. A number of policy questions in this coordination scheme must be answered for each application such as, which data should be carried along with the object as opposed to being stored at the initiating agent or being stored redundantly at several agents. Similarly, should the rules be carried along with an object as opposed to being executed remotely or duplicated at multiple agents.

In PAGES, all information appears as forms; migrating objects are complete application-specific forms with rules and data, whereas the monitor objects and the coordination messages are forms of standard classes known to all agents. This approach implies that (1) the coordination forms flowing between a monitor form and its migrating target form consist of plain data and that (2) the monitor forms of a given agent are able to present a uniform up-to-date overview of its migrating forms. The standard information contains the path of each form, i.e. a list of agents and dates.

5. NEGOTIATION PARADIGMS

We define a *negotiation* as a coordinated goal-oriented set of message interchanges between user agents. A consistent negotiation proceeds from a start state into a well-defined end state so that the process involves a finite set of agents, message types, and messages. Considering the message paradigms described above, we assume here that negotiations employ structured

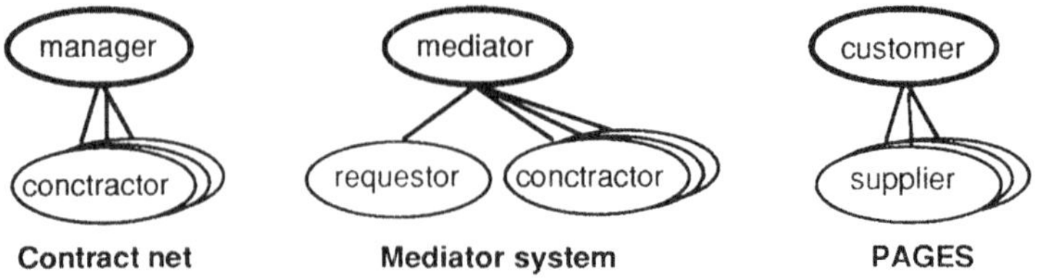

FIGURE 4. Examples of centralized multilateral control.

The Mediator system [18] based on the Amigo Activity model [3] illustrates the approach with a specialized group agent (fig. 4). The system supports users to agree upon, for instance, dates of business meetings. A *mediator* is a specialized intelligent agent which coordinates negotiations based on simple user agents, e.g. mail box programs. The user acting as a requestor initiates a negotiation by interacting with the mediator. The mediator then interacts with the desired participants called contractors. The designers of the system have formalized their multilateral model by considering it as a set of bilateral negotiations, each of which appears as a high-level Petri net, i.e. Predicate/Transition net.

5.2.3. Decentralized control

A pure decentralized control implies that no single agent holds a perfect view of the complete state of a negotiation. The concept of role in a business organization illustrates this approach nicely. Each negotiating agent plays a permanent or temporary *role* which specifies the local tasks, goals and inter-role relationships with the assumption that a feasible result is achieved if each player follows its role rationally. Consequently, the negotiation can be locally optimal for each agent relative to some goals, but if a *global goal* for a negotiation exists, there is no way to guarantee its optimal solution provided that it may differ from the Pareto optimal one. We characterize decentralized multilateral control with unstructured, non-conflict and conflict-oriented models.

An *unstructured negotiation* involves a loose dynamic group of agents without explicit computerized roles or goals. Such a negotiation is created when some agent starts it, expanded when a participant sends a message to a new agent, and terminated when the last active participant considers it finished. In PAGES, this flexible approach has proved useful as a generalized book-keeping mechanism for user-driven manual negotiations. Moreover, it provides the user with additional uniform overviews of his negotiations by listing the forms, senders and recipients coupled through a negotiation.

The *non-conflict models* are multilateral extension to the request-response model. Agents playing well-defined roles under imposed benevolence handle common tasks without having to resolve conflicts. This approach is followed in the information flow models of office systems [34]. The related operations are often well-structured which implies a high degree of automation in user agents. PAGES supports such applications well except that atomic multi-agent transactions, which are necessary in shared multi-user systems, do not fit well into the framework of asynchronous parallel agents.

Finally, the multilateral *conflict-oriented models* derived from the simple bilateral negotiation involve agents with well-defined roles prepared to handle conflicting situations successfully. The agents must negotiate, either with or without imposed benevolence, about some goals and scarce resources which appear for instance as temporal, financial or material constraints. Due to the laboriousness of the implementation of multilateral negotiation mechanisms, this framework is likely to be relevant only in applications with rather permanent and well-organized topological relationships between roles. An example of a problem which might satisfy the conditions, is the scheduling of manufacturing in a single factory. The scheduling problem can be decomposed for a hierarchy of agents which negotiate vertically. Some recent implementations, e.g. BOSS [13], extend the vertical control with horizontal interaction between peer agents. A similar approach can be applied in the inter-site management of order changes along the supply chain in distributed manufacture which has been prototyped with PAGES [33]. It must be emphasized, though, that the automation of negotiations between user agents seems to be far less important than the user friendly interactive coordination of those negotiations.

6. CONCLUSIONS

We have attempted to characterize the modeling aspects of autonomous user agents by reviewing the concepts employed in the DIMUN project. Clearly, user agents are still far from mature as a field of research, which can be seen from the multitude of existing alternative approaches in organizing the inter-agent cooperation. One obvious reason is the subtle and varying nature of human cooperation, which should be intimately reflected in the functions of user agents.

Our pilot experiments on applications of distributed change management indicate that a user agent should support simultaneously several roles involving different modes regarding the message paradigm, topology and control of cooperation. In fact, the semi-automated cooperative aspect of user agents should be an integral part of the other functions of a personalized desktop. In order to achieve this integration, information must be represented semiformally in a way that people and agents can operate intelligently; natural language and computerized knowledge must be combined into some easily accessible uniform templates, e.g. form classes. In trying to break the old rule of the thumb which says that the potential benefits of automation may surpass the risks of misinterpretation only in secondary tasks, the uniform representation is a necessity. This approach helps to avoid the obstacles of automation by allowing agents to transfer tasks flexibly into manual control whenever necessary.

The understanding and testing of the behaviour of complex semi-automated multi-agent systems is difficult. PAGES makes the implementation and maintenance of such systems easier, but does not support the necessary planning, verification and simulation aspects. Our modest experiences achieved in building pilot applications suggest that separate tools are needed for designing complex interactions. Yet, compared with fully automated agent systems, semi-automatic cooperation based on user agents can manage potential conflicts better by necessarily relying on human assistance. Nevertheless, formal methods are required in verifying the correctness of negotiations, including deadlock freeness and consistent termination. Formalisms such as finite state machines [23], state transition diagrams [31] and various versions of Petri nets [18] have been applied in the modelling of cooperative inter-agent work patterns, but the practical usability of these methods is still limited to rather simple situations.

ACKNOWLEDGEMENTS

The authors gratefully acknowledge the valuable comments by Eero Eloranta, Esko Pohjanpalo, and the enthusiastic participants of the workshop on Modelling Autonomous Agents in a Multi-Agent World.

REFERENCES

[1] Chang E.: Participant Systems for Cooperative Work, in Distributed Artificial Intelligence, ed. Huhns M. (Pitman Publishing, London, 1987)

[2] Chang S.-K., Leung L.: A Knowledge-Based Message Management System, ACM Transactions on Office Information Systems, Vol. 5, No. 3, (July 1987), pp.213-236
[3] Danielsen T., Pankoke-Babatz U.: The Amigo Activity Model, proc. of EUTECO'88, Research into Networks and Distributed Applications, ed. Speth R., (North-Holland, 1988)
[4] Davis R., Smith R.G.: Negotiation as a Metaphor for Distributed Problem Solving, Artificial Intelligence, No. 20, (1983)
[5] DIMUN: Distributed International Manufacturing Using Existing and Developing Public Networks, Project deliverable, Project R-1039, RACE Programme (1988)
[6] Ellis C.A.: An Office Information System Based on Intelligent Forms, internal memorandum, Office Research Group, Xerox PARC (not published)
[7] Eloranta E., Hämmäinen H., Alasuvanto J., Malmi L., Doumeingts G.: An evaluation of expert system design tools, in Knowledge-based systems in manufacturing, ed. A.Kusiak, (Taylor&Francis, 1989)
[8] Galliers J.: The Positive Role of Conflict in Cooperative Multi-Agent Systems, this volume
[9] Gold E.: Envoys in Electronic Mail Systems, ACM Transactions, ACM 0-89791-210-1/86/1000-0002 (ACM, 1986)
[10] Goodman D.: The Complete HyperCard Handbook, ISBN 0-553-34391-2, (Bantam Computer Books, 1987)
[11] Hogg J.: Intelligent Mail System, Office Automation - Concepts and Tools, ed. D.Tsichritzis, (Springer-Verlag, 1985)
[12] PAGES User's Manual, Department of Computer Science, (Helsinki University of Technology, 1989)
[13] Hynynen J.: A Framework for Coordination in Distributed Production Management, PhD thesis, Department of Computer Science, (Helsinki University of Technology, 1988)
[14] Hämmäinen H., Eloranta E.: Object-Oriented Data Communication for Loosely Coupled Control, Computers in Industry, Vol. 9, No. 4, December (1987)
[15] d'Inverno M., Campbell J., Pankhurst G.: Knowledge Interchange Protocols, Proc. of the European workshop on Modelling an Autonomous Agent in a Multi-Agent World, Cambridge, England, August 16-18, (1989)
[16] ISO: Information Processing - Tect and Office Systems - Office Document Architecture (ODA) and interchange format, ISO/DIS 8613, (1986)
[17] ISO: Electronic data interchange for administration, commerce and trade (EDIFACT) - Application Level Syntax Rules, ISO/DIS 9735, (1987)
[18] Kreifelts T., Victor F., Woetzel G., Woitass M.: A Design Tool for Autonomous Group Agents, proc. of EC-CSCW '89, London, (September 1989)
[19] Lai K.-Y., Malone T., Yu K.-C.: Object Lens: A "Spreadsheet" for Cooperative Work, ACM Transactions on Office Information Systems, Vol. 6, No. 4, (October 1988), pp.332-353
[20] McCarthy D., Dayal U.: The Architecture of an Active Database Management System, Proc. of the International Conference on the Management Data, eds. Clifford J., Lindsay B., and Maier D., Portland, Oregon, May 31-June, 1989, ACM SIGMOD RECORD, vol. 18, no. 2., (June 1989)
[21] Malone T., Grant K., Turbak F., Brobst S., Cohen M.: Intelligent Information-Sharing Systems, Communications of the ACM, Computing Practices, Vol. 30, no. 5, (May 1987), pp.390-402
[22] Muller J.-P., Demazeau Y.: Decentralized Artificial Intelligence, this volume
[23] Nierstrazs O.: Message Flow Analysis, Office Automation - Concepts and Tools, ed. Tsichritzis D., (Springer-Verlag, 1985)
[24] Pollock S.: A Rule-Based Message Filtering System, ACM Transactions on Office Information Systems, Vol. 6, No. 3, (July 1988), pp.232-254
[25] RACE: R&D in Advanced Communications in Europe, RACE '89, Commission of the European Communities, OTR 202, (March 1989)
[26] Schumann M.: Eingangspostbearbeitung in Bürokommunikationssystemen, Expertensystemen-ansatz und Standardisierung, (Springer-Verlag, 1987)

[27] Searle J.: A taxonomy of illocutionary acts, in Language, Mind and Knowledge, ed. K. Gunderson, (University of Minnesota Press, 1975)
[28] Shepherd A., Mayer N., Kuchinsky A.: Strudel: An Electronic Conversation Toolkit, Software Technology Laboratory, Hewlett-Packard Laboratories, Report STL-89-04, (March, 1989)
[29] Sulonen R., Pietikäinen P.: Forget-Me-Not, A System Controlling Inter-Company Operations by Intelligent Mail, HICS '90, Hawaii, (January 1990)
[30] Tsichritzis D., Fiume E., Gibbs S., Nierstrasz O.: KNOs: Knowledge Acquisition, Dissemination and Manipulation Objects, in Objects and Things, ed. Tsichritzis D., Centre Universitaire d'Informatique, (Universite de Geneve, 1987)
[31] Winograd T.: A language/action perspective on the design of cooperative work, STAN-CS-87-1158, Department of Computer Science, (Stanford University, 1987)
[32] Hämmäinen H.: An Object-Oriented Approach to Distributed Production Management Systems, Licentiate thesis, Department of Computer Science, Helsinki University of Technology, 1987
[33] Hämmäinen H., Eloranta E., Pohjanpalo E.: Intelligent User Agents in Distributed Change Management, Department of Computer Science, Helsinki University of Technology (to appear)
[34] Ellis C.A.: Formal and Informal Models of Office Activity, in Proc. of the Information Processing '83 Conference, ed. R. Mason, (North-Holland, 1983)

type of agents considered by AI researchers differs depending on the type of problems addressed. At one extreme are *neural networks* that constitute the fine-grained multi-agent systems. They are composed of a set of tightly-coupled, simple, and unintelligent processing elements or units that represent a piece of knowledge (e.g., a symbol, a feature, or a concept), and maintain an internal potential or activation level [Addanki, 1987]. By acting asynchronously and by communicating through their connections, the cooperating units can respond flexibly to data so that their overall behavior can be viewed as being intelligent. At the other extreme are *distributed problem-solving systems* that constitute the coarse-grained multi-agent systems. They are loosely-coupled distributed networks of semi-autonomous problem-solving nodes that are capable of sophisticated problem-solving [Lesser and Corkill, 1987]. Each node is a complex problem-solver that can modify its behavior as circumstances change and plan its own communication and cooperation strategies with other nodes.

1.2 Blackboard Systems

The research reported in this paper falls between the two extremes. It concerns *blackboard systems*, a kind of medium-grained multi-agent systems, in which the agents are cooperating closely-coupled knowledge sources (KSs) that interact through a global database called the blackboard [Nii, 1986a; Nii, 1986b; Engelmore, 1988; Jagannathan, et al. 1989]. A KS monitors a portion of the blackboard, waiting for particular patterns of data. When such a pattern occurs, the KS takes the data and processes it, typically forming new combinations of data which it places on other portions of the blackboard.

In a blackboard system, knowledge is compartmentalized so that each KS is a specialist in one particular aspect of the overall problem-solving task. The cooperative behavior exhibited from these systems stems from a sophisticated scheduling mechanism that controls KSs' activities. Effective scheduling is crucial to the efficiency and flexiblity with which blackboard systems have to solve problems. Of the three defining architectural components (blackboard, knowledge sources, and scheduler), the scheduler shows the greatest variety among blackboard systems and poses the greatest technical challenge during the design of these systems.

In the remainder of this paper, we present a meta-level blackboard shell for building blackboard systems, ATOME, we have developed at CRIN/INRIA-LORRAINE. ATOME integrates different types of control in attempting to achieve two important and often conflicting behaviors of blackboard architectures: *flexibility* and *efficiency*. Flexibility is achieved when the system is able to: (1) explicitly represent domain and control problems, knowledge and solutions, (2) modify and adapt its own behavior to dynamic problem-solving situations, and (3) integrate various schemes of control and knowledge representation. Efficiency is concerned with: (1) the ability of the system to achieve high-speed computation, and (2) the rapidity of the control component to select knowledge sources. Unfortunately, these two fundamental goals often conflict while building blackboard systems, and the system designer is therefore led to make compromises.

The second section of this document describes ATOME's blackboards, domain and control knowledge organization. Section 3 emphasizes how ATOME achieves both flexibility and efficiency in an effective manner. In section 4, we present a comparison with other works in this field. Finally, we conclude by an overview of ATOME's current state and use.

2 ATOME Case Study

This section defines the implementation of ATOME basic blackboard components and its additional control structures.

2.1 The Blackboards

Many blackboard systems use multiple panels or blackboards to organize their knowledge. For instance, in the DVMT system [Lesser and Corkill, 1983] the data-blackboard stores hypotheses, the goal-blackboard memorizes goals as intentions to abstract and extend these hypotheses, while the abstract-blackboard groups together related hypotheses based on their blackboard level, their time, and their region characteristics. The VISIONS system [Hanson and Riseman, 1978] defines a STM (Short Term Memory) blackboard as a related collection of information representing an interpretation of a specific image, and a LTM (Long Term Memory) blackboard as a general visual model knowledge.

In addition, a subset of KSs can require a private data region where they can easily interact before communicating their results to the entire community. This can be done by defining local and global blackboards. A local blackboard provides local privileged interaction between a subset of KSs whilst a global blackboard serves as a communication area of leading results of the overall problem.

To cope with such needs, ATOME provides the use of multiple blackboards. Each level in a blackboard is represented as an object class in the sense of object oriented languages and is characterized by a set of attributes and links. A hypothesis corresponds to an instance of one of these classes. A hypothesis attribute can have various alternative values resulting from the action of diverse specialist KSs. Each value is weighted by a certainty coefficient (i.e., a number or the symbol *undefined*) and, if necessary, by a validation period of time which indicates the portions of time during which the value is valid [Maître, et. al 1987]. Links between two hypotheses of the same blackboard or of different blackboards are also represented as attributes. A hypothesis link contains the hypotheses with which it is linked, and has automatically a reverse link.

2.2 Specialist Knowledge Sources

These are interdependent modules which include domain-dependent knowledge linked to the subject under consideration. Each specialist (KS) is an expert for a specific problem in the domain of application.

The activation of a specialist provokes a series of actions in the blackboards: creations of new hypotheses, modifications or deletions of old ones. If the actions are judged as being important enough to be indicated to the control mechanism then they generate events. The problem-solver will not waste one 's time by useless events describing intermediate blackboards changes that appear unnecessary to trigger KSs: the number of events to be processed by the control component is decreased. Whether an action should or should not be indicated to the control mechanism is part of the specialist's expertise provided by the designer. Relevant events are placed on the top, on the queue or at a specific rank in the event-lists depending on their importance (cf. 2.3.2).

The precondition of an ATOME specialist KS is a blackboard state-based predicate required for execution. The action of an ATOME specialist KS can be either a set of production rules according to the ATOME's formalism or a program written in various languages (LISP, C...) as well as an expert system developed with other shells.

Depending on the formalism it respects, a specialist can have a local working-memory on which it can consult and/or post some specific or private information. That case relates to a specialist as an expert system or as a program for which the blackboard serves only to memorize global information needed to be shared between specialist KSs. Consequently the number of useless hypotheses on the blackboards is dramatically reduced, and the specialists are less distracted to process unnecessary information.

2.3 Control Knowledge Sources

The control in ATOME is carried out by *control* KSs which work as meta-knowledge sources. Organizing control knowledge in this way defines what we refer to as *meta-level blackboard architecture.*

2.3.1 Meta-Level Blackboard Architecture

Meta-level blackboard architecture [Nii, et. al 1982; Terry, 1983; Lâasri, et. al 1987] distinguishes between domain KSs and meta-level KSs (control KSs which select domain KSs). Continuing the progression, meta-meta-level KSs select among meta-level KSs, and so forth. Control within a meta-level blackboard architecture called *hierarchical control* proceeds in a top-down manner. The highest level consists of a single control KS which examines the blackboards and selects a KS or a set of KSs to invoke at the next lower level. This process is then repeated, the execution of a KS at one level causes KSs at the next lower level to be invoked, until the lowest level which constitutes the application domain KSs is encountered. The main difference between this architecture and the blackboard control architecture is that the former uses control KSs to accomplish scheduling while the latter uses them to manipulate the objects on the control blackboard, which serve for KSARs scheduling [Hayes-Roth, 1985].

Some of the advantages of the meta-level architecture over other approaches are that, in the presence of a large number of KSs that can be invoked at any point in the problem-solving task, it is possible to reduce the number of competitive KSs and to reorder them so as to improve the efficiency of KS invocations. This is achieved by considering only a subset of knowledge sources at each phase of the problem-solving process: each knowledge source located at one level has to manage only a restricted set of knowledge sources at the next lower level; therefore, when actived, the system takes into account only this subset of knowledge sources. Moreover, the representation of control heuristics as rules contributes to the clarity since they are written in a highly constrained representation and tend to be concise [Terry, 1988].

ATOME's controller is hierarchical; it is made up of two levels: *task* level and *strategy* level.

2.3.2 Task Control Level

They are meta-knowledge sources which contain knowledge linked to control. A task (KS) enables local control to coordinate the work of a set of specialists in order to solve a specific part of the problem.

As such, each task has a local control structure called *event-list* where the blackboard changes with which it is concerned are kept. Most meta-level blackboard systems post all blackboard changes into the same global event-list. The control KSs scan the entire event-list to test the appearance of some specific events and are often distracted by events not in their own area of interest. ATOME has corrected this drawback by allocating a local event-list to each task. When a task is activated it tries to match only the blackboard changes that have occurred in its area. For instance, in a speech understanding application a task whose work is located at the signal level does not have to try to examine events which occurred at the sentence level. Thereby, local event-lists provide tasks with more autonomy so that they can be viewed with their specialists as semi-autonomous subsystems.

According to its event-list, each task selects a set of specialists and an order in which they will be carried out. To do this, a task is composed of production rules. Their left hand side tests the appearance of particular events in the task event-list and the state of global variables or task bindings (i.e., the left hand side of a task rule is an event-based predicate for triggering a la BB-1), whilst their right hand side contains a list of one or several specialists to be executed *sequentially* or *opportunistically* depending on the task type of control.

Each event-list is updated when its corresponding task terminates its work: all events which participated in the problem-solving process (i.e., those that served to trigger specialist KSs) are deleted from the event-list of the activated task without disturbing the others. Consequently, we have eliminated the inherent problem encountered (in earlier ATOME versions [Haton, et. al 1987]) with a shared global event-list: a task removing an event from the event-list disabled potential activities of successive tasks interested by this event making them more concurrent than cooperative.

ATOME provides three types of tasks:

1. *Event-driven tasks*

   The task takes the event with the highest priority (i.e., the first event) of its local event-list and scans the entire task rules in attempting to fire them.

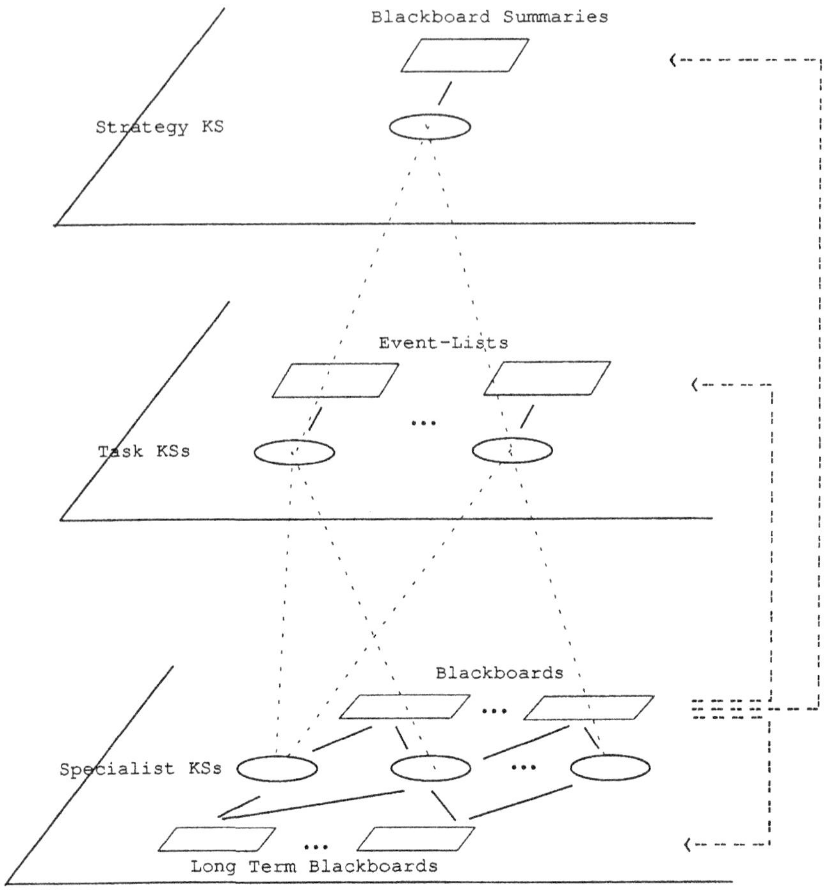

Figure 1: ATOME's Architecture.

task being activated consults its event-list, chooses a set of specialists and activates them according to its type of control. The specialist being activated consults the blackboard regions with which it is concerned and creates new hypotheses, modifies or deletes existing ones according to the state of the previous regions. Then the event-lists as well as the blackboard summaries are updated and the cycle starts again.

The following paragraph describes in more details a problem-solving cycle of an ATOME-system, a system developed with the ATOME tool:

1. The strategy KS chooses the most important rule with its left hand side satisfied: in order to do this, it scans the BSs to find important hypotheses which meet the rule left hand side conditions.

   When a rule fires, the strategy activates *sequentially* the tasks whose names are specified in the rule right hand side, executes LISP functions and/or requests the system to stop. The activated tasks can focus on events associated with hypotheses selected by the strategy KS.

2. The current task activates *sequentially* or *opportunistically* specialist KSs depending on its type (event-driven, rule-driven or agenda-based task), executes LISP functions and/or stop itself.

   The activated specialist KSs can access to hypotheses selected by the strategy and to those associated with events selected by the current task.

3. The current specialist action is executed: it can create, modify or delete hypotheses on the blackboards, execute programs (LISP, C...) and/or stop itself.

4. Goto 1.

The system stops when no strategy KS rule fires or when a strategy rule explicitly calls for this stop.

The user can specify for each domain or control KS that only the first rule that matches is to be fired (Single-hit), all rules that match on a top to bottom pass are to be fired (Multiple-hit), or rules are to be fired in successive passes until none matches (Cyclic-hit).

For more details on the ATOME control component see [Lâasri and Maître, 1989].

3 On Efficiency and Flexibility

In this section, we discuss how ATOME can conciliate the efficiency and flexibility needed in blackboard real applications:

1. *Efficiency:*

   ATOME reduces the emission of events and consequently it reduces equally the reasoning time of tasks by:

(a) storing in the local event-lists of tasks only those blackboard changes considered useful by the specialists which have generated them;

(b) synthesizing events having a bearing on similar types of changes of the same hypothesis.

It also reduces the amount of data stored into the blackboards by:

(a) allowing each specialist to dispose of a private working-memory where it memorizes its private information and stores in the blackboards only data needed to be shared;

(b) associating to each blackboard a *long term blackboard* (LTB) which contains old hypotheses (not processed since a long application-dependent time). The blackboard is regularly scanned in order to locate old entries and translate them to the LTB. The specialist KSs can consult these LTBs to retrieve information when necessary.

It also reduces the work-space of KSs, be they of the domain or of control by:

(a) associating to each blackboard a blackboard summary which contains only hypotheses considered important as regards the pursuit of the system activities;

(b) associating to each task a local event-list which contains only relevant events for the considered task. Each task defines a filter on the generated events that allows to determine its area of interest;

(c) associating to each specialist a *working-context* evaluated at each activation of the latter. It can in fact define a filter on the blackboards that allowed it at each activation to determine this working-context (subset of blackboard hypotheses). Thus instead of reasoning on all blackboards, the specialist orients its activities towards the region of the data that it must process.

It finally permits the KSs to focus on specific data by:

(a) notifying to the tasks the important hypotheses of blackboard summaries thus making for their activation. These hypotheses are transmitted by the strategy to the activated tasks as focalization of control;

(b) notifying to the specialists the events thus making for their activation. These events are transmitted by the tasks to the activated specialists as focalization of control. In fact, hypotheses associated to these events are transmitted.

2. *Flexibility:*

ATOME addresses flexibility in a number of ways:

(a) the three types of tasks make possible the testing and the combination of different types of control. Thus the problem-solving process can be subdivided into a succession of stages for which the designer will choose the most appropriate control;

(b) it allows multiple specialist formalisms to appropriately represent the various domain expertises;

(c) it is an open system: other task control schemes or specialist formalisms can easily be added.

4 Comparison with Other Works

Since many blackboard systems do not provide a balance between the two behaviors described earlier, they do not support large-scale applications in an effective manner.

For example, BB-1 provides a powerful architecture for applications in which control knowledge has to be frequently updated. This architecture offers a fully flexible and modular environment for experimental development, but it suffers from high overhead, combining computational and storage costs. Therefore, BB-1 architecture is not suitable to applications that need high execution performance [Hayes-Roth, 1985].

On the other hand, a procedural architecture like HEARSAY-II is suitable for applications that prefer performance running over flexibility. Major weaknesses of this architecture are its lack of clarity, and its difficulty for maintenance [Garvey, 1987].

In order to address the problem of reconciling efficiency and flexibility, the GBB shell [Corkill, et. al 1986] provides an efficient blackboard database kernel with primitives for inserting and retrieving blackboard objects, and it also provides pattern matching capabilities. The application developer is free to implement a specific control mechanism. The implementation of a hybrid multi-stage control (similar to ATOME 's controller) within GBB would significantly improve its efficiency and flexibility.

5 Conclusion

Blackboard systems constitute medium-grained multi-agent systems in the sense that agents have no understanding of the problem outside of their own area of expertise, cannot be suspended during execution, and keep no history of their actions. Thus, a sophisticated control mechanism is needed for coordinating the cooperative behavior of the agents.

In this paper, we presented a hybrid multi-stage controller that organizes and controls reasoning in a flexible and efficient manner. This control architecture integrates the opportunism that exists in blackboard control architectures like BB-1, BBB [Benda, et. al 1986], and GBB-1 [Johnson, et. al 1987] and the efficiency that appears in solution-based focusing architectures like HASP/SIAP and CRYSALIS.

An implementation of these ideas was realized within ATOME, a shell for building blackboard systems. ATOME is developed in a LISP environment. It runs on SUN workstation under the UNIX system and on SYMBOLICS Machine [Brunessaux, et al. 1989]. At present, it serves for the development of systems in several advanced application areas (e.g., character processing and recognition [Belaïd, et al. 1988] and complex decision-making [Ferraris, et al. 1989]). It also serves as a framework for implementing temporal and hypothetical reasoning tools [Lâasri, et. al 1988]. The

ATOME-style control was also used to implement a blackboard architecture for automatic labeling of speech [Juncqua, 1989].

Acknowledgments

Parts of this work are reproduced from *Blackboard Architectures and Applications* (edited by V. Jagannathan, R. Dodhiawala, and L. S. Baum) with the permission of the publisher (Academic Press, Inc., 1989).

References

Addanki, S. (1987) Connectionism. In: *Encyclopedia of Artificila Intelligence*, Volume 1, John Wiley and Sons.

Belaïd, A., Chenevoy, Y., Lâasri, H., and Maître, B. (1989) Vers un système à base de connaissances pour la compréhension de l'écriture. *Actes du Septième Congrès AFCET/RFIA* (RFIA-89), Paris.

Benda, M., Baum, L.S., Dodhiawala, R.T., and Jagannathan, V. (1986) Boeing blackboard system. Presented at *AAAI Sponsored Workshop on High Level Tools.*

Brunessaux, S., Lâasri, H., and Maître, B. (1989) *ATOME Version Common Lisp 3.0 : Manuel d'utilisation.* Rapport technique 89-R-032, CRIN/INRIA-LORRAINE.

Corkill, D.D., Gallagher, K.Q., and Murray K.E. (1986) GBB: A generic blackboard development system. In: *Proceedings of the Fifth National Conference on Artificial Intelligence* (AAAI-86), pp. 1008-14.

Engelmore, R. and Morgan, T. (eds) (1988) *Blackboard Systems.* Addison-Wesley.

Ferraris, C., Haton, M.C., Davaine, J.J., Cuchet, P., and Cornu, G. (1989) Le diagnostic en voirie urbaine : Utilisation d'un système expert. *Actes des Journées Européennes sur la Ville et les Nouvelles Technologies*, Nancy.

Garvey, A. (1987) *Implementing Diverse Forms of Control Knowledge in Multiple Control Architectures.* Technical Report KSL-87-40, Stanford University.

Hanson, A.R. and Riseman, E.M. (1978) VISIONS: a computer system for integrating scenes. In: *Computer Vision Systems*, pp. 303-33. Hanson, A.R. and Riseman, E.M. (eds), Academic Press, New York.

Haton, J.P., Maître, B., Lâasri, H., and Mondot T. (1987) ATOME: Another TOol for developing Multi-Expert systems. Presented at *AAAI-87 Workshop on Blackboard Systems*, Seattle, WA.

Hayes-Roth, B. (1985) A blackboard architecture for control. *Artificial Intelligence* **26(2)**, 251-321 (previous version in Technical Report HPP-83-38, Stanford University).

Jagannathan, V., Dodhiawala, R., and Baum, L.S. (eds) (1989) *Blackboard Architectures and Applications.* Academic Press.

Johnson, P.M., Corkill, D.D., and Gallagher, K.Q. (1987) Integrating BB1-style control into the generic blackboard system. Presented at *AAAI-87 Workshop on Blackboard Systems*, Seattle, WA.

Juncqua, J.C. (1989) A blackboard architecture for automatic labeling of speech. In: *Proceedings of the Ninth International Workshop on Expert Systems and Their applications* (AVIGNON-89), General Conference, Volume 2, pp. 853-64.

Lâasri, H., Maître, B., and Haton, J.P. (1987) ATOME : outil d'aide au développement de systèmes multi-experts. *Actes du Sixième Congrès AFCET-RFIA* (RFIA-87), tome 2, pp. 749-59.

Lâasri, H., Maître, B., Mondot T., Charpillet F., and Haton, J.P. (1988) ATOME: a blackboard architecture with temporal and hypothetical reasoning. In: *Proceedings of the Eighth European Conference on Artificial Intelligence* (ECAI-88), pp. 5-10 (extended version appeared as INRIA Technical Report no. 855).

Lâasri, H. and Maître, B. (1989) *Coopération dans un univers multi-agents basée sur le modèle du blackboard : Etudes et réalisations.* Thèse de l'université de Nancy 1, rapport technique 89-T-028, CRIN/INRIA-LORRAINE.

Lesser, V.R. and Corkill D.D. (1983) The Distributed Vehicle Monitoring Tested: a tool for investigating distributed problem solving networks. *AI Magazine* **4(3)**, 15-33.

Lesser, V.R. and Corkill D.D. (1987) Distributed problem solving. In: *Encyclopedia of Artificial Intelligence*, Volume 1, John Wiley and Sons.

Maître, B., Lâasri, H., and Mondot, T. (1987) *Manuel d'utilisation d'ATOME : Version 1.1.* Rapport technique 87-T-110, CRIN/INRIA-LORRAINE.

Nii, H.P., Feigenbaum, E.A., Anton, J.J., and Rockmore, A.J. (1982) Signal-to-symbol transformation: HASP/SIAP case study. *AI Magazine* **3**, 23-35.

Nii, H.P. (1986a) Blackboard systems (Part 1), *AI Magazine* **7(2)**, 38-53.

Nii, H.P. (1986b) Blackboard systems (Part 2), *AI Magazine* **7(3)**, 82-106.

Terry, A. (1983) *The CRYSALIS Project: Hierarchical Control of Production Systems.* Technical Report HPP-83-19, Stanford University.

Terry, A. (1988) Using explicit strategic knowledge to control expert systems. In: Engelmore and Morgan (1988), pp. 159-88.